IMAGES
of America

SAN JACINTO

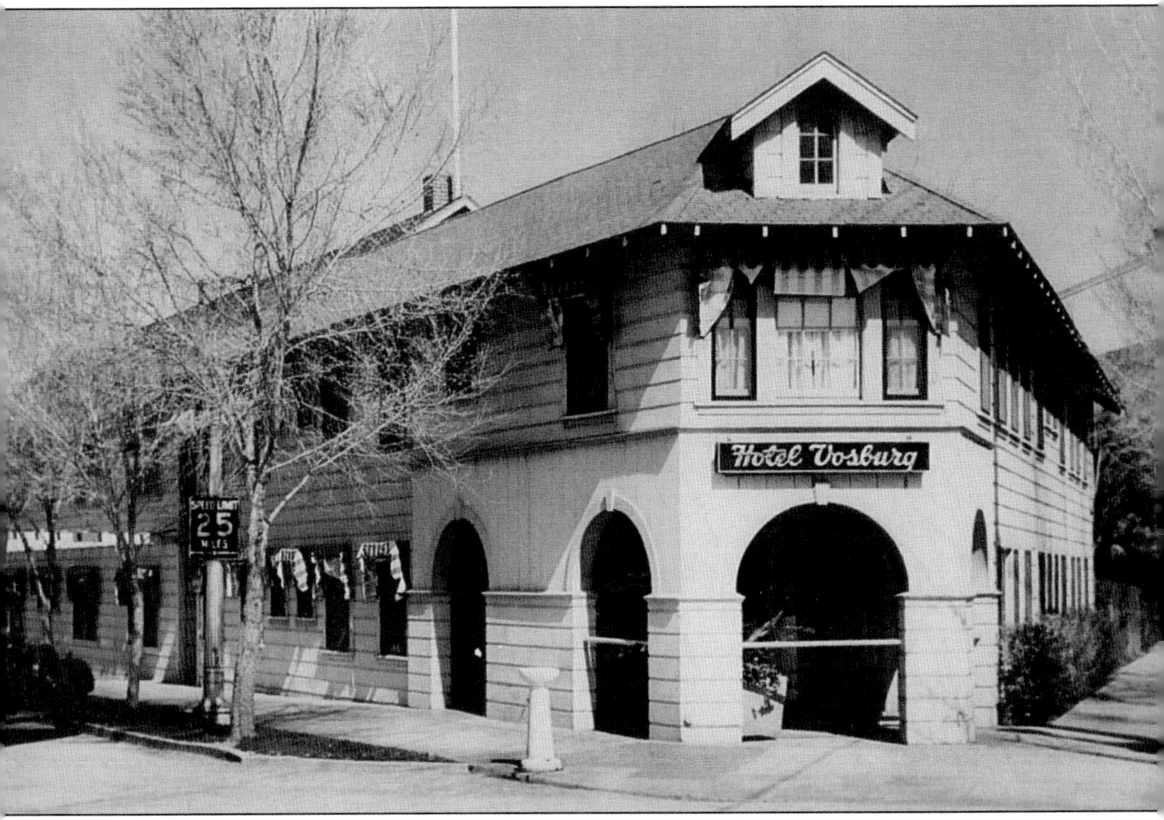

The Vosburg Hotel is the focal point of the five-corner intersection at San Jacinto Avenue and Ramona Boulevard. The final addition to the hotel was completed in the 1930s when the owners acquired the San Jacinto Library and incorporated it into the original hotel structure. New owners are now restoring the building. The neon sign is on display in the San Jacinto Museum.

ON THE COVER: This view of the city of San Jacinto looks east along Main Street toward the San Jacinto Mountain Range, with Mount San Jacinto in the center. A covering of snow extends down to 3,000 feet. The photograph was taken around 1890, after San Jacinto's 1888 incorporation and before the installation of electric power poles in 1897. At the time, the city population was about 800. (Courtesy San Jacinto Museum.)

IMAGES
of America

SAN JACINTO

Jack Warneke, Kenneth M. Holtzclaw,
and the San Jacinto Valley
Museum Association

ARCADIA
PUBLISHING

ISBN 978-0-7385-5842-4

Published by Arcadia Publishing
Charleston, South Carolina

Printed in the United States of America

Library of Congress Control Number: 2007943613

For all general information, please contact Arcadia Publishing:
Telephone 843-853-2070
Fax 843-853-0044
E-mail sales@arcadiapublishing.com
For customer service and orders:
Toll-Free 1-888-313-2665

Visit us on the Internet at www.arcadiapublishing.com

Contents

Acknowledgments 6

Introduction 7

1. Native American Culture 9

2. Early San Jacinto 21

3. Hotels and Resorts 53

4. 20th-Century San Jacinto 67

5. Agriculture 87

6. Special Events 111

ACKNOWLEDGMENTS

The principal source of these images was the collection in the San Jacinto Museum. Charles Van Fleet, a 1913 graduate of San Jacinto High School, started taking photographs before 1910 and continued into the 1970s. As his reputation grew, people donated their own images from the 1800s. After his death in 1980, his widow, Marvel, sold the collection to Harley Garbani, who in time gave the collection to the San Jacinto Museum.

We also thank the following individuals for loaning photographs: Pam Hubble, curator of the Clarence Swift photograph collection at the Hemet Library; Marjorie Quandt Goodwin for the images of the Quandt ranch; Bill Corwin for those of the Corwin ranch; Betty Jo Dunham for family photographs; and Mildred Ferrett Dummer for the Ferrett family album. We are grateful to Charlene Ryan, Evelyne Burke, Mary Grace Hurst, Joan O'ostram, Becky Rose Schlosser, Ignacio Cordero, Mary Collier, Russ Jacobs, and the Warneke family members. Betty Jo Dunham and James and Barbara Dunham Walsh helped identify people in the photographs.

The following references were used to compile the captions: *The Friendliest Valley*, published in 1990 by the San Jacinto Valley Museum Association; *San Jacinto Valley Past and Present*, published in 1989 by the Hemet-San Jacinto Genealogical Society; *The Hyatt Legacy*, republished in 1992 by the San Jacinto Valley Museum Association; *The Pictorial History of Hemet and San Jacinto Valley*, published in 1995; the *Hemet News*, edited by Merriam Hamilton; the *San Jacinto Valley Register*, which in 1984 published a 26-part series of articles written by Mary Whitney and then a special centennial edition in August 1984 in commemoration of the first issue; and the 1988 *Press-Enterprise* centennial edition in commemoration of the founding of the city of San Jacinto.

INTRODUCTION

The history of Native American culture goes back centuries before recordings were made. At least two maze stones have been found in the San Jacinto Valley, but no one has been able to identify the precise date of the carvings. The maze stone carvings pre-date the most recent Native Americans to inhabit the valley, the Luisenos. Though seven villages of Luiseno Indians existed in the early 1800s, now only the Soboba Band remains. It has 900 members, most of whom live on the Soboba Reservation on the east edge of the San Jacinto city limits.

The first Spanish explorer, Juan Baptista de Anza, arrived in the San Jacinto Valley in 1774 on an exploration of a route from Arizona to San Francisco. From his diary, he called the valley San Jose, which translated to San Jacinto. Another version is that the Catholic priest in his group named the valley in honor of St. Hyacinth, a name that also translates into San Jacinto from Spanish. When Mexico won independence from Spain in 1822 and issued land grants to the Estudillo family of San Diego, two of the sons settled in the valley in the mid-1800s to raise cattle. Both brothers had two-story brick houses built in 1885. Francisco Estudillo's house, at the corner of Main and Seventh Streets, is designated on the National Register of Historic Places and is currently being restored. The San Jacinto Museum is now located on the grounds of Francisco Estudillo Heritage Park.

After California gained statehood in 1850, it was still a while before other settlers found the San Jacinto Valley. Henry T. Hewitt was the first to develop businesses and begin farming there. Francisco Estudillo started selling off his land, and the San Jacinto Land Company parceled most of what is now San Jacinto. The railroad brought a spur line into the city in 1888, with the spur terminating near Francisco's house. Hewitt's "Old Town" San Jacinto, which was two miles from the railroad, stopped developing. Businesses cropped up in a new area along Main Street in San Jacinto, on the other side of the river—the beginning of the 1880s building boom. Devastating earthquakes in 1899 and 1918 each destroyed all the brick businesses along Main Street; the city did not fully recover until recently. The population was at about 2,000 in 1910, but by 1920, after the second earthquake, it had dropped down to 945. The city housed 1,353 people in 1930 and 1,760 in 1950. Growth continued at a slow pace until the building boom in the late 1980s, when population went from 5,000 to more than 30,000 in 2007.

For over 100 years, San Jacinto was primarily an agricultural community. Cattle ranching gave way to grain farming in the 1800s, and after 1900, many different crops were being grown. In the eastern area were acres of apricot and walnut groves. Grapes were a major crop from 1900 to 1920 but then just disappeared. The small dairies that started up in the early 1900s had formed a major industry by the 1980s, with 31 dairies owning a total of 22,700 cows. From the 1930s until 1990, several Thoroughbred horse ranches were located in the area. Much of the acreage was then devoted to raising alfalfa for the cows and horses. Potato growing began in the 1930s and continues on what land is still available today. Other vegetables grown in the valley have been onions, carrots, watermelons, pumpkins, cantaloupe, and cabbage. The raising of roses and ornamental plants for landscaping has been in operation since the early 1900s.

Another large source of income in the San Jacinto Valley was tourism, particularly from around 1900 until the 1930s. Mineral hot springs had formed naturally along the foothills to the north of the city, prompting the creation of three hot springs resorts: Eden, Gilman, and Soboba. The trains that started in 1888 brought tourists from Los Angels to San Jacinto. The hot springs dried up after the Metropolitan Water District dug a tunnel through an adjacent mountain to deliver water from the Colorado River to Southern California in 1937. The underground vein of water now drains into the tunnel.

The final chapter recounts some of the interesting events that have happened in San Jacinto over the past 100 years. The biggest was when a Russian plane landed in a dairy pasture along Cottonwood Avenue in 1937. The crew had just set a long-distance record by flying nonstop from Moscow over the North Pole and down to San Diego—6,305 miles in 62 hours. San Diego and the coast were foggy, so the plane flew inland and found San Jacinto.

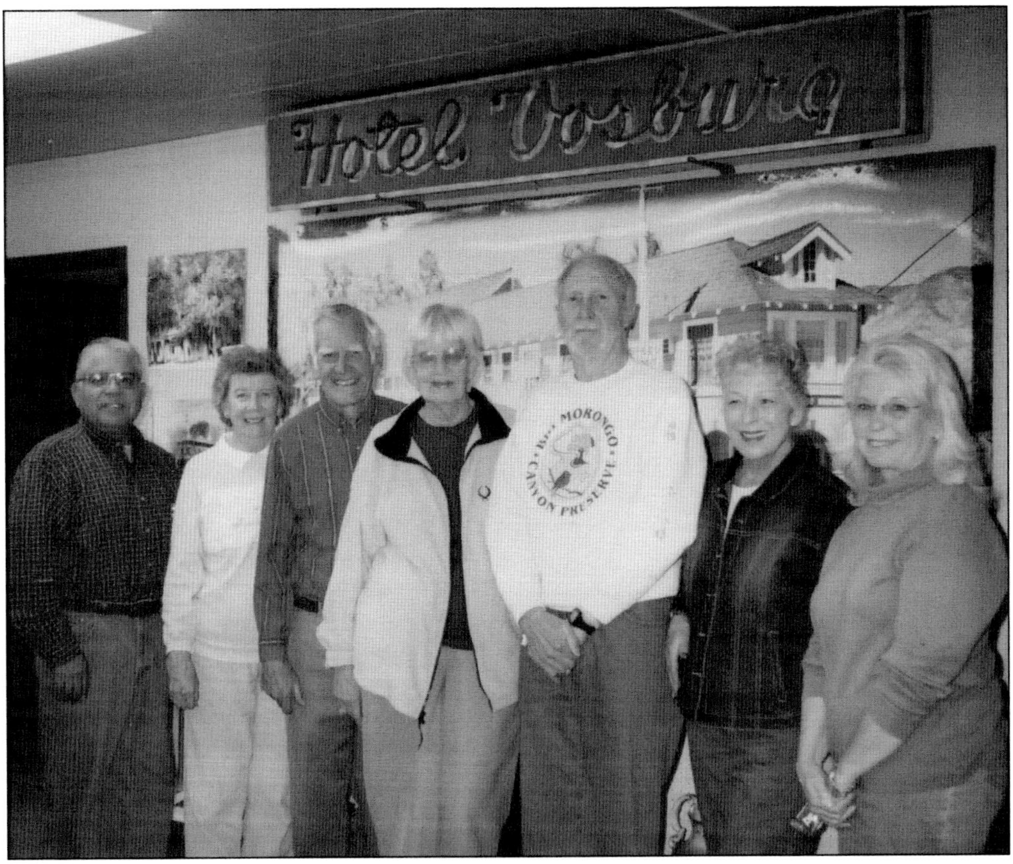

Members of the 2008 board of directors of the San Jacinto Valley Museum Association gather for a photograph. Shown from left to right are director Robert Garcia, vice president Nancy Warneke, president Jack Warneke, treasurer Betty Jo Dunham, director Russ Jacobs, historian Gwen Schlick, and secretary Mary Collier. Board members not pictured are newsletter editor Sharon Terricciano and directors Del Kroker and Charlene Ryan. The officers are standing in the San Jacinto Museum against a backdrop of the Vosburg Hotel's original sign and an enlarged early photograph of the hotel. (Courtesy Ken Holtzclaw.)

One

NATIVE AMERICAN CULTURE

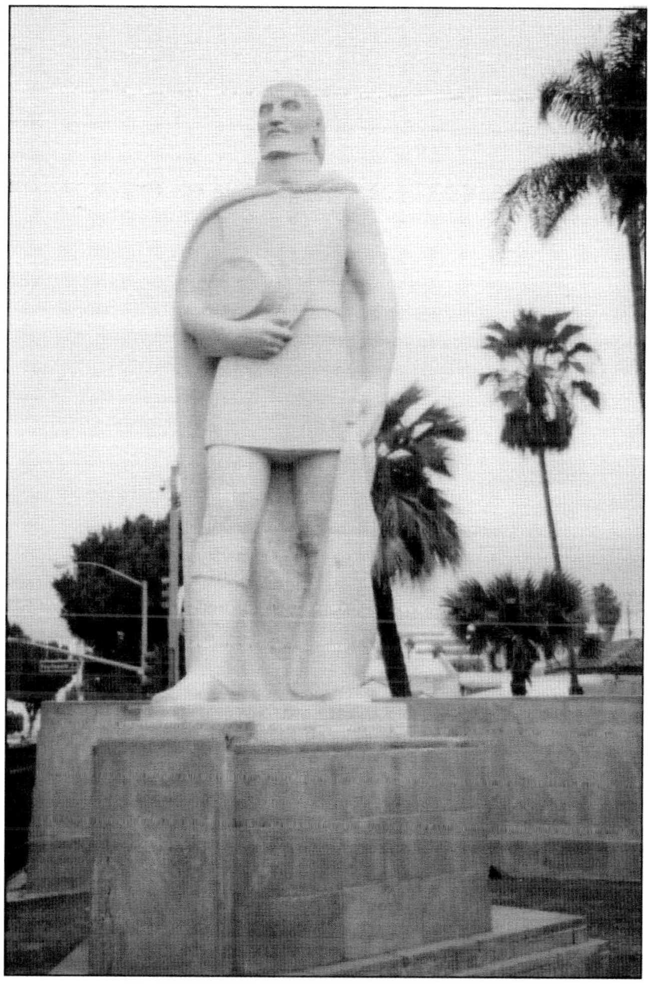

The Don Juan Baptista de Anza Memorial Statue in Riverside, California, is located at the intersection of Magnolia Avenue and Fourteenth Street. De Anza was a Spanish explorer and captain of the cavalry at Tubec, 40 miles south of present-day Tucson, Arizona. He set out to explore a new route to Alta California in 1774. From the Borrego Valley, west of the Salton Sea, he crossed the San Jacinto Mountains at San Carlos Pass, traveled down Bautista Canyon to the San Jacinto River, and then arrived at present-day Valle Vista. On March 18, 1774, his party camped at San Jose, which translated to the name *San Jacinto*. The explorers continued west to the Santa Ana River at Riverside and then turned north to the San Francisco Bay area. In 1776, he led a group of settlers on the same route. (Courtesy Jack Warneke.)

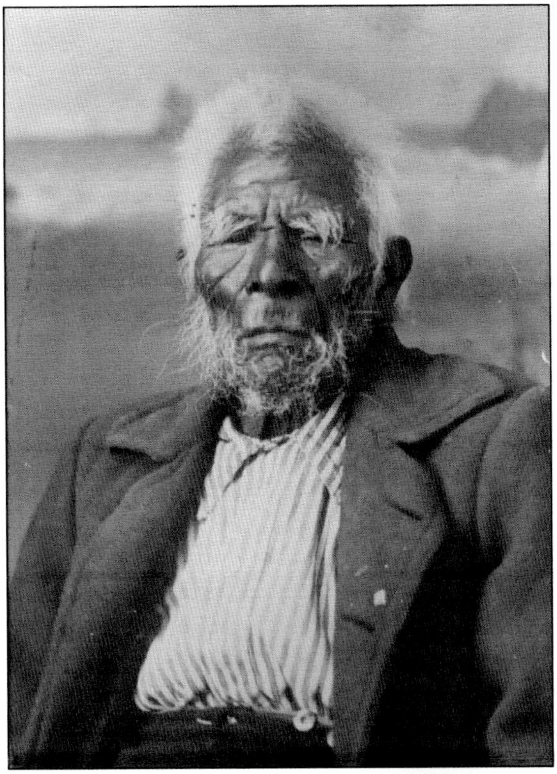

Chief Victoriona died in August 1888 at the age of 132. The chief, representing the Sobobas, signed a peace treaty at Temecula in 1852. The Soboba Reservation was formed in 1883, but land developers were still intruding on Native American land. In the early 1880s, Helen Hunt Jackson was in the valley researching the plight of the Native Americans for her book *Ramona*. She was appointed by the government to intervene on behalf of the tribe and was ultimately able to secure the Soboba land. (Courtesy San Jacinto Museum.)

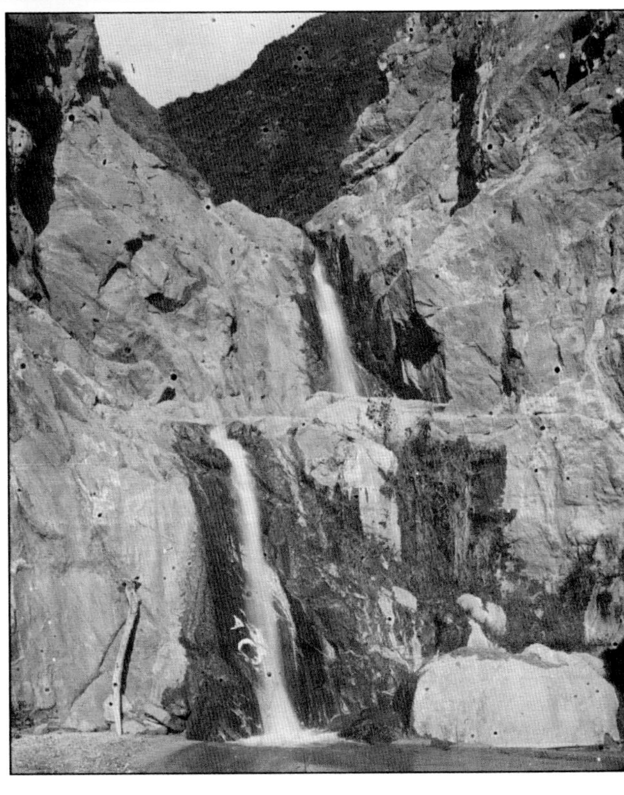

The Portero Creek waterfalls in Massacre Canyon are active when it rains. They are located north of the Gillman Hot Springs road and east of Lamb Canyon Road, only a few miles north of San Jacinto. The name is derived from a battle fought between two villages of Luiseno and Temecula Indians: the Ivahs and Temeculas. The Temeculas drove the Ivahs, who lived in the area, up the box canyon and killed them all in order to acquire their chia supply. (Courtesy San Jacinto Museum.)

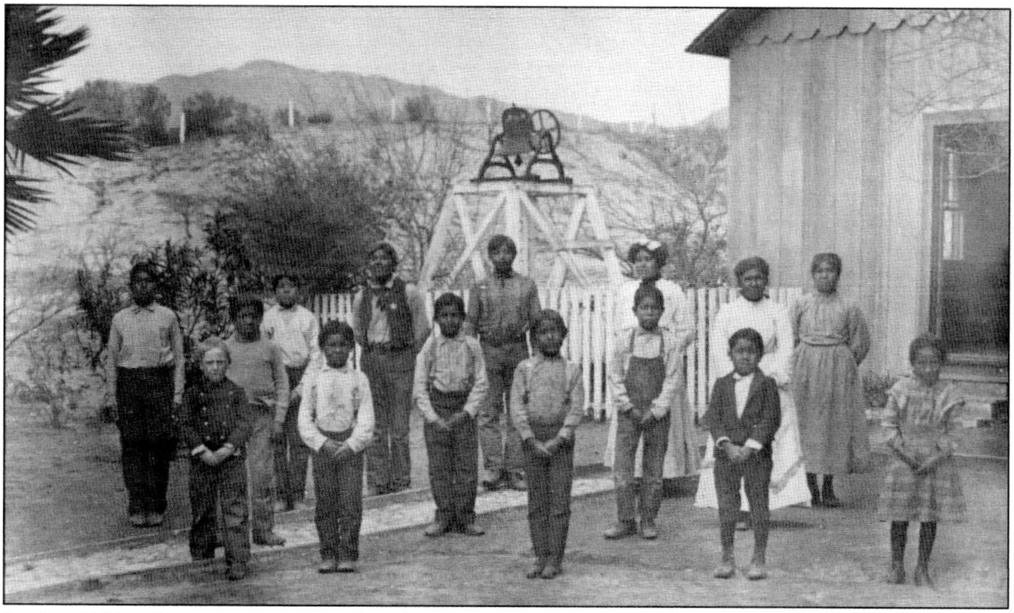

In the 1880s, this structure served as the elementary school in Soboba. The first teacher sent to the Soboba Indian Reservation by the government was Mary Sheriff. San Diego records show an 1889 enrollment of 28 students taught by a Mary Noble. Students also attended boarding schools in surrounding Perris and Banning. They later went to the Sherman Indian School in Riverside, which opened in 1901 and is still operating. (Courtesy San Jacinto Museum.)

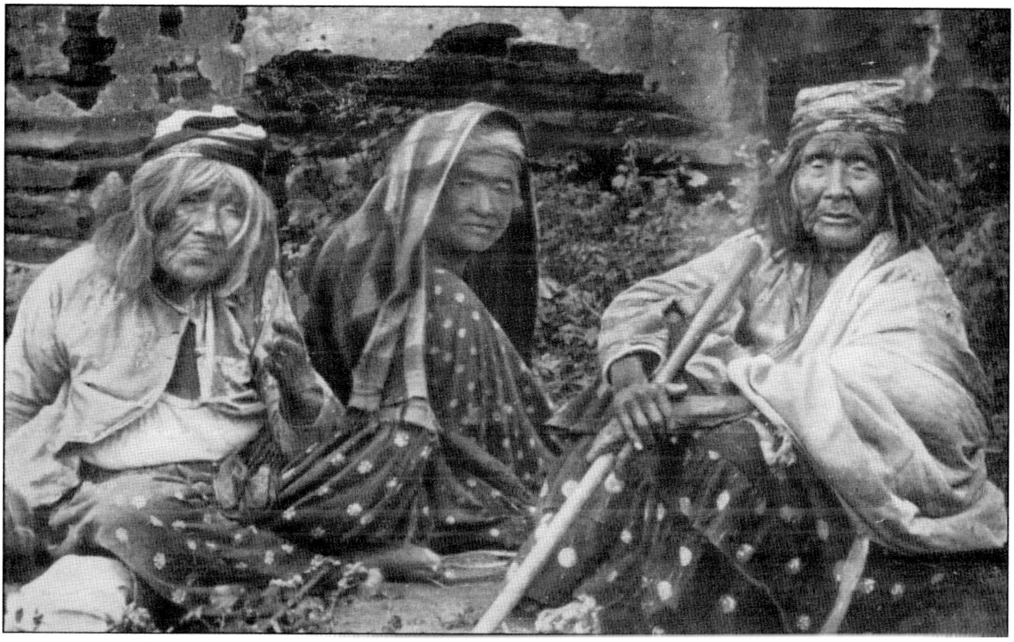

The first inhabitants of the San Jacinto Valley were the Luiseno Indians, three of whom are pictured here. Seven known villages originally existed in the valley: the Ararah, Corova, Huachippah, Ivah, Pahstnah, Pochea, and Soboba tribes. The Ivahs were subsequently killed by the Temeculas at Massacre Canyon, leaving only six villages. When a sailor from San Diego introduced smallpox into the valley in 1862, the Soboba village was the only one to survive. (Courtesy San Jacinto Museum.)

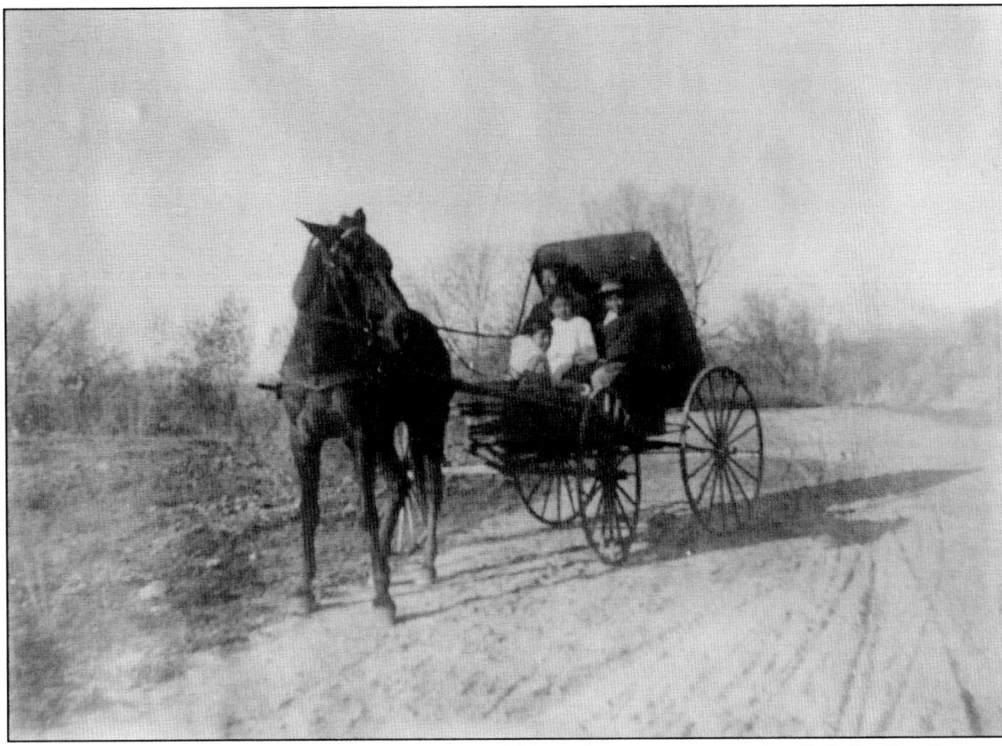

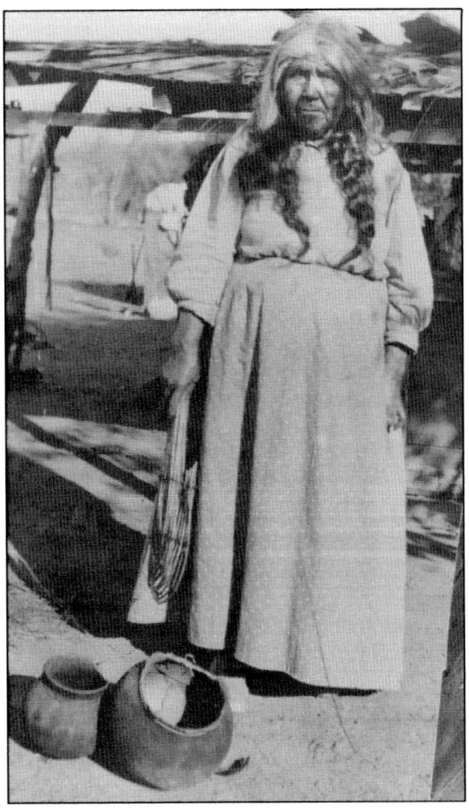

Although transportation by Soboba families was mostly achieved via horseback or foot during the 1880s, some families were fortunate enough to incorporate a horse-drawn buggy. The Soboba Indian Reservation is situated at the east end of Main Street in San Jacinto and on the northeast side of the San Jacinto River; from there, tribe members traveled in order to barter and secure food. (Courtesy Charles Van Fleet.)

A Soboba Indian woman stands beside two earthenware Olla cooking vessels in 1900. Today the Soboba Band of Luiseno Indians has about 900 members. The 1883 executive order that established the Soboba Reservation set aside 3,172 acres extending from the northern ridge of the San Jacinto River up into the foothills of the San Jacinto Mountains. (Courtesy Charles Van Fleet.)

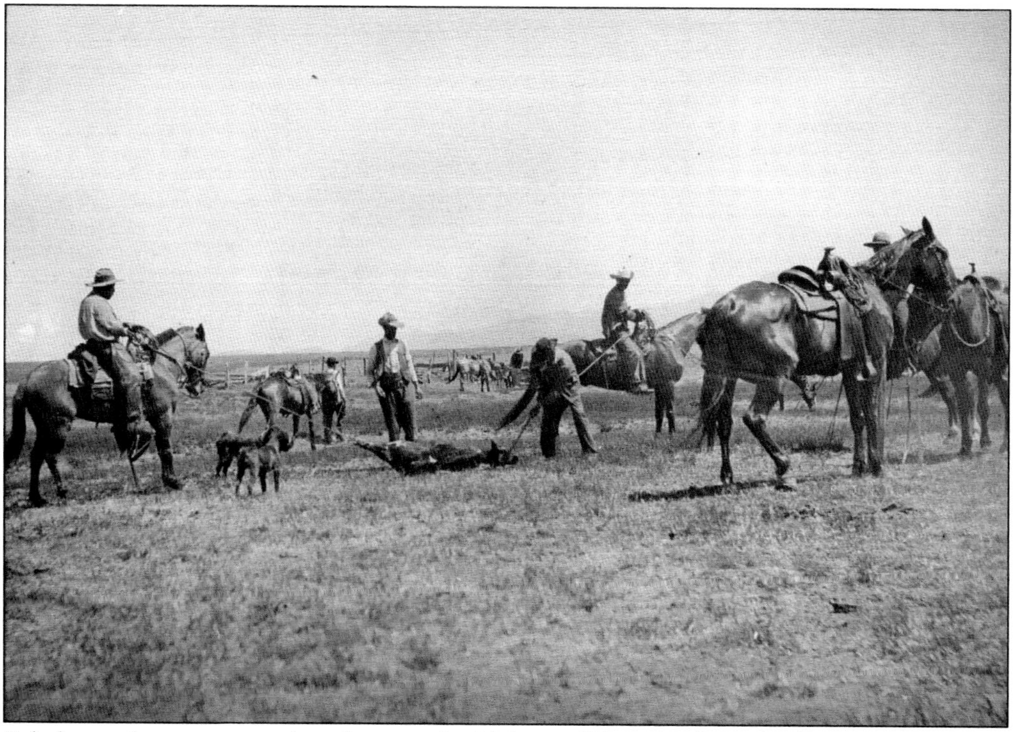

Soboba cowboys are at work with a roped calf they will brand. The Cahuilla, Santa Rosa, and Soboba Indians sometimes helped each other during roundups and brandings and also performed labor outside their tribes. For instance, the Estudillo family hired Sobobas to maintain its cattle ranching operation in the 1880s. (Courtesy Charles Van Fleet.)

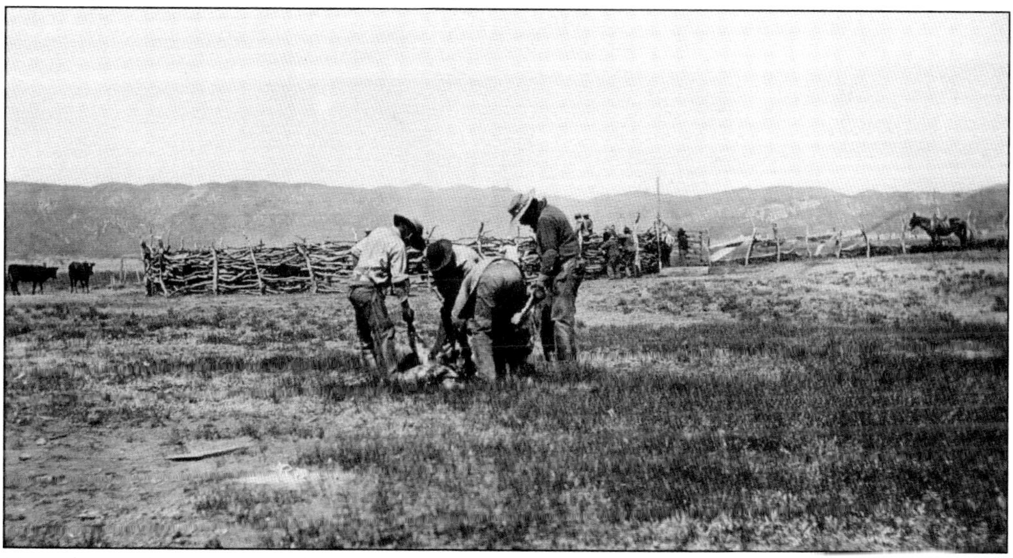

Here the cowboys are branding a calf. The Native American experience with cattle led to the Indian Cattleman's Association, which continued until the 1970s. The Soboba tribe shared pastures with the Cahuilla and Santa Rosa tribes. For breeding purposes, all three rotated registered bulls in order to guard against inbreeding and keep genetic strains sound. (Courtesy Charles Van Fleet.)

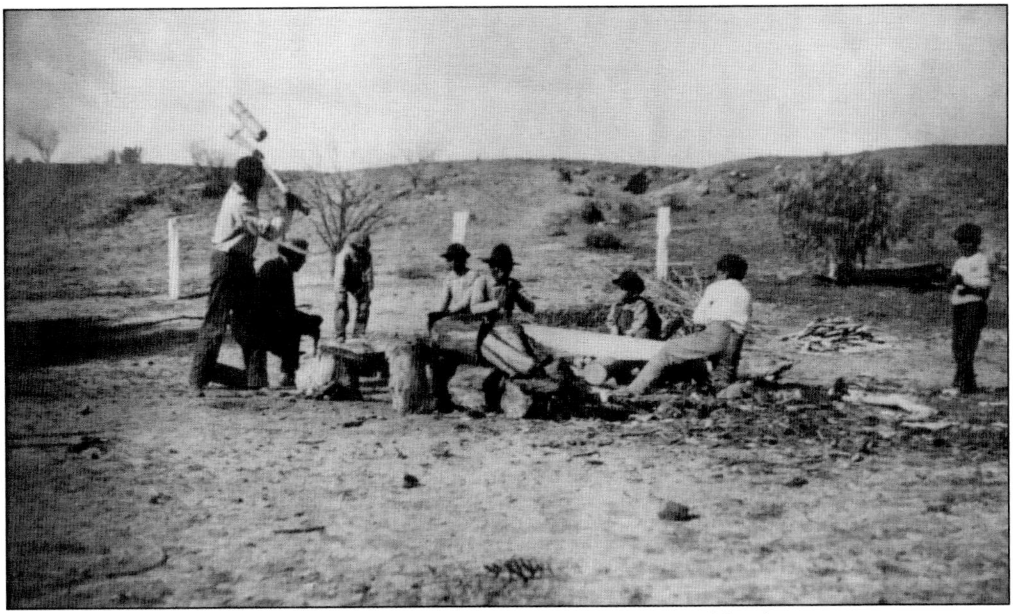

Because Soboba Indians used wood for heating and cooking, scenes like this were quite common. Here a man and a boy prepare wood—often a joint effort between the young and old. Large logs are cut into convenient segments with the cross saw and then passed to an ax man at the side, who splits them on a chopping block. (Courtesy San Jacinto Museum.)

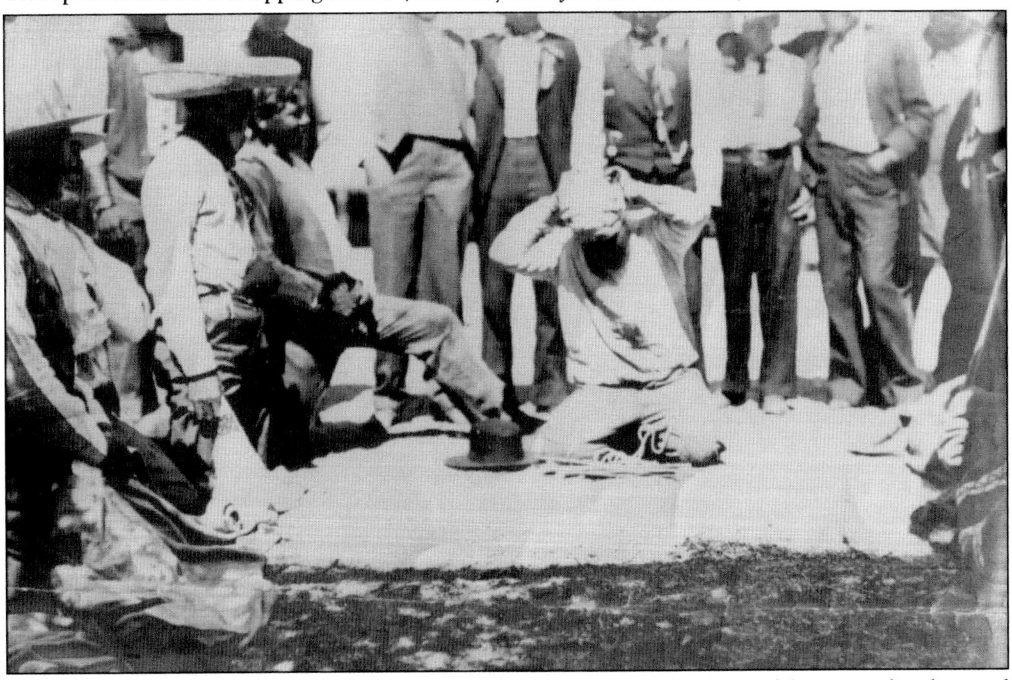

The game of Peon involves teams of up to four players sitting on the ground facing each other and a referee in the center. Those on the active team hold a blanket with their teeth while passing two bones under the blanket—one black and one white. The other team has to guess which hand holds the white and which one the black. Women sing "The Peon Song" during the game and money is wagered on the outcome. (Courtesy Charles Van Fleet.)

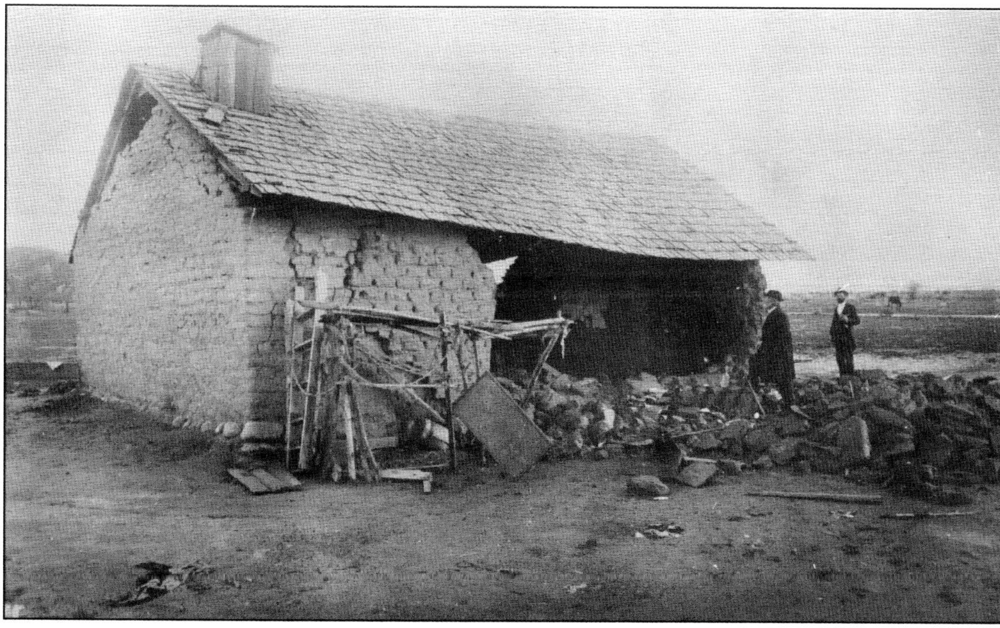

This Soboba building was severally damaged in the 1899 earthquake, which also destroyed most of the brick structures in San Jacinto. During the Christmas morning earthquake, six Soboba women died in the building. Businesses in San Jacinto were closed; therefore, there were fortunately no casualties in the city. (Courtesy San Jacinto Museum.)

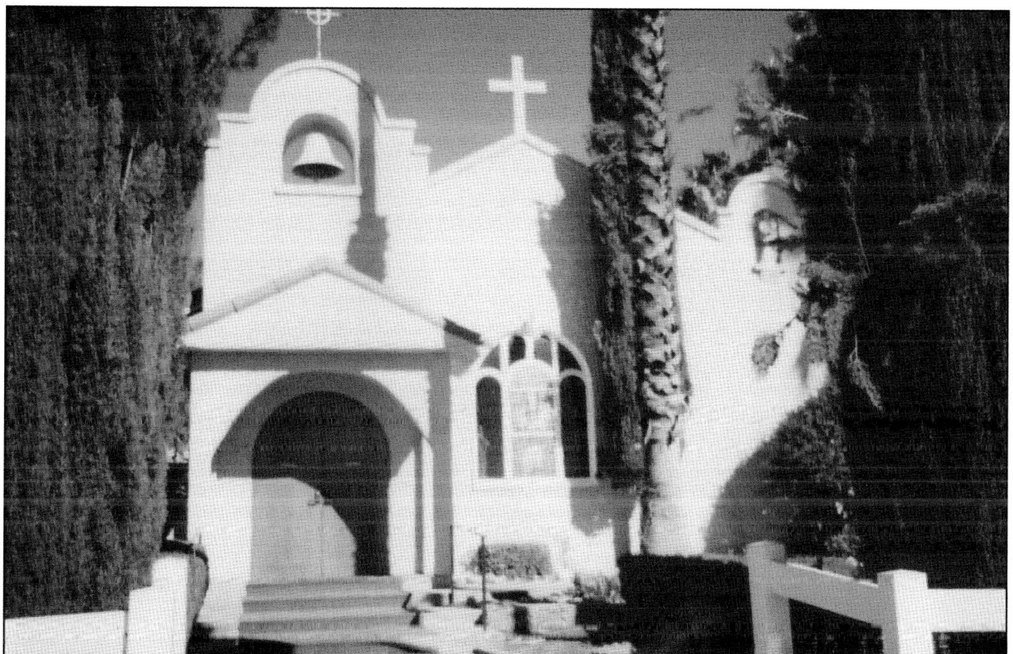

St. Joseph's Catholic Church was established on the Soboba Reservation in 1888 with a full-time priest. The present structure, built in 1910, became a popular church for Sobobas. A cemetery for the reservation is located directly on the grounds behind the building. (Courtesy Jack Warneke.)

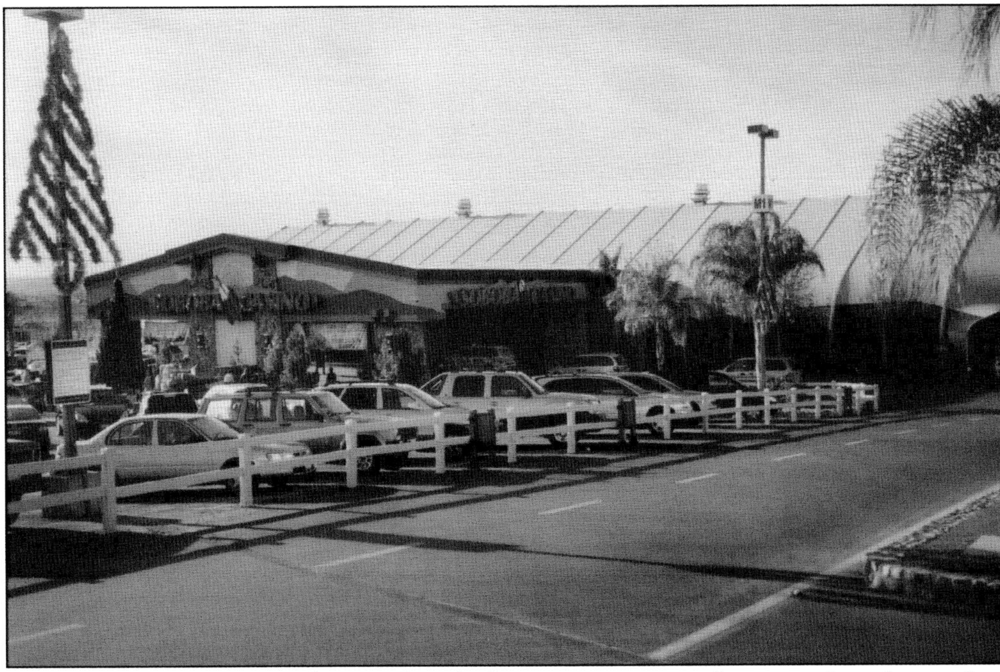

The Soboba Casino opened in 1995 with three restaurants and a sports bar. An outdoor entertainment complex with seating for 12,000 guests is located adjacent to the large casino. The adjoining Soboba Resort was purchased by the Soboba Reservation in 2005 and features a championship golf course. (Courtesy Jack Warneke.)

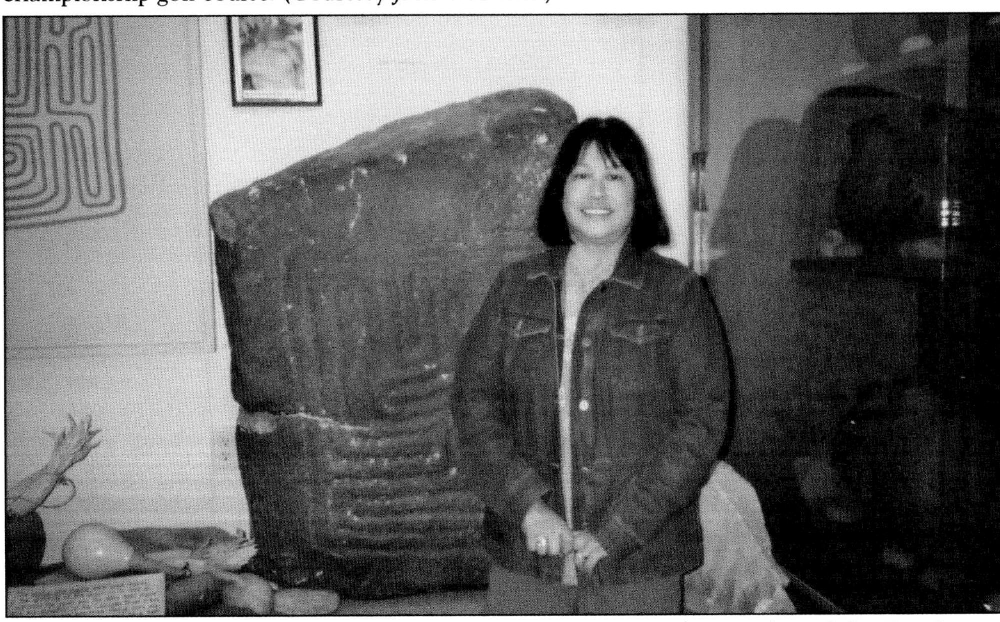

Charlene Ryan, the director of the Soboba Culture Center and a member of the San Jacinto Museum Board of Directors, stands by a replica of the San Jacinto maze stone found on the Hafliger Dairy. A nearby museum display features Ollas, which the Sobobas used to prepare and store food. Another case exhibits a large collection of handwoven Native American baskets. (Courtesy Nancy Warneke.)

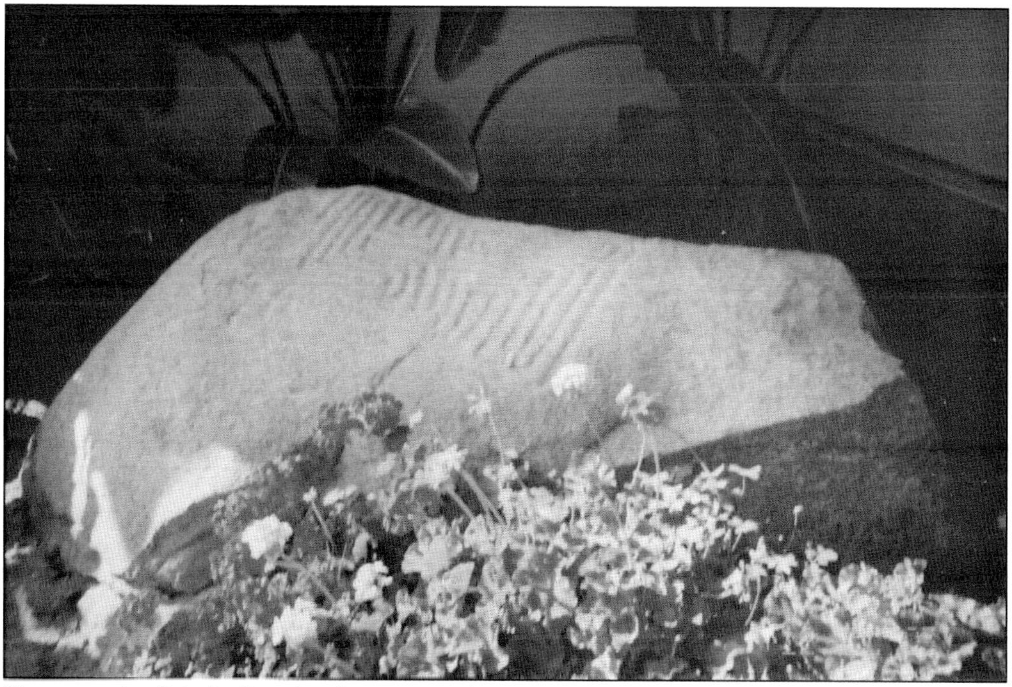

Shown at the Soboba Preschool entrance, this maze stone was discovered in the 1980s on the Henry Hafliger Dairy, along Warren Road southwest of San Jacinto. Hafliger, with the aid of local paleontologist Harley Garbani, removed the stone and had it transported to the Soboba Reservation. A similar maze stone is located about three miles south of the original site of the removed stone. Their meaning remains a mystery, but the stones are believed to pre-date the Luiseno Indians in the valley. (Courtesy Jack Warneke.)

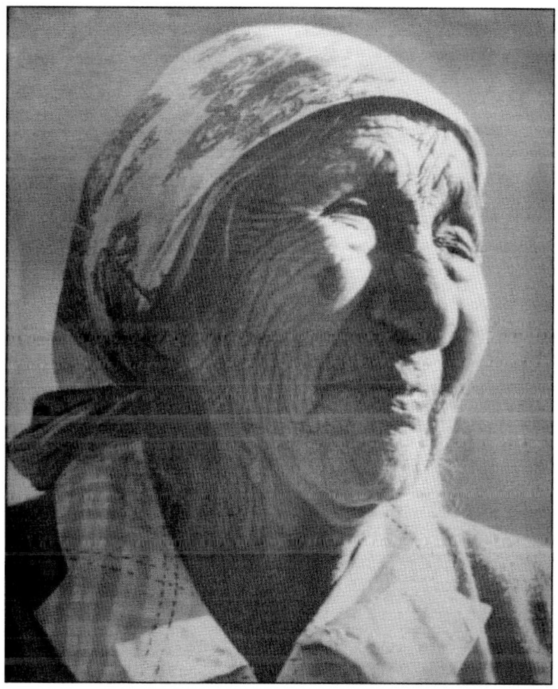

Carlotta Lubo of the Santa Isabel tribe married Monty Lubo, a Soboba. Prior to her death in 1968, she had reportedly lived for 120 to 130 years, surpassing all of her 12 children. She was the great-grandmother of Charlene Ryan, the director of the Soboba Culture Center. (Courtesy Charlene Ryan.)

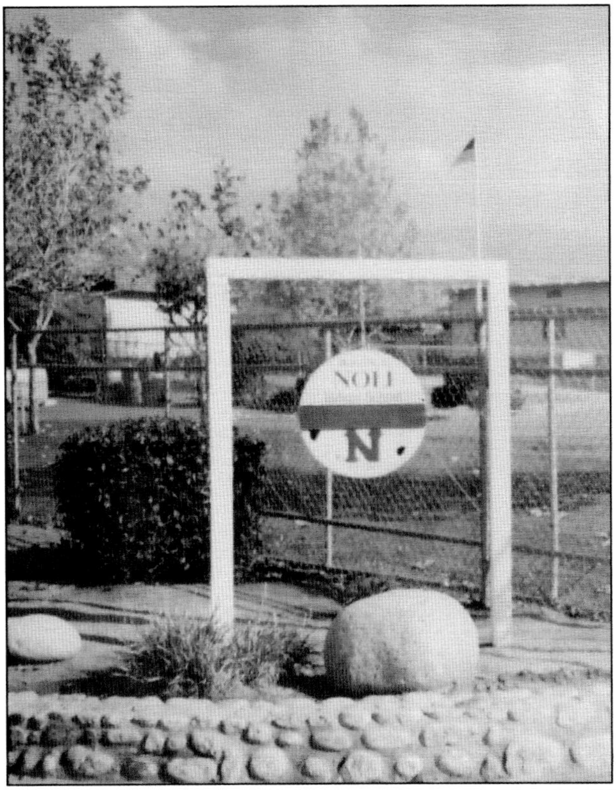

When it was established on the Soboba Reservation in 1992, the Noli Indian School became the first tribal middle school in California. Students from other reservations in Riverside and San Diego Counties also attend Noli. A large sports complex located next to the school provides activities such as softball, baseball, basketball, and swimming. (Courtesy Jack Warneke.)

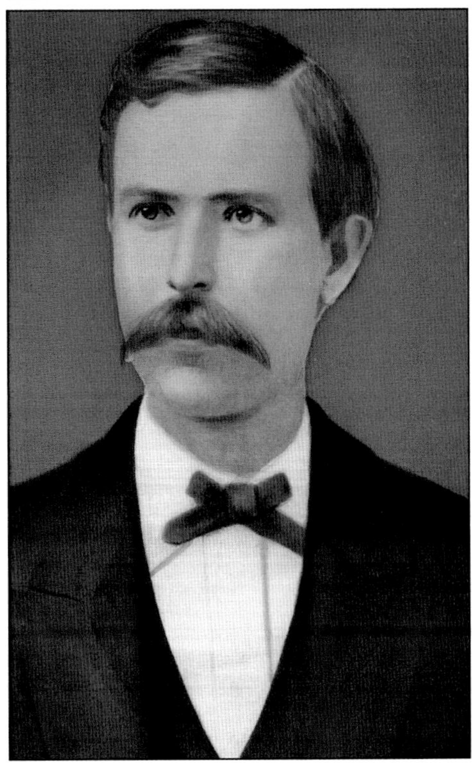

Francisco Estudillo was born in San Diego in 1845. His father, Jose Antonio, worked as an official in San Diego from 1828 to 1840. In 1835, he also served as administrator of the Mission San Luis Rey properties. The Estudillo family received land grants that included San Jacinto Nuevo y Potrero, totaling 48,861 acres. Two of Jose's four sons, Francisco and Jose Antonio, settled in the San Jacinto Valley to begin a cattle business. (Courtesy San Jacinto Museum.)

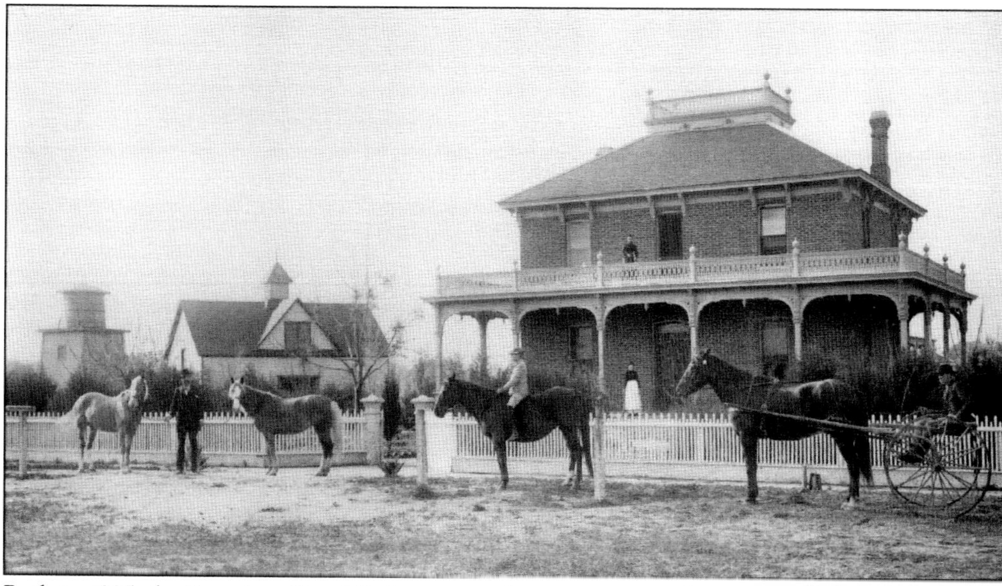

Built in 1885, the Francisco Estudillo house stands on six acres at the corner of Main and Seventh Streets. After serving as the first postmaster in the 1870s, Francisco was elected to the school board in 1890, became San Jacinto's second mayor in 1892, and was appointed mission Indian agent over 32 reservations in Southern and Central California. He sold most of his property during the land boom of the 1880s. Francisco lost his house in foreclosure in 1901 and moved to Los Angeles, where he died in 1921. (Courtesy San Jacinto Museum.)

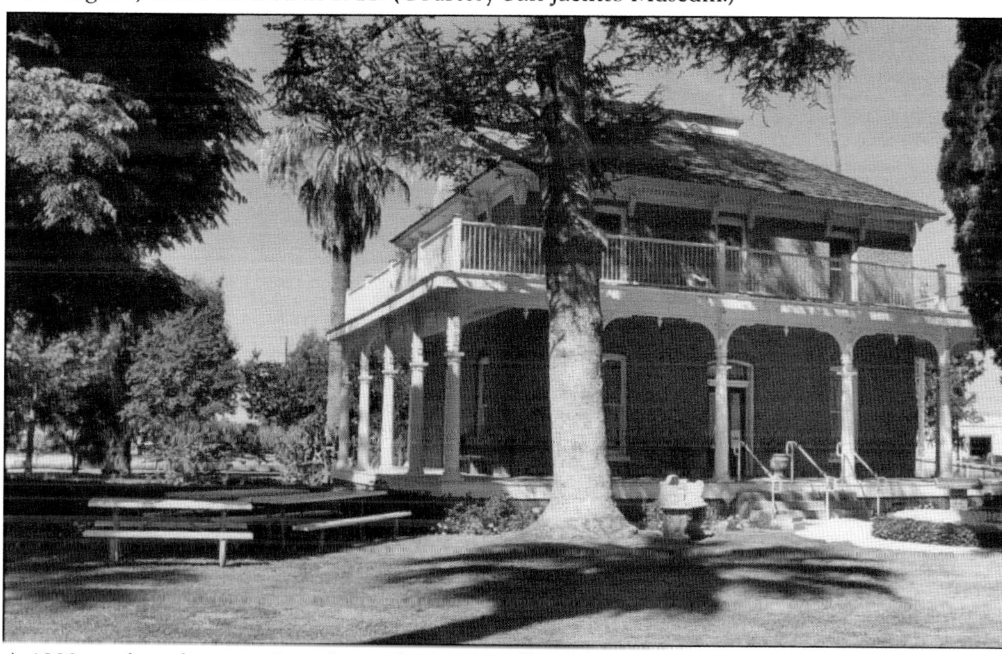

A 1992 earthquake caused cracks in the brick walls of the Estudillo Mansion, but the home was restored in 2007, as pictured here. The Riverside County Parks Department bought the property, thereby giving title to the City of San Jacinto, in 1998. In 2001, the mansion was designated on the National Register of Historic Places as well as the California Register of Historic Resources. (Courtesy Mary Collier.)

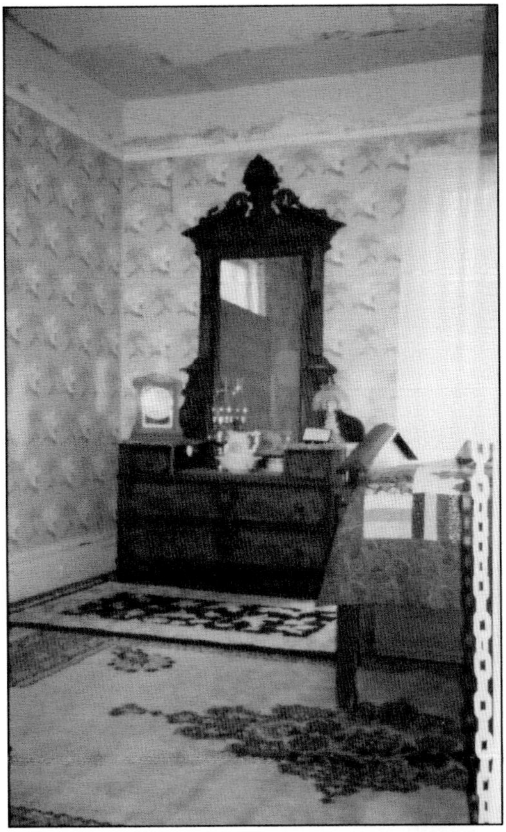

An upstairs bedroom at the Estudillo Mansion is pictured in this view. Helen Shadwick, a member of the Soboba Chapter of Colonial Dames of the Seventeenth Century, donated this bedroom furniture of the late 1800s. In the future, all of the rooms will be decorated with pre-1900 furniture for public viewing. (Courtesy Jack Warneke.)

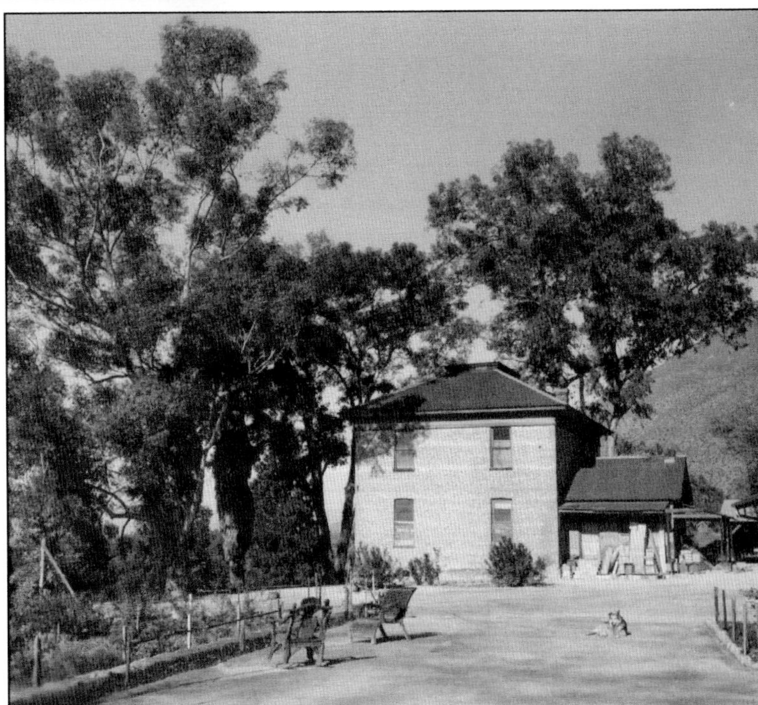

Shown here is the other Estudillo house, near the east end of Main Street next to the Soboba Reservation. This residence has the same floor plan as Francisco's house, built in San Jacinto at the same time. Owner Jose Antonio Estudillo, son of Francisco Estudillo, was born in 1840 and died in 1901. He married a Soboba Indian woman, and his children were the grandchildren of Chief Victoriona. (Courtesy San Jacinto Museum.)

Two

Early San Jacinto

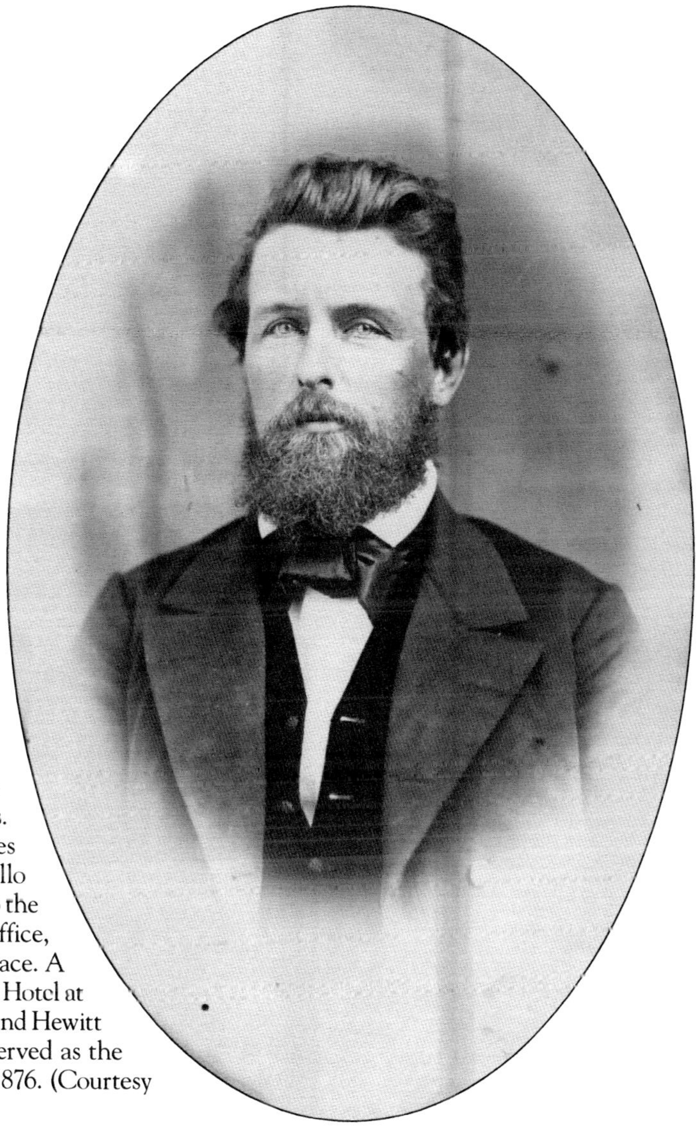

Henry T. Hewitt (1829–1898) is credited with being the founder and "merchant prince" of early San Jacinto. He purchased the trading post that Russian exile Procco Akimo had built in the 1860s. Hewitt also bought 8,000 acres of land from Francisco Estudillo in 1871. In 1879, he added on to the adobe store to include a post office, a courtroom, and a meeting place. A year later, he opened the Palma Hotel at the same location, First Street and Hewitt Avenue. Francisco Estudillo served as the first postmaster from 1871 to 1876. (Courtesy San Jacinto Museum.)

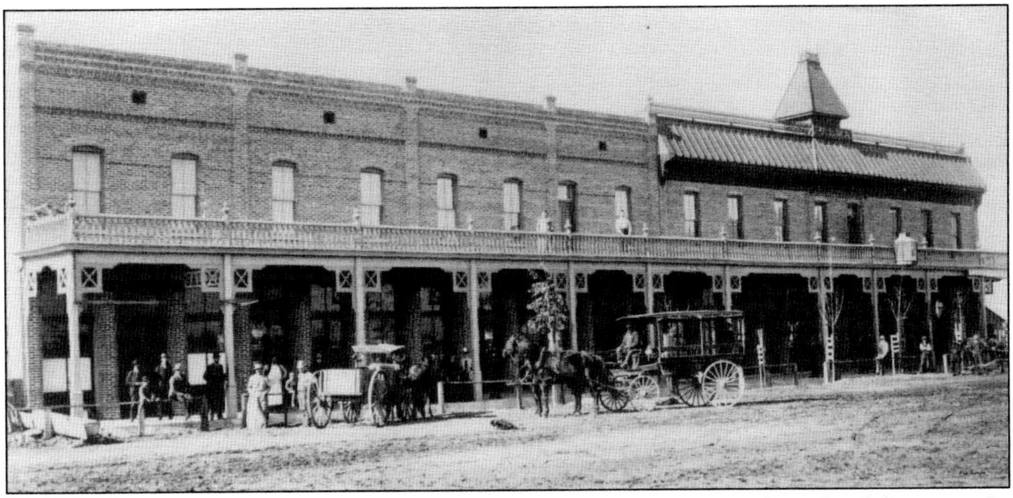

Ray Stout sits on a wagon by the Palma Hotel. Five businesses were on this side of the street. In addition to running the hotel, Henry Hewitt grew 1,200 acres of grain, owned a flour granary, and operated a livery stable with Daniel Clark. He sold the Palma to Julius Brown in 1890. (Courtesy San Jacinto Museum.)

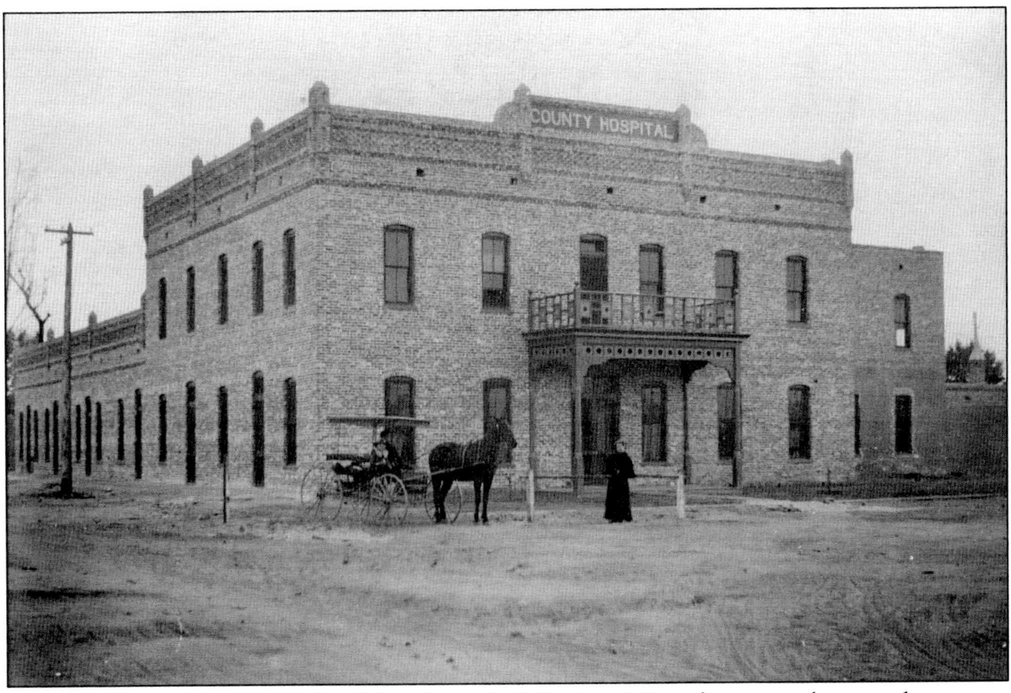

Riverside County purchased the Palma Hotel building in 1897 and converted it into the county hospital. A fire in 1898 caused a temporary closure. Then, on Christmas Day in 1899, a major earthquake struck the valley. (Courtesy Charles Van Fleet.)

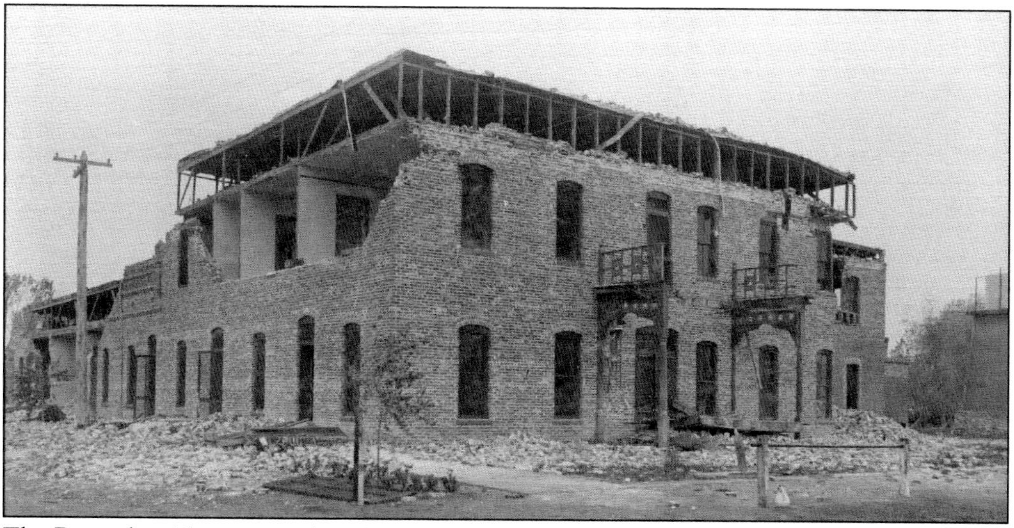

The December 25, 1899, earthquake hit at a magnitude of 6.8, damaging the Riverside County Hospital in old town San Jacinto, as seen here. The building was then torn down completely and not rebuilt. The county constructed a new hospital on Magnolia Avenue in Arlington, now Riverside. (Courtesy Charles Van Fleet.)

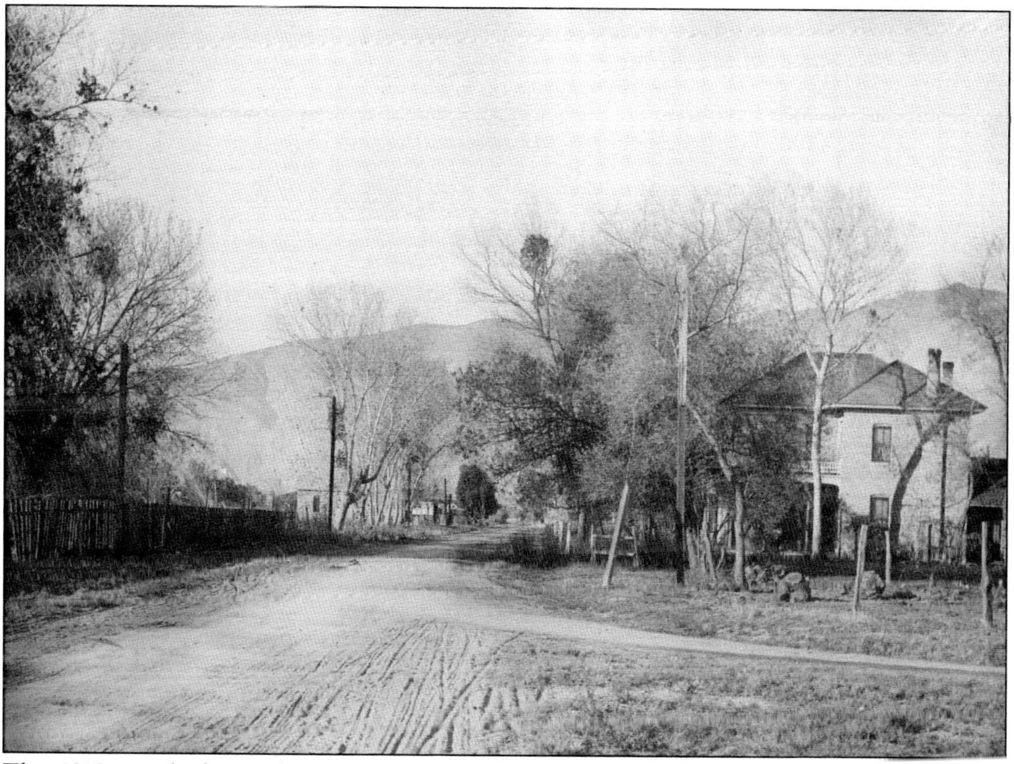

This 1910 view looks north on Hewitt Avenue in old town San Jacinto, with the Jordan House on the right. A friend of Helen Hunt Jackson, Emmaline Jordan lived here and was referred to as "Aunt Ri" in Jackson's *Ramona*. The book was made into a movie, and the citizens of San Jacinto Valley adapted it into a play in 1923. It is presented each year at the Ramona Bowl in Hemet. (Courtesy Charles Van Fleet.)

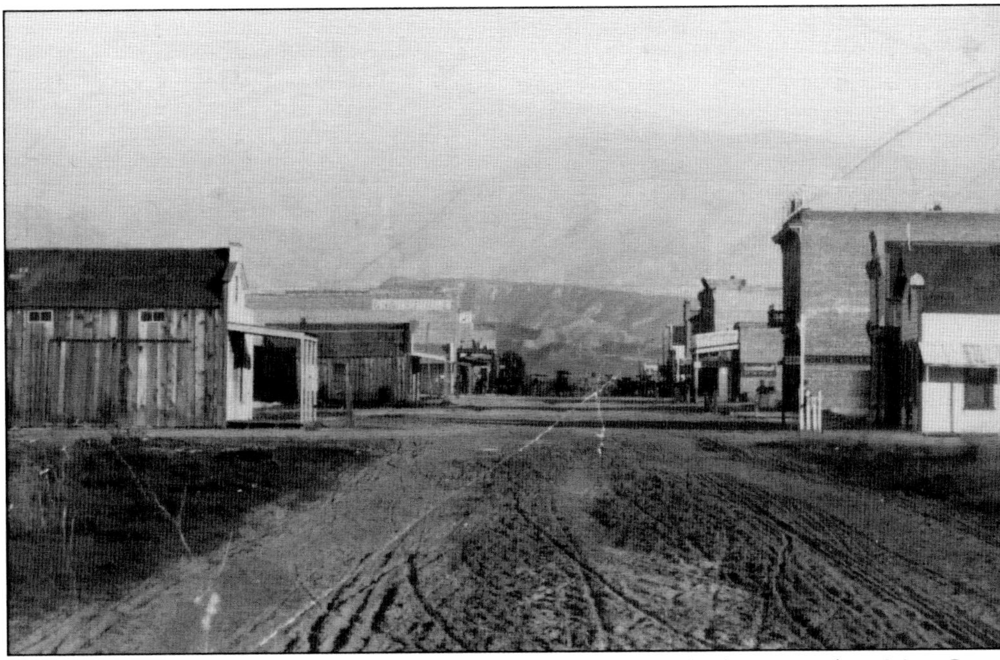

The city of San Jacinto, incorporated in 1888, is seen in this view looking east along Main Street toward Mount San Jacinto. The photograph was taken before the 1897 installation of electric lines and the advent of the automobile. When cars did arrive, the dust they created promoted the paving of city streets. (Courtesy Diane Barnes Miller.)

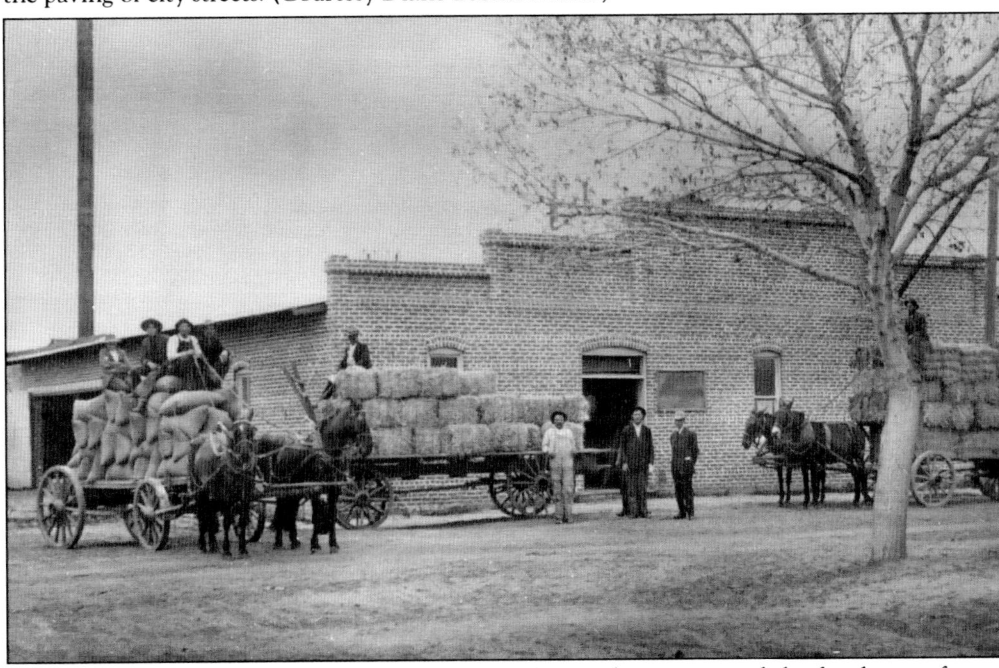

Grain and hay farming were prevalent during the late 19th century, and the freighting of cargo to local farms and supply centers became an important enterprise. In this 1897 photograph, the wagon on the left is loaded with 100-pound burlap sacks of grain. The other two are carrying bales of hay. (Courtesy San Jacinto Museum.)

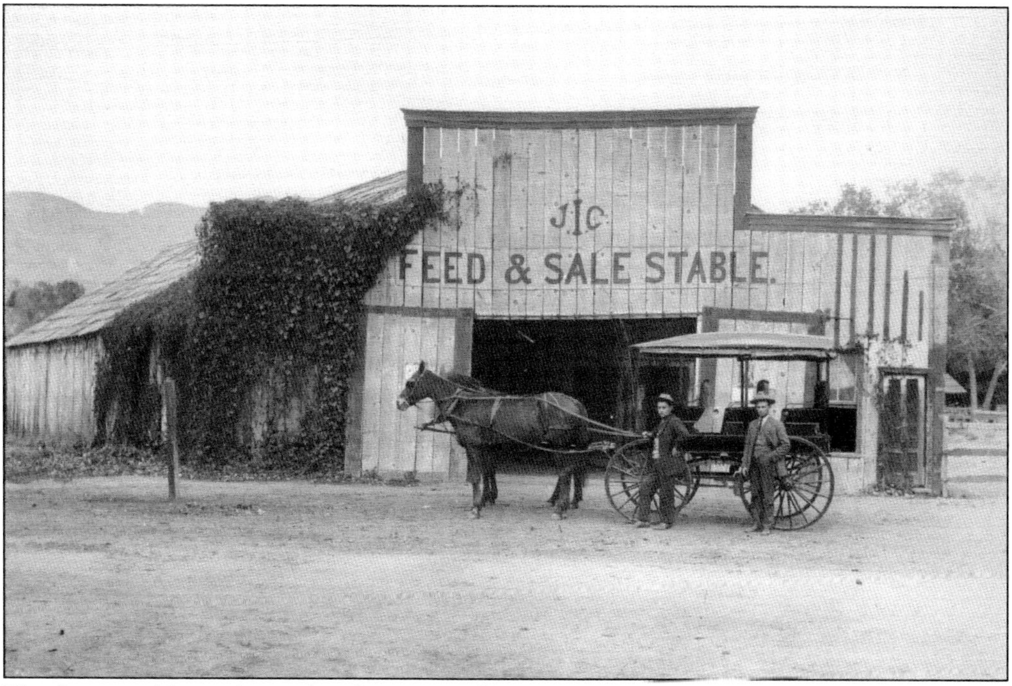

This livery stable was located at the corner of Pico and Central (now Ramona Boulevard), next to the Farmer House Hotel. Proprietors Ralph and Louis Williams stand next to a carriage that was used to transport people from the depot to the hotel. (Courtesy Charles Van Fleet.)

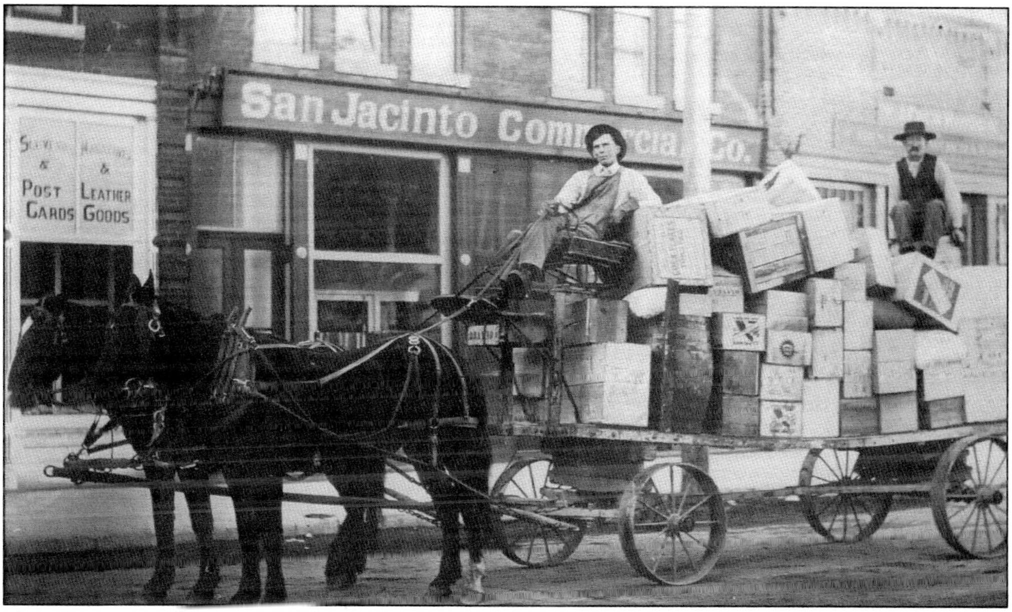

Vern Scranton, the owner of the San Jacinto Transfer Company, transports a load of merchandise from the San Jacinto depot to various stores in the city. Vern, a drayman, leans his arm on a large box of toasted corn flakes. He is denoted a drayman because the iron-wheeled wagon is called a dray. (Courtesy San Jacinto Museum.)

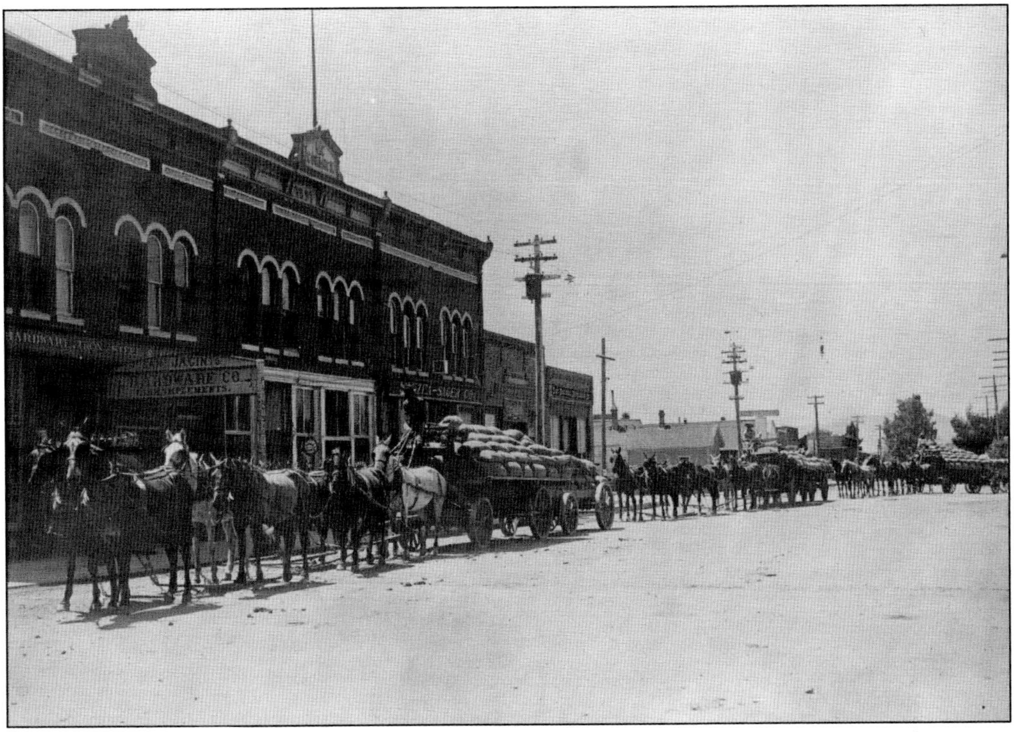

This photograph reveals the extreme importance of cargo transport during this era. The wagon train is lined up on the south side of Main Street in San Jacinto heading east. The wagons are loaded with sacks of grain that have just been harvested to the west of town. The first team stands in front of the San Jacinto Hardware Store. (Courtesy San Jacinto Museum.)

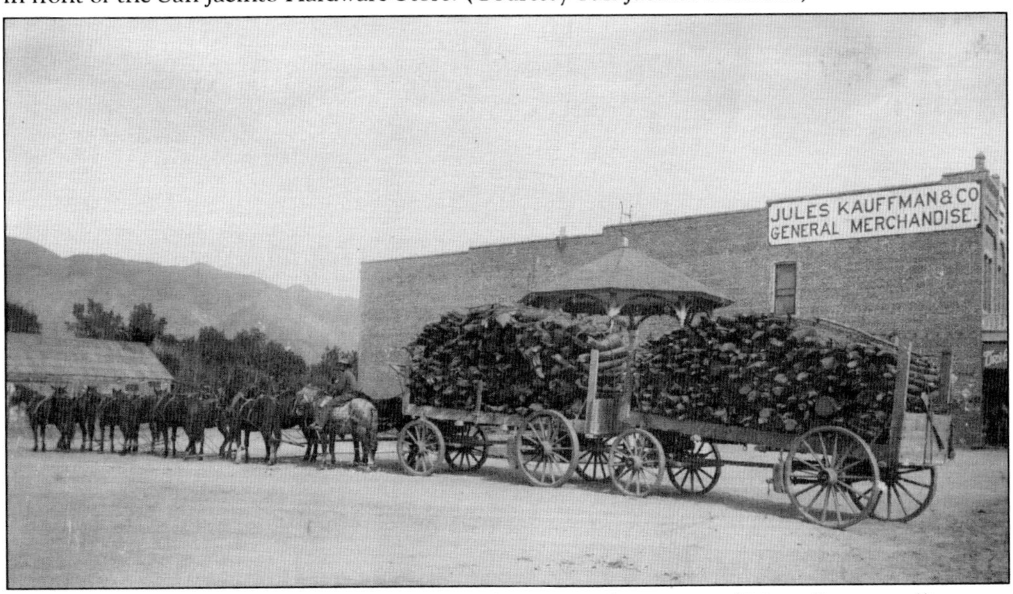

A 10-horse team heads north on San Jacinto Avenue at the corner of Main Street, pulling two wagons heavily loaded with wood. The team driver rides on the last horse on the left, in front of the lead wagon. Judging by size and length, the logs may be used as fence posts, although dry wood was also a popular commodity for fuel. (Courtesy San Jacinto Museum.)

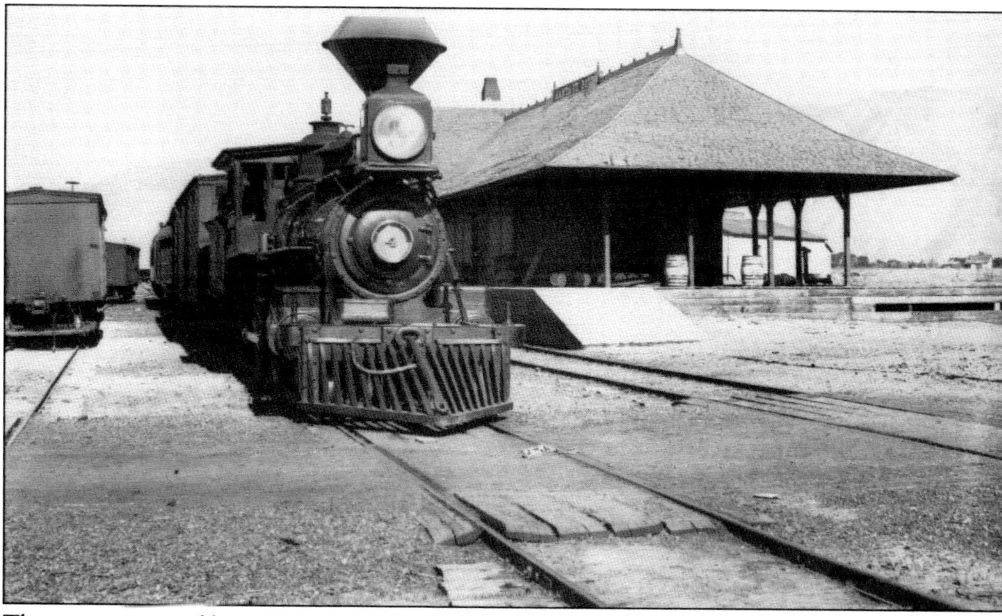

This steam-powered locomotive was one of many used to pull trains to San Jacinto in the 1890s. The first trains arrived in 1888, operating on a line from Riverside via Perris with the terminus at San Jacinto. Diesel replaced steam in the 1950s. Freight trains still come to San Jacinto today, mainly to pick up potatoes from the large Agri-Empire packinghouse. (Courtesy San Jacinto Museum.)

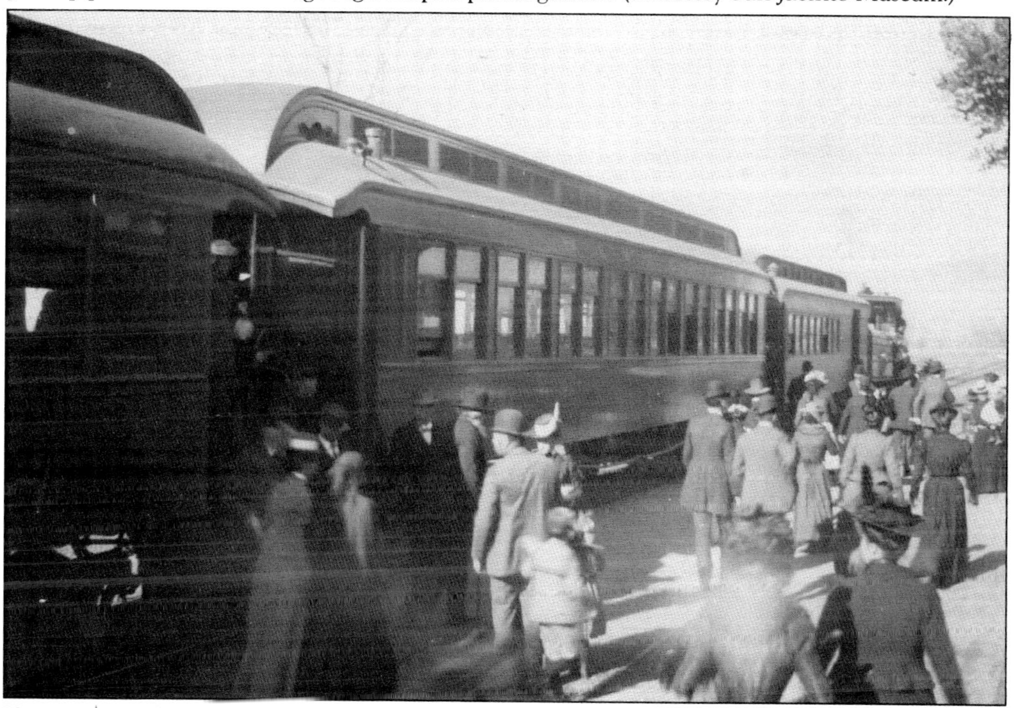

During the railroad peak around 1920, two daily trains brought visitors to the San Jacinto Valley. Travelers had a choice of hot spring resorts at Eden, Gilman, or Soboba and a choice of either the Lockwood or Vosburg Hotel. Some came from Los Angeles just for a day outing in the country. The California Central was the first train in 1888. (Courtesy San Jacinto Museum.)

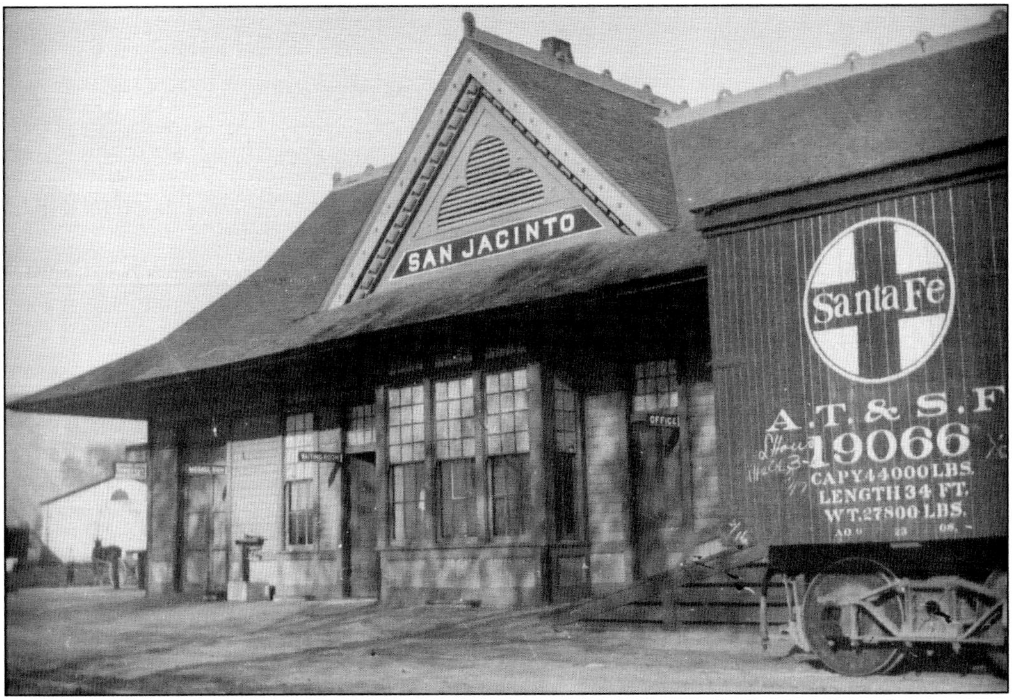

The San Jacinto depot was the terminus of this branch of the Santa Fe Railroad. Both passenger and freight trains used the station. Products leaving the valley between the 1880s and the 1920s were fruits and vegetables, grain, lumber from the San Jacinto Mountains, and lime from the kilns north of town. (Courtesy San Jacinto Museum.)

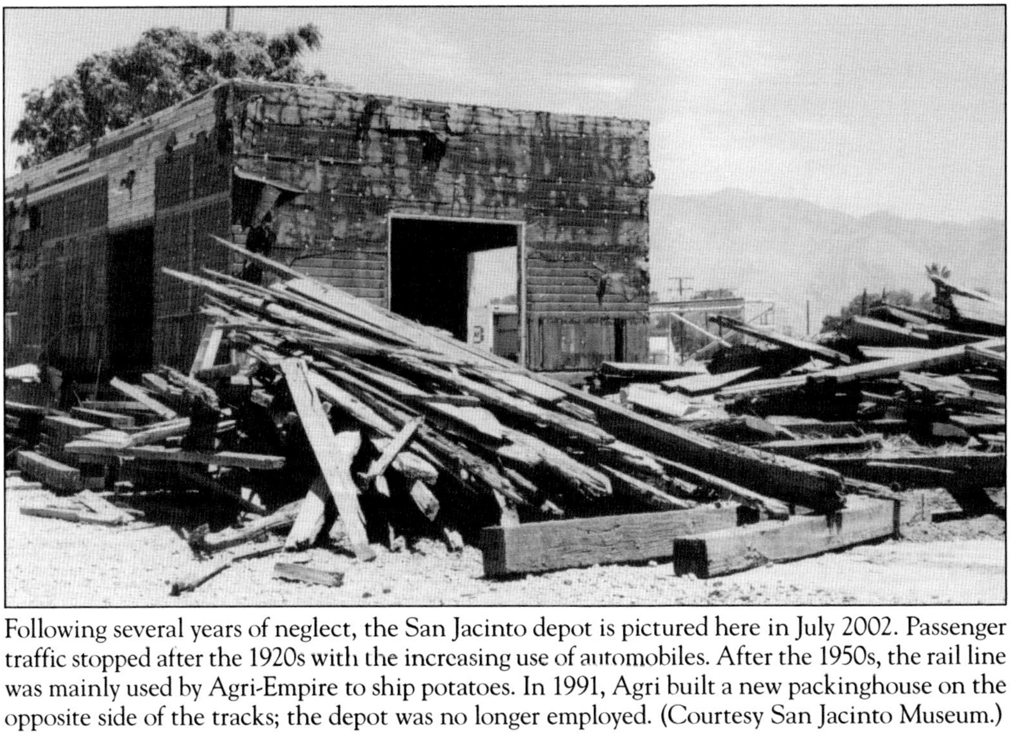

Following several years of neglect, the San Jacinto depot is pictured here in July 2002. Passenger traffic stopped after the 1920s with the increasing use of automobiles. After the 1950s, the rail line was mainly used by Agri-Empire to ship potatoes. In 1991, Agri built a new packinghouse on the opposite side of the tracks; the depot was no longer employed. (Courtesy San Jacinto Museum.)

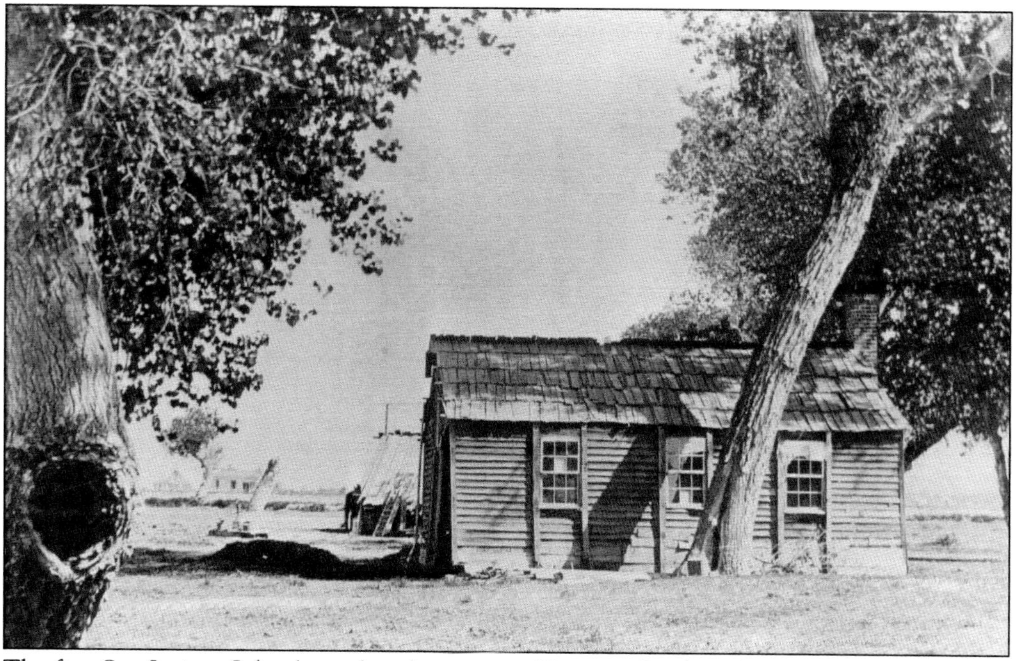

The first San Jacinto School stood at the corner of Ramona Boulevard and Young Street, at the same location as the present-day Mountain View Continuation High School. Classes started in 1869 with only eight students, made up of the Estudillo families and their workers. Previously, from 1865 to 1868, children had been taught in the Estudillo home. In just two years, the San Jacinto School enrollment increased to 45, deeming a larger school imperative. (Courtesy San Jacinto Museum.)

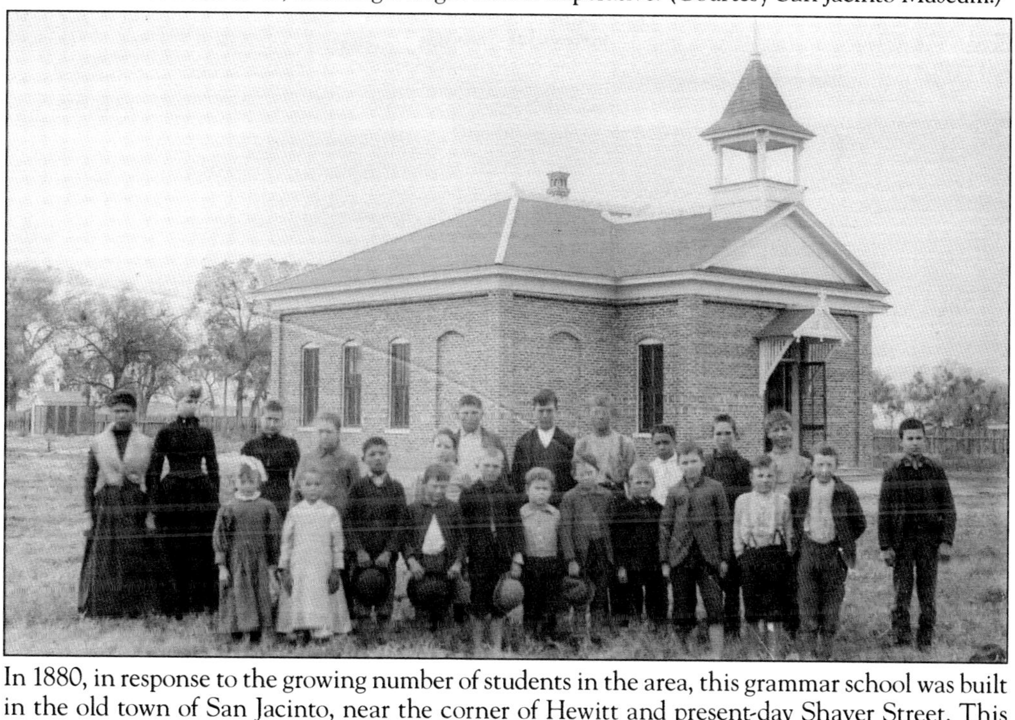

In 1880, in response to the growing number of students in the area, this grammar school was built in the old town of San Jacinto, near the corner of Hewitt and present-day Shaver Street. This structure replaced the one at Ramona and Young. (Courtesy Clarence Swift collection.)

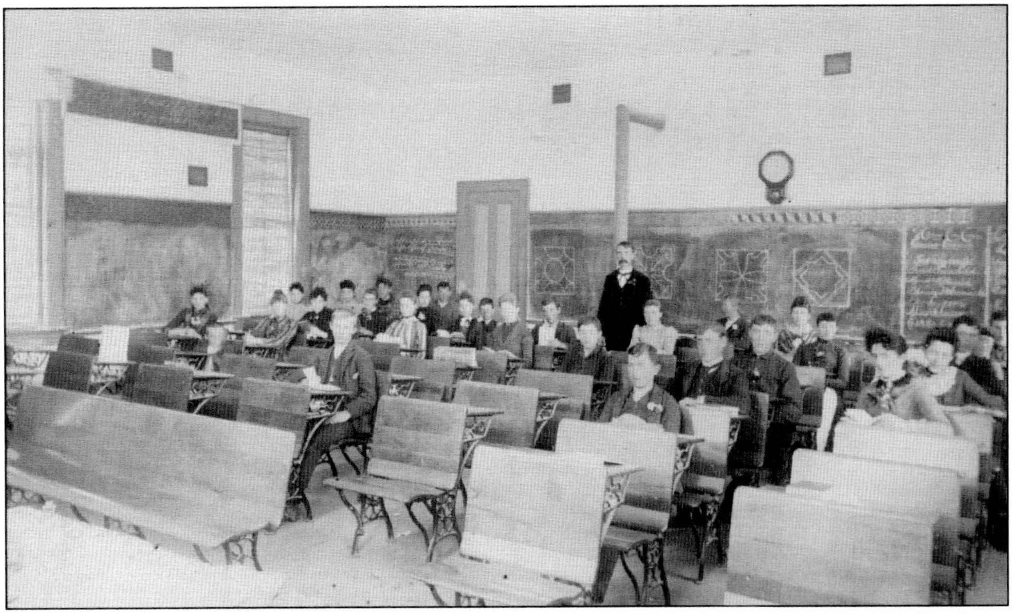

Edward Hyatt stands in the back of a classroom about 1888. The 1885 two-story brick school was located at the corner of San Jacinto Avenue and First Street. Arriving in 1884, Hyatt championed that education be adapted for the individual child. He began teaching at the high school level, graduating the first three students in 1886. His wife, Maggie, taught classes when he was attending meetings for the San Diego Board of Education. (Courtesy San Jacinto Museum.)

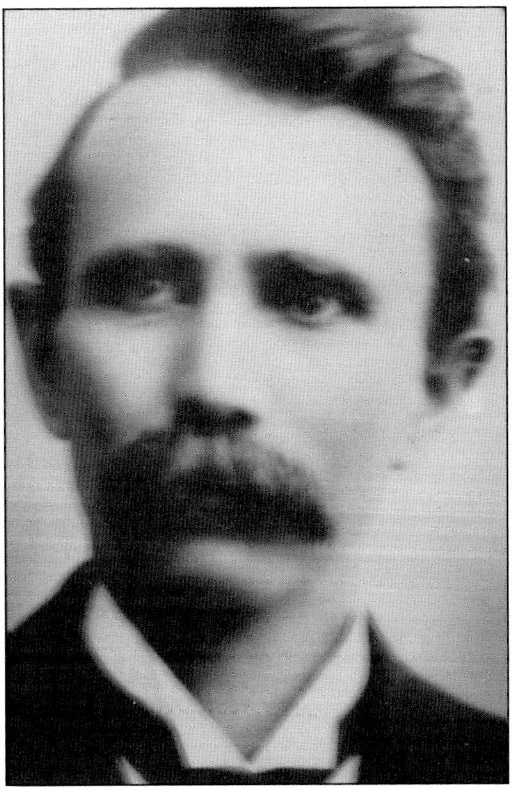

A year after Riverside County's formation in 1893, Edward Hyatt (1858–1919) was elected the county's superintendent of schools. He had sat on the San Diego Board of Education from 1887 to 1893 and had served as California state superintendent from 1906 to 1917. His major accomplishments include establishing a law to enable districts to bear the cost of children's school transportation and the authorization of night school. (Courtesy Linda Ward Skipworth.)

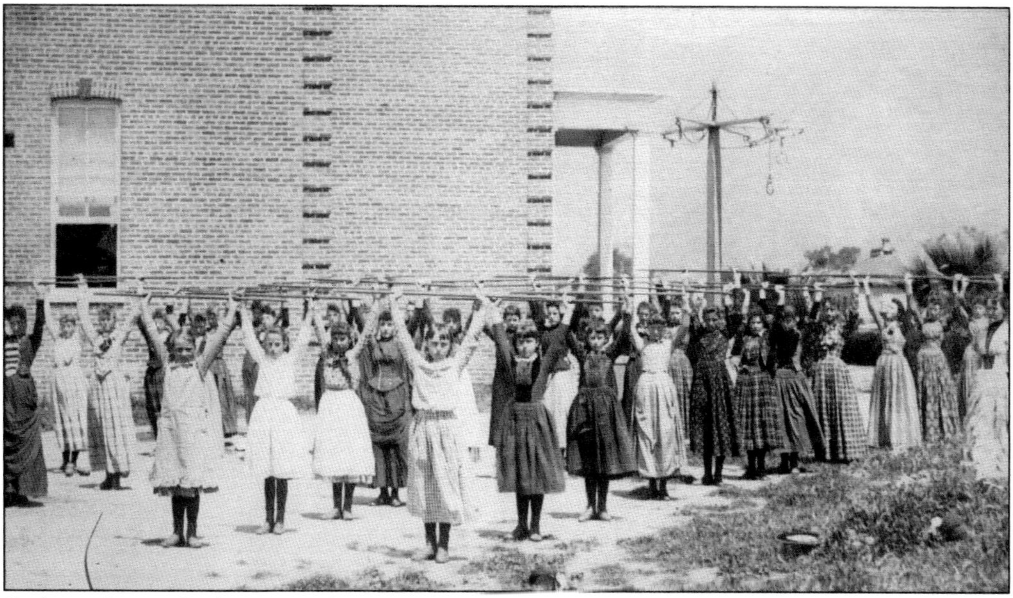

Girls perform calisthenics at the San Jacinto School in the 1880s. Edward Hyatt strenuously promoted physical training for all grades and for both boys and girls. The school had previously been concerned only with the three Rs: reading, 'riting, and 'rithmetic. Hyatt introduced the teaching of natural sciences. While he was state superintendent, he passed a law establishing free schoolbooks for elementary children in 1911. (Courtesy San Jacinto Museum.)

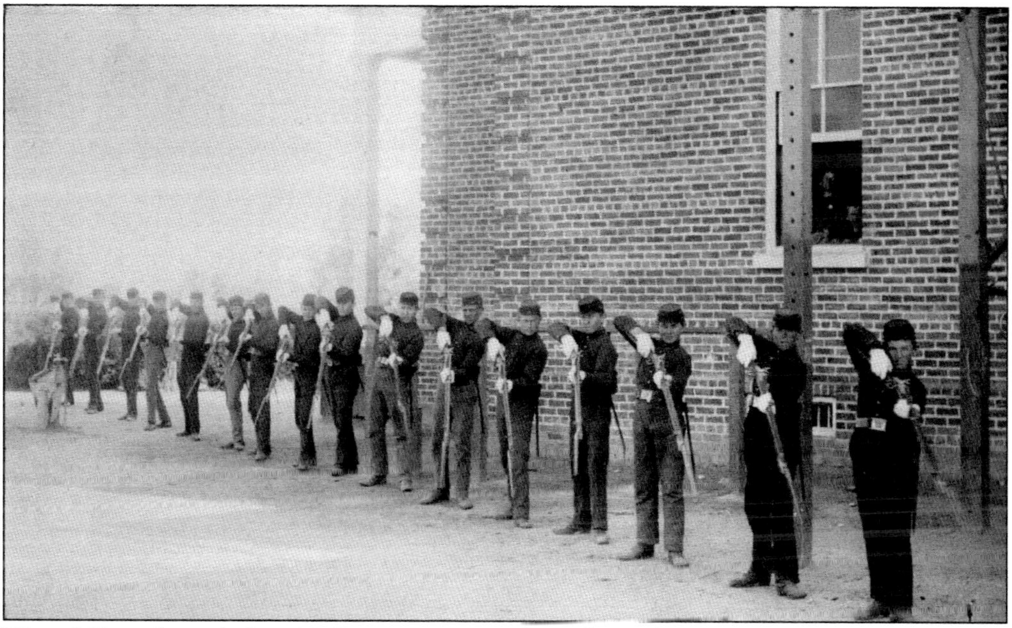

Edward Hyatt formed a boys' drill team using wooden rifles and invited the community to see the boys perform. When they gave the flag salute, however, there was no flag. The board of trustees acted quickly, authorizing funds for 20 Winchester rifles plus an American flag. The student leader was Miguel Estudillo, the son of Jose Antonio Estudillo, one of the original land grant owners. The drill team marched in the Decoration Day Parade, which was led by the GAR and included children from all the San Jacinto Valley schools. (Courtesy San Jacinto Museum.)

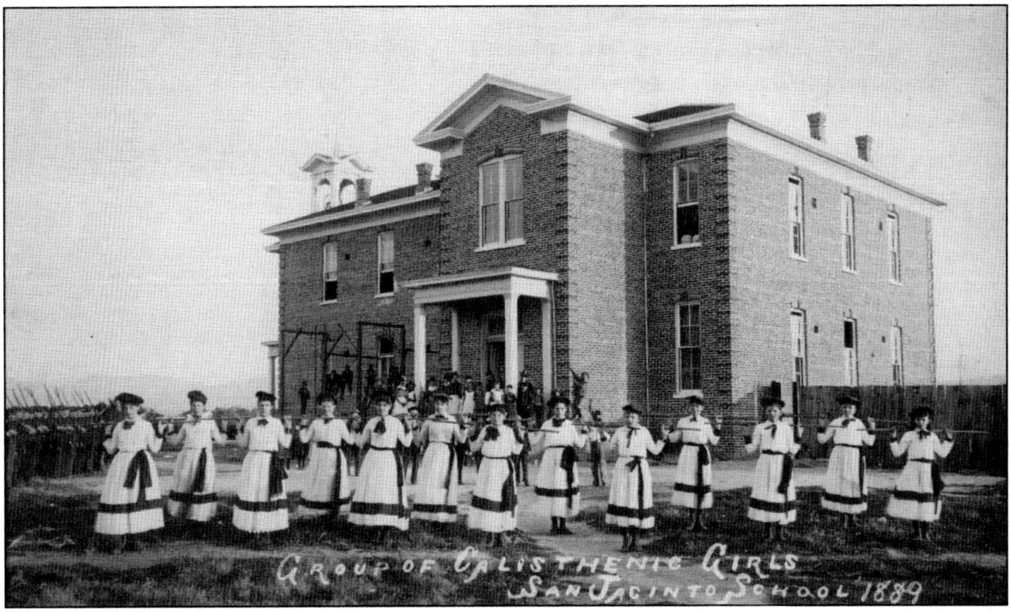

These girls are in special dress to perform for the parents and citizens of San Jacinto. To the left, members of the boys' drill team stand in formation with their rifles, waiting for their turn. Linda Skipworth, a teacher at Hyatt Elementary School, portrays Edward Hyatt for the schoolchildren today, so they will have knowledge of the educator who made many improvements to the system more than 100 years ago. (Courtesy San Jacinto Museum.)

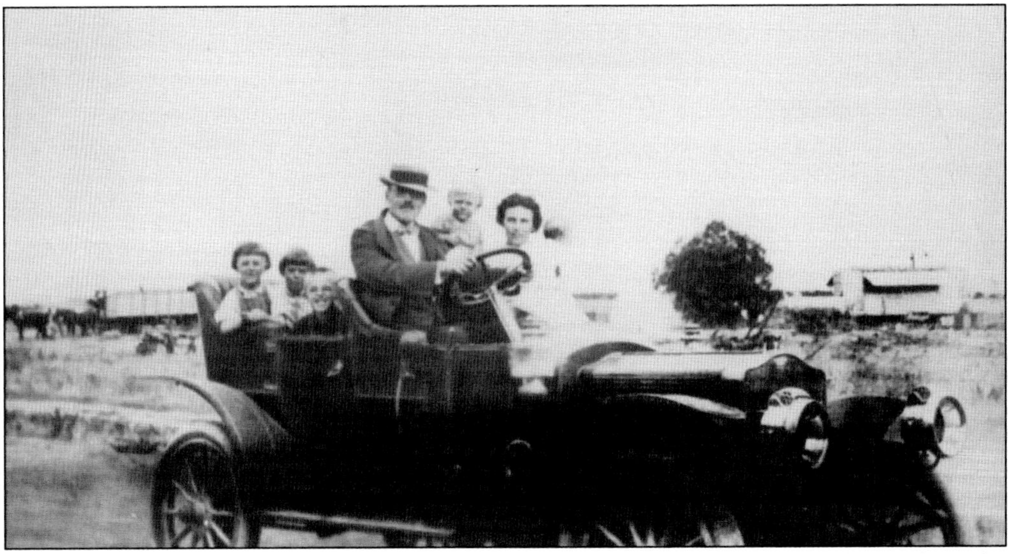

James B. Maxwell came to the San Jacinto Valley to farm. Here he sits beside his wife, Myrtle, at the wheel of his touring car. The couple's children are, from left to right, Robert, Langdon, Kenneth, Margaret, and Naomi (held by Myrtle). Myrtle, a member of the Wardrobe family, lived next door to the Hyatts in the 1880s and played with the Hyatt children. In fact, Edward Hyatt resided with the Wardrobes until buying the adjacent house. Sometime after marriage, the Maxwells moved to the Moreno Valley but still farmed in San Jacinto. (Courtesy Jim Maxwell.)

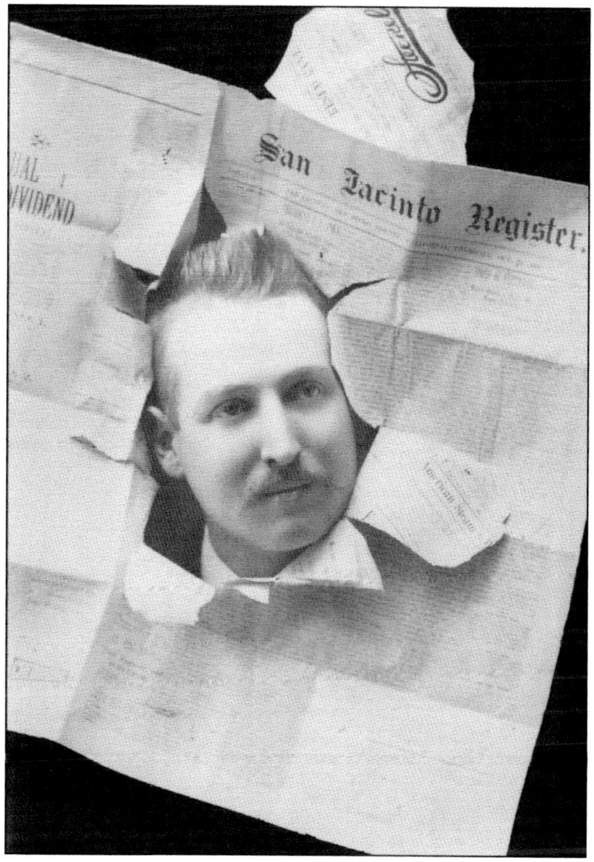

Arthur "Archie" Munn, depicted in this unique photograph, was the owner and editor of the *San Jacinto Register* from 1884 to 1912. The San Jacinto Museum owns a complete collection of *Register* issues from 1884 to 1989, when the newspaper was sold. The papers are available to the public for historical and genealogical research. (Courtesy San Jacinto Museum.)

In 1898, the *San Jacinto Register* office was located on the north side of Main Street and east of San Jacinto Avenue. This newspaper was the first published in what is now Riverside County. Chester Kline bought it in 1912 and served as editor until 1947. Archie Munn, who founded the *Register* in 1884, is seen sixth from left, beside the man at far right. (Courtesy San Jacinto Museum.)

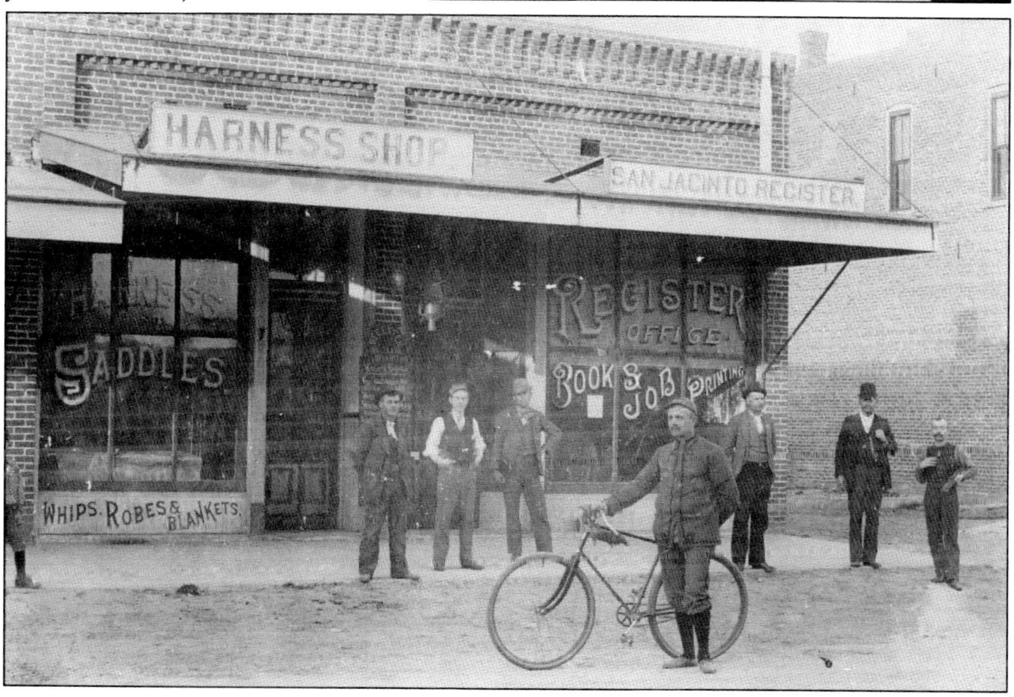

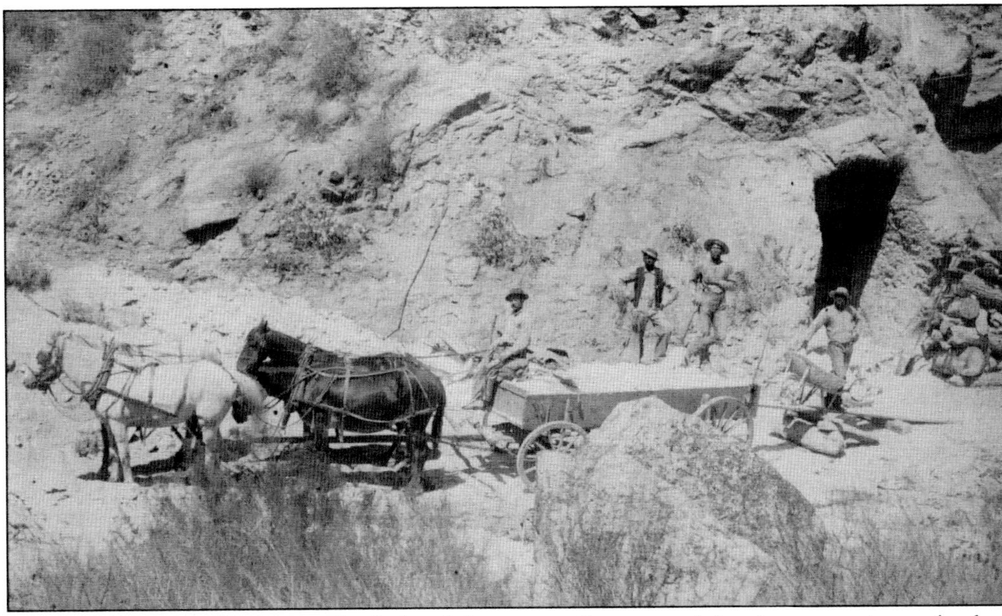

A team of horses pulls a wagon loaded with limestone from one of the three quarries at the foot of the mountains north of San Jacinto, along Gilman and Soboba Roads. When the railroad came to San Jacinto in 1888, it greatly enhanced the ease and effort of moving large quantities of lime to Los Angeles and the surrounding areas. (Courtesy San Jacinto Museum.)

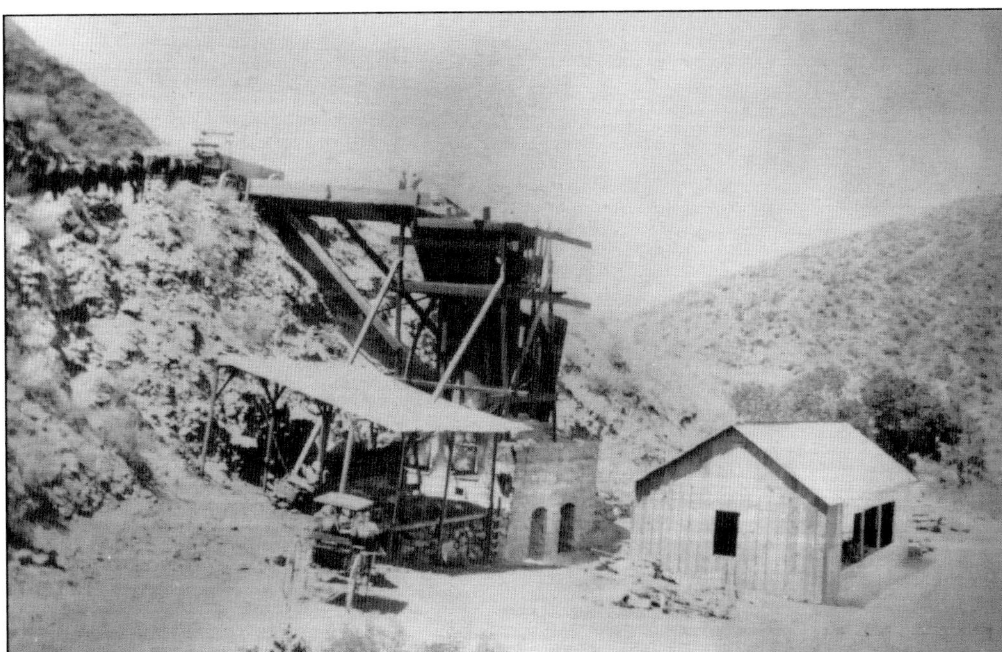

Here limestone rock from the quarry above is dumped into the rock mill below. Once crushed, the rock was heated in nearby kilns to form lime for use in the building industry. This kiln was located along Portero Creek at the entrance of Massacre Canyon. (Courtesy San Jacinto Museum.)

Ferdando Snyder and his son may have started the lime kiln business in San Jacinto as early as the 1870s. They operated the kiln at Massacre Canyon and also owned one at Tehachapi, north of Los Angles. Ferd Snyder said that the San Jacinto lime was the best in the state of California. (Courtesy Clarence Swift collection.)

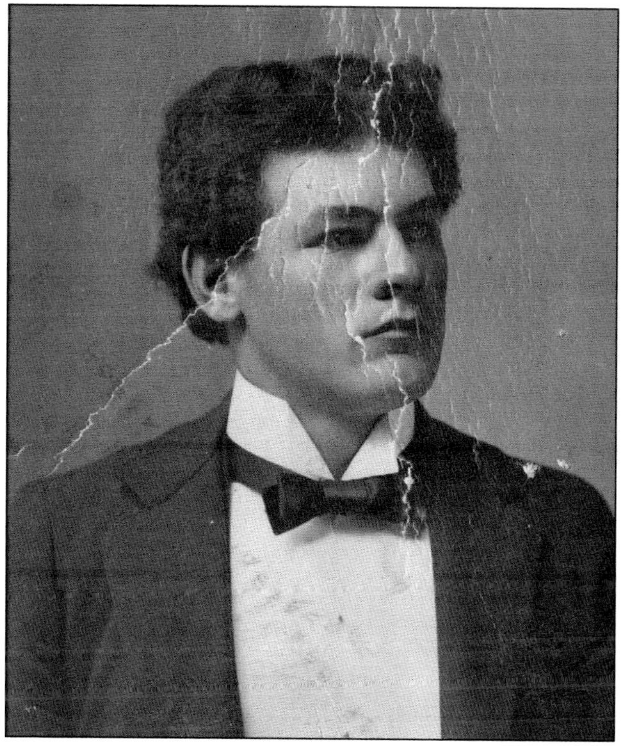

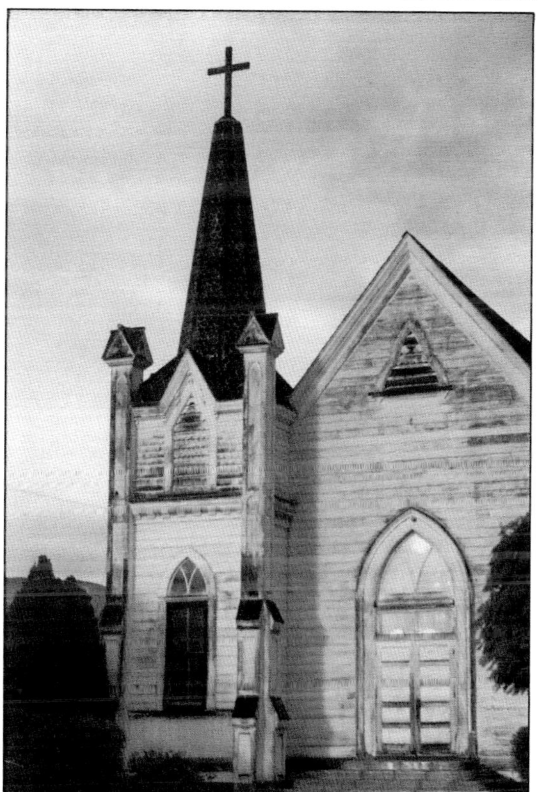

Construction on St. Mary's Catholic Church began at the corner of Santa Fe and Seventh Streets in 1889. In 1905, the church reached parish status, and the name was changed to St. Anthony. Services were held until 1940. (Courtesy San Jacinto Museum.)

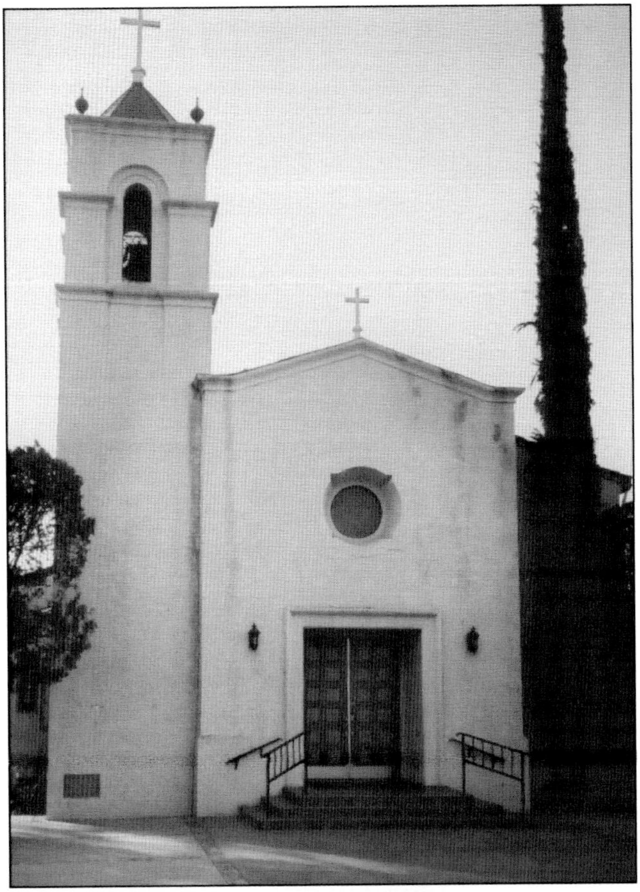

In 1940, the new St. Anthony's Catholic Church replaced the 1889 structure at the corner of Santa Fe and Seventh Streets in San Jacinto. The well-respected parish now has a school on its grounds that accommodates children from kindergarten through eighth grade. (Courtesy Ken Holtzclaw.)

This 1917 Methodist church replaced the one built on the same site in 1884. The original congregation gave financial support to start up Methodist churches in several outlying areas: Valle Vista in 1886, Winchester in 1889, and Hemet in 1902. Electricity was obtained at the original San Jacinto church in 1898. (Courtesy Jack Warneke.)

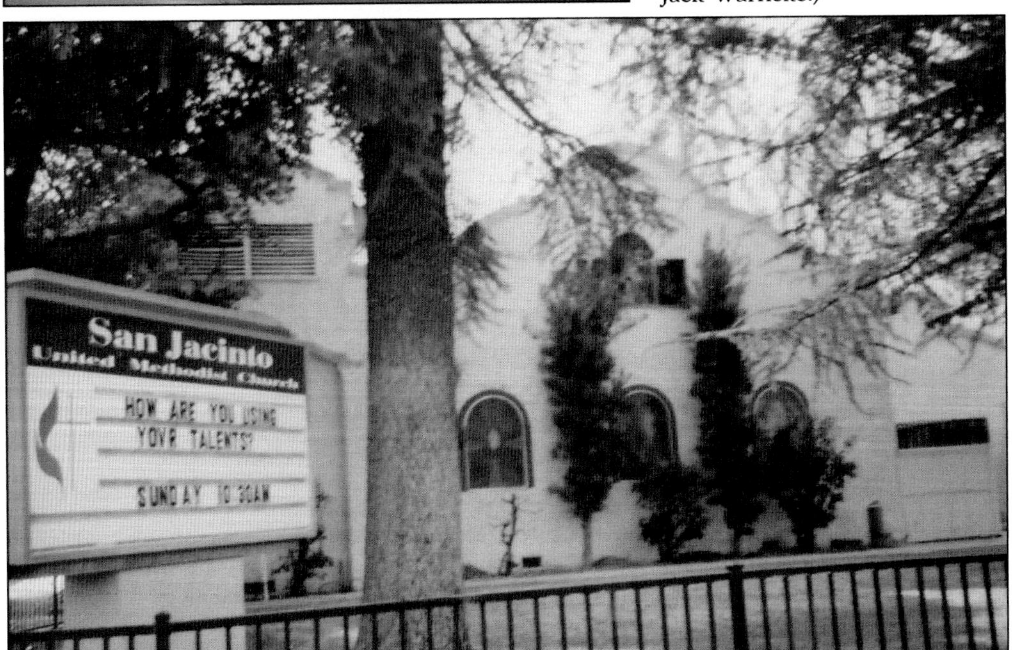

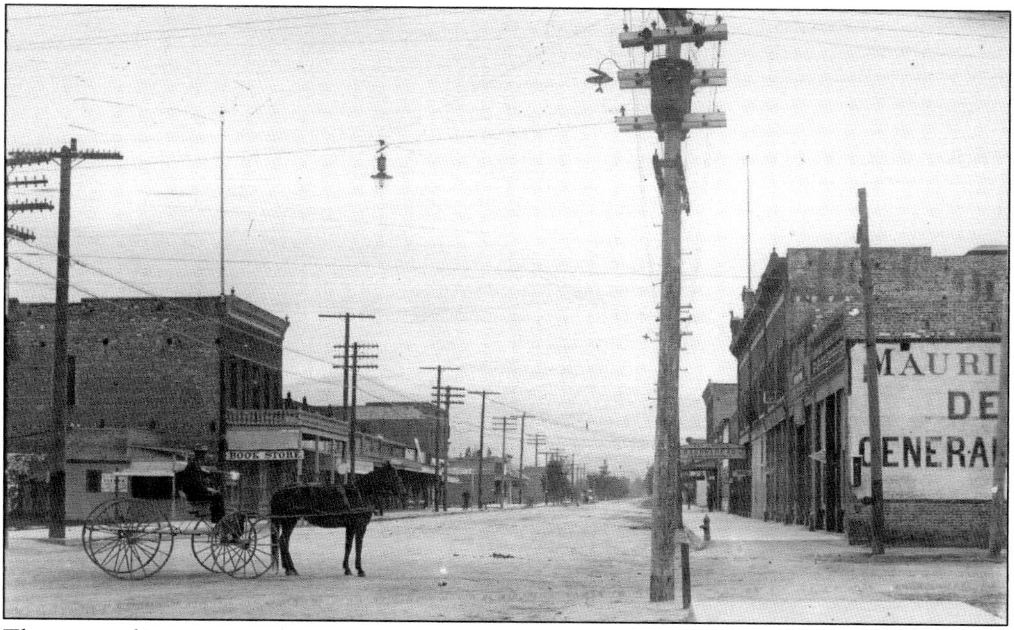

This view of Main Street looks east from San Jacinto Avenue. Electrical service was started in San Jacinto with the incorporation of the city's own power plant near Fifth and Pico Streets in 1897. This photograph was taken sometime after the introduction of electricity, as evidenced by the power pole and transformer on the right side. (Courtesy San Jacinto Museum.)

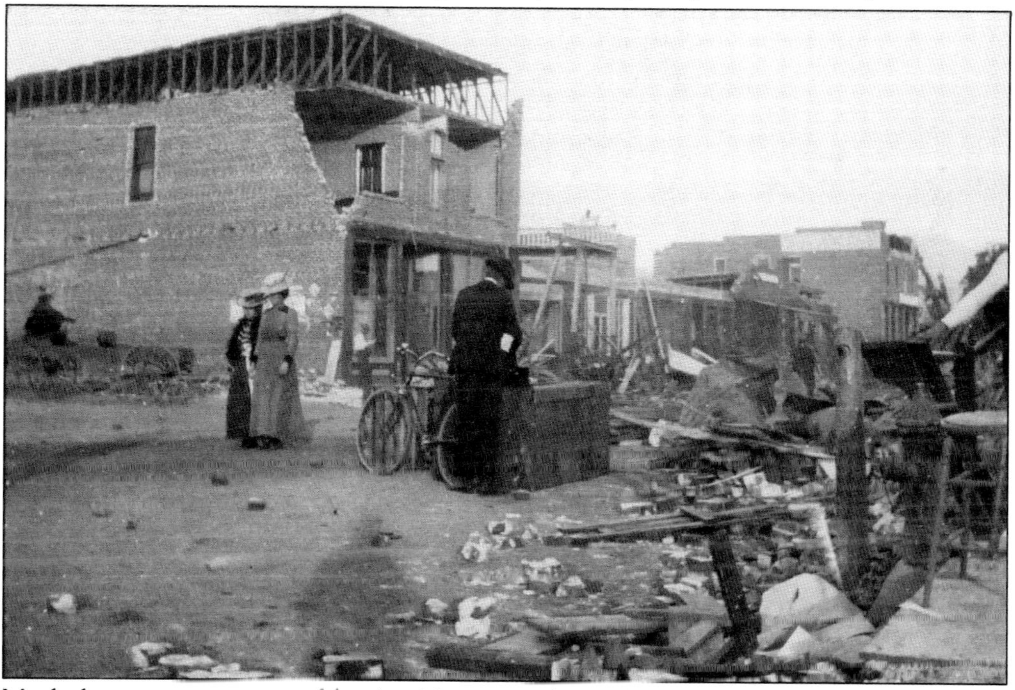

Much devastation was caused by the 6.8-magnitude earthquake that hit San Jacinto on the morning of December 25, 1899. The earthquake lasted only 13 seconds but destroyed nearly all of the brick buildings in the city. Fortunately, both the Francisco and Jose Estudillo landmark houses were spared. (Courtesy San Jacinto Museum.)

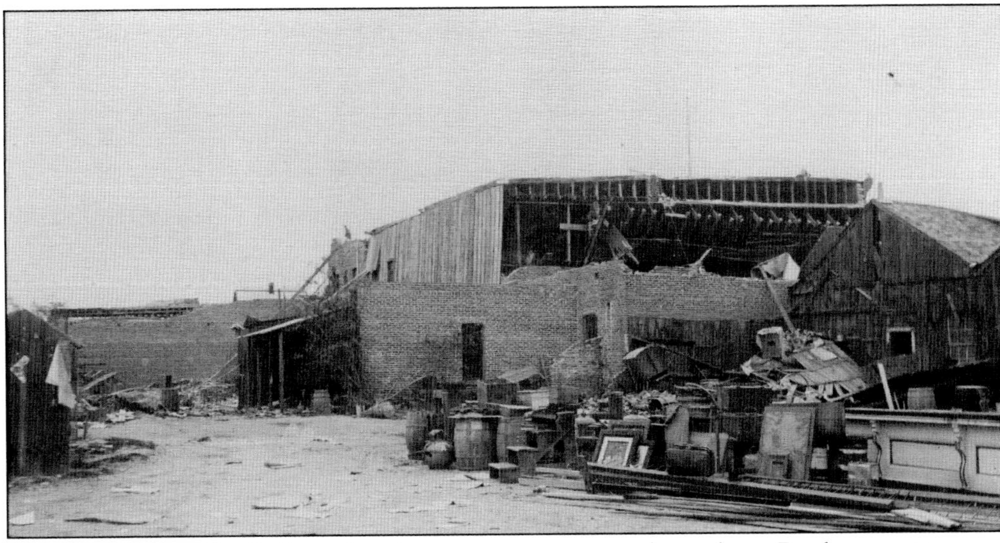

The damage from the 1899 earthquake was very severe, as shown here. But because it was on Christmas Day and all the businesses were closed, the loss of life was fortunately avoided in San Jacinto proper. The only fatalities were on the nearby Soboba Reservation, where six Soboba women were killed when an adobe structure collapsed. (Courtesy San Jacinto Museum.)

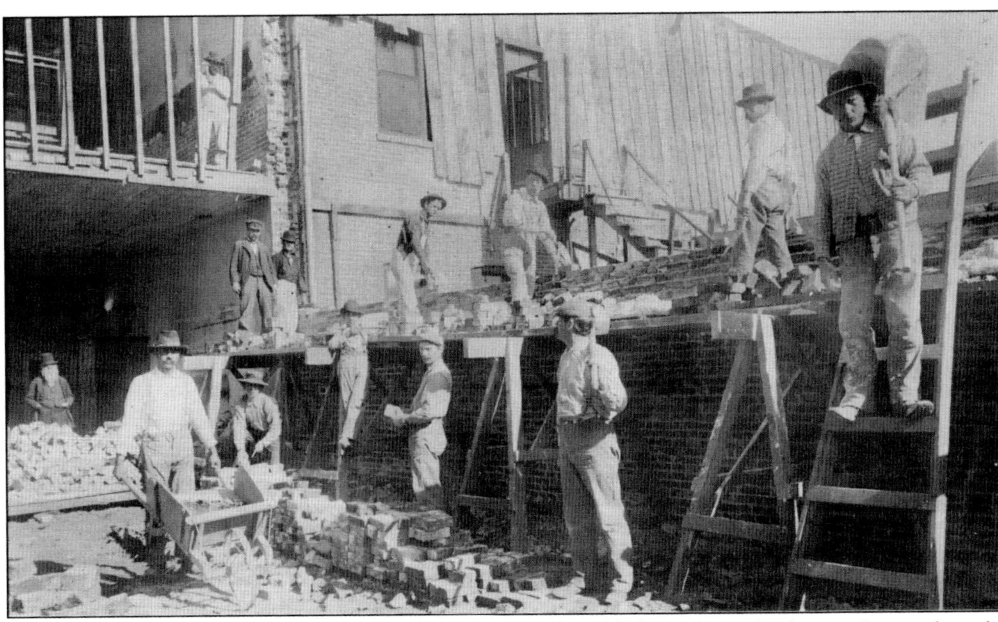

Workers rebuild a structure in San Jacinto with bricks that fell from the walls during the earthquake of 1899. At this point, they are still not using steel reinforcing to prevent structural failure. Consequently, the workers will see the devastating results again in another earthquake in 1918. (Courtesy Fredie H. Ropers.)

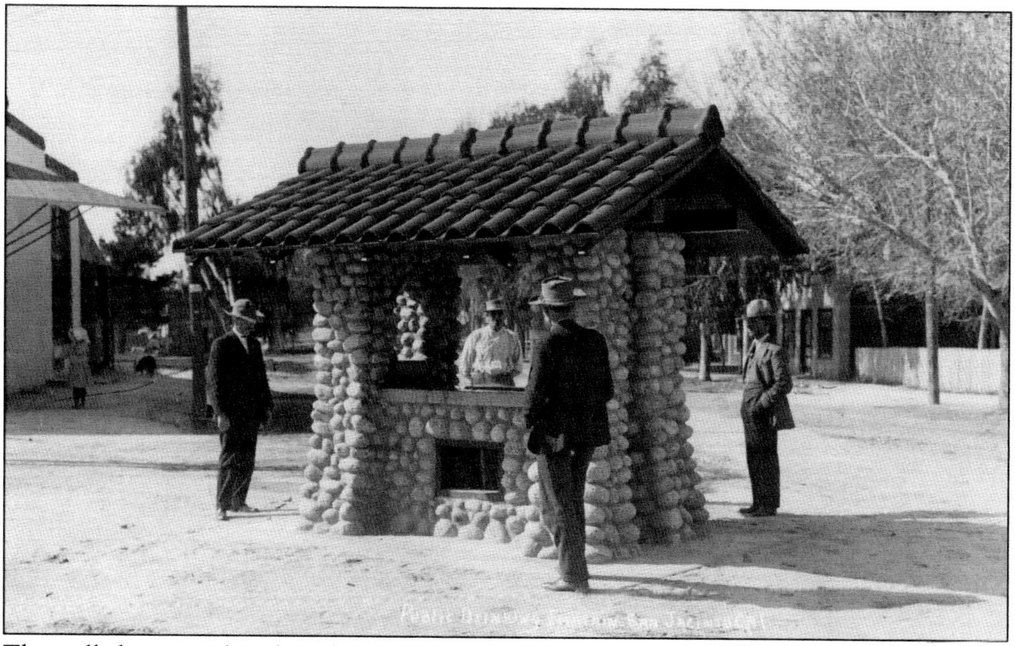

The well that was placed in the middle of the five-corner intersection of Main Street, San Jacinto Avenue, and Central (Ramona) Boulevard is pictured in 1910. Reportedly donated to the citizens of San Jacinto by the Women's Christian Temperance Union, the well was a landmark for more than 50 years. The Vosburg Hotel is visible in the right background. (Courtesy San Jacinto Museum.)

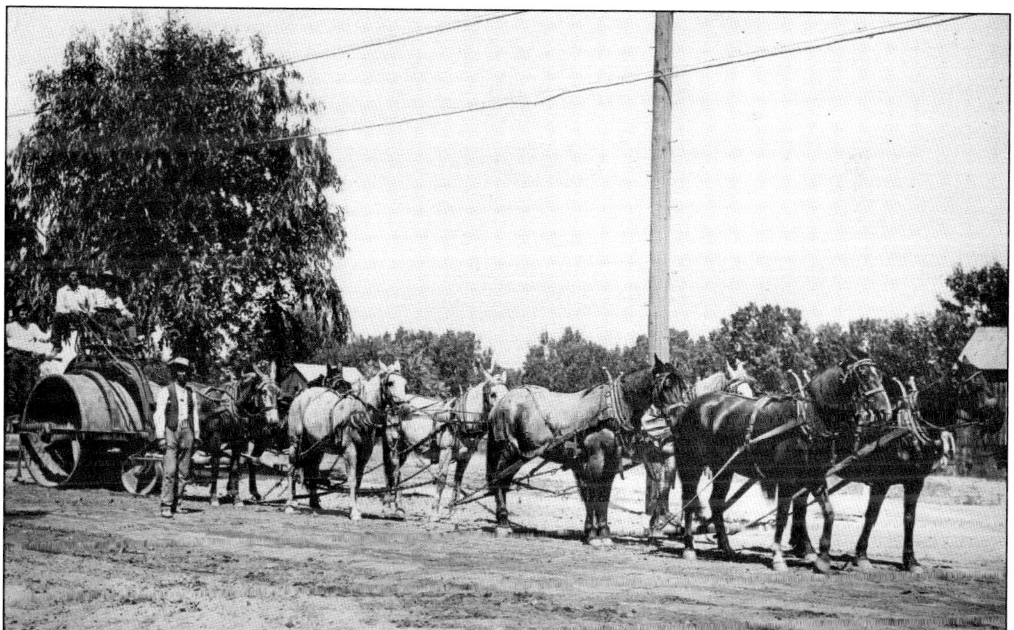

At the end of the 19th century, horses and mules still proved important entities for farming, hauling cargo, traveling, and other tasks. They would remain so until some time after the advent of the automobile and the sophistication of farm machinery. Here a team of eight horses pulls a roller machine to pack the roadbed. (Courtesy San Jacinto Museum.)

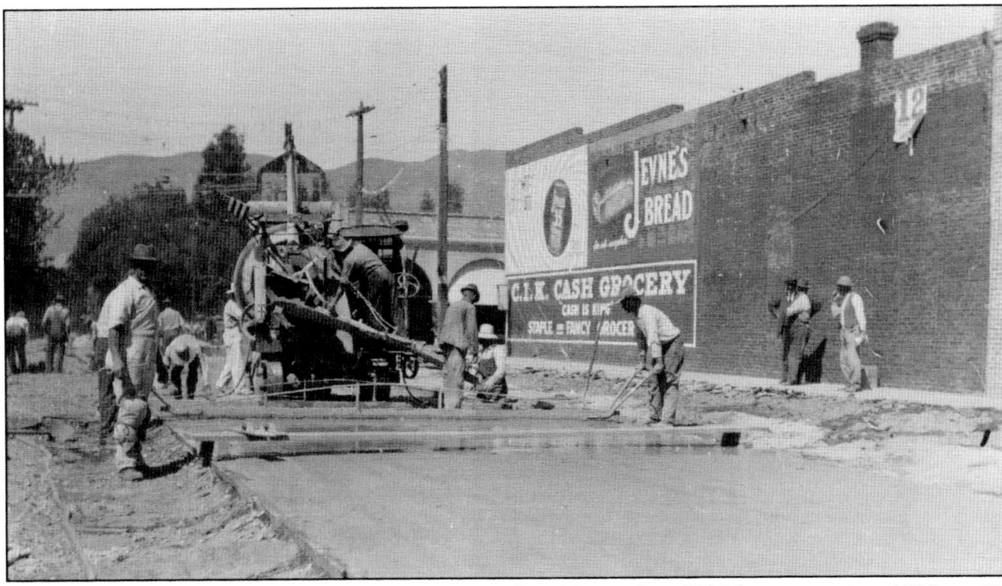

A bond to pave San Jacinto's streets was passed in November 1916 by a margin of 333 to 33. It became prudent to pave at this time, not only for ease in travel, but also to control the dust caused by the faster-moving automobiles. Concrete is poured for road construction on San Jacinto Avenue near the corner of Main Street. (Courtesy San Jacinto Museum.)

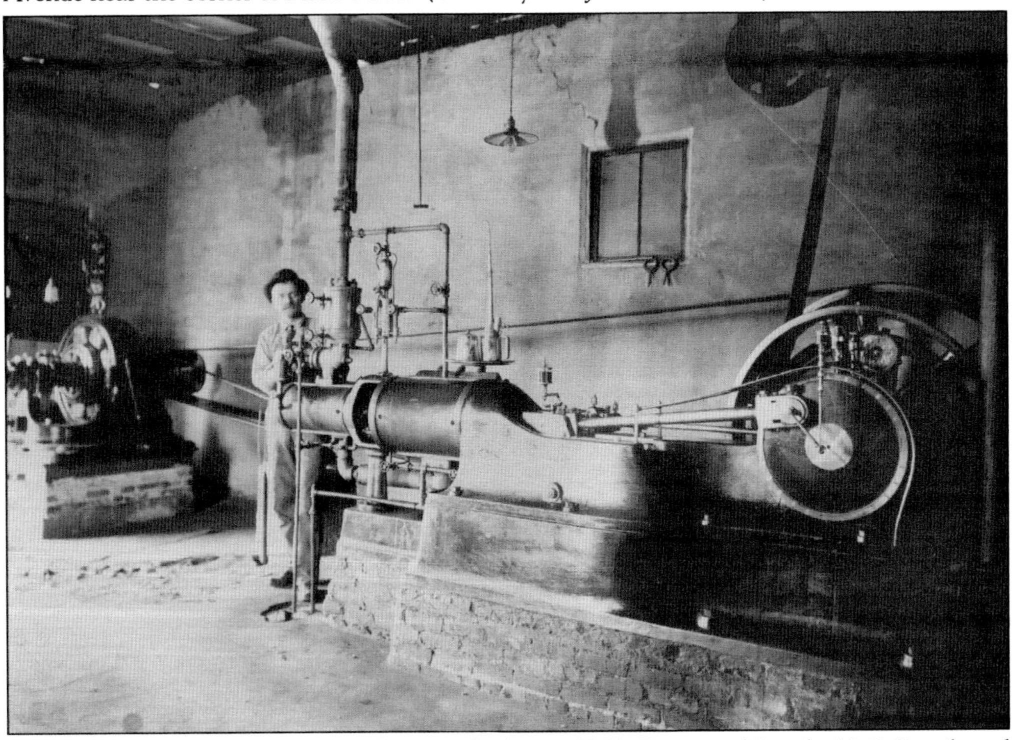

In 1897, San Jacinto's first electric plant was built near Fifth Street and Pico by H. S. Roach and Charles Chambers. The plant, which was updated in 1905, provided electricity for the city. This photograph of the generator was taken inside the electric plant building in 1910; an unidentified maintenance man stands to the side. (Courtesy Charles Van Fleet.)

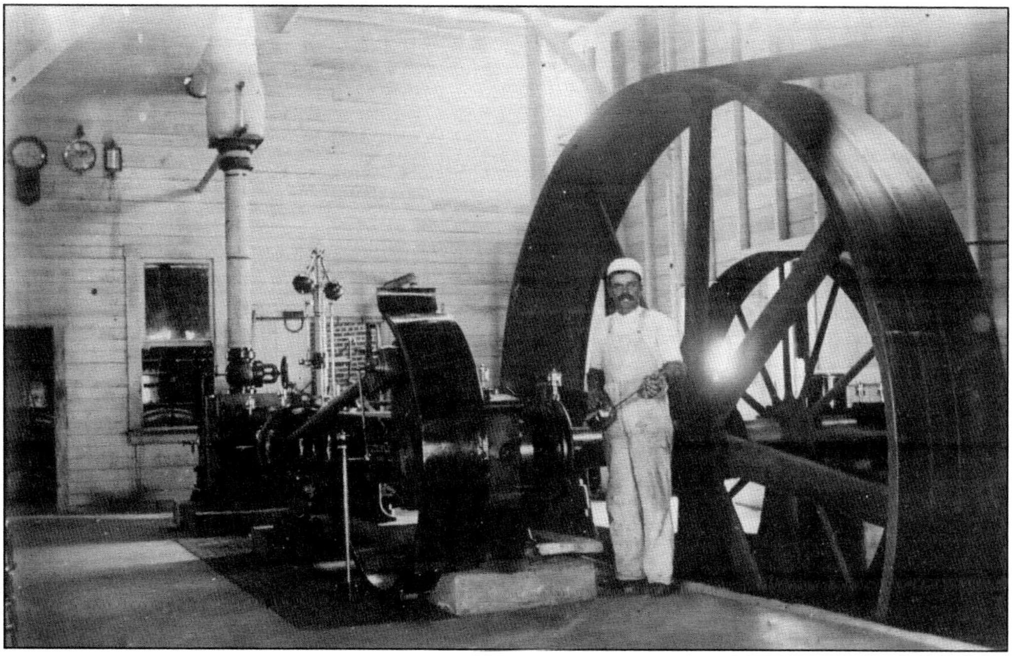

This 1910 view of the electric plant reveals the mechanical extensity of the operation. An unidentified operator stands by with an oil can in his hand. Due to this plant, the first electric streetlights were installed in 1912. Charles Van Fleet, who took this photograph, operated equipment in the plant while attending San Jacinto High School. (Courtesy Charles Van Fleet.)

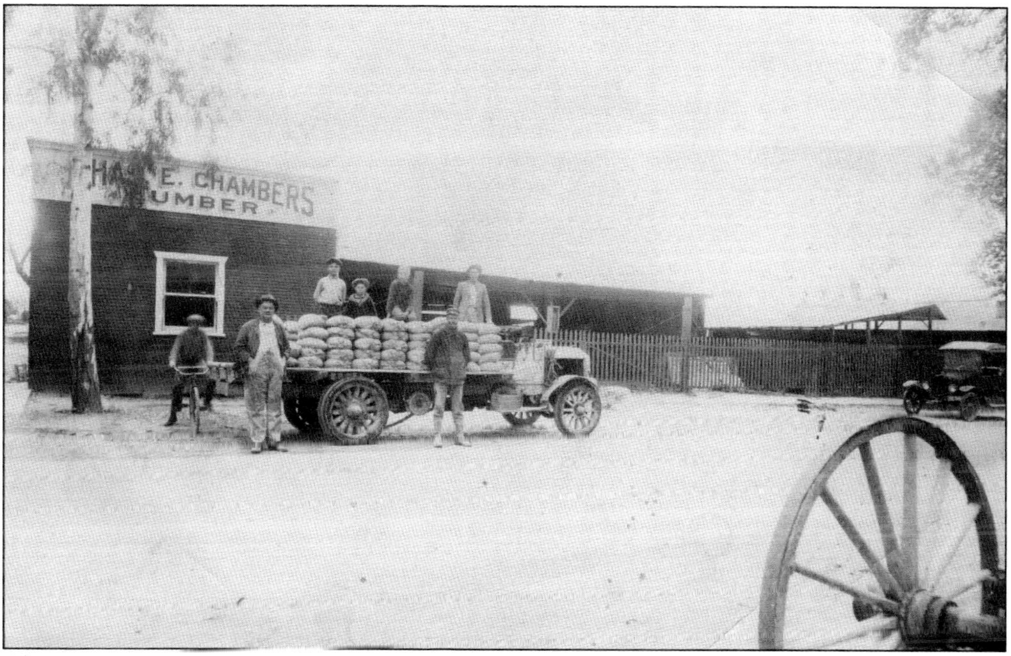

Charles E. Chambers owned the Charles E. Chambers Lumber Company in San Jacinto and co-owned the electric company. He also started the San Jacinto Ice Company. The lumberyard was located on the east side of San Jacinto Avenue between Fifth and Sixth Streets. Chambers, in overalls, stands at the rear of the loaded truck. (Courtesy San Jacinto Museum.)

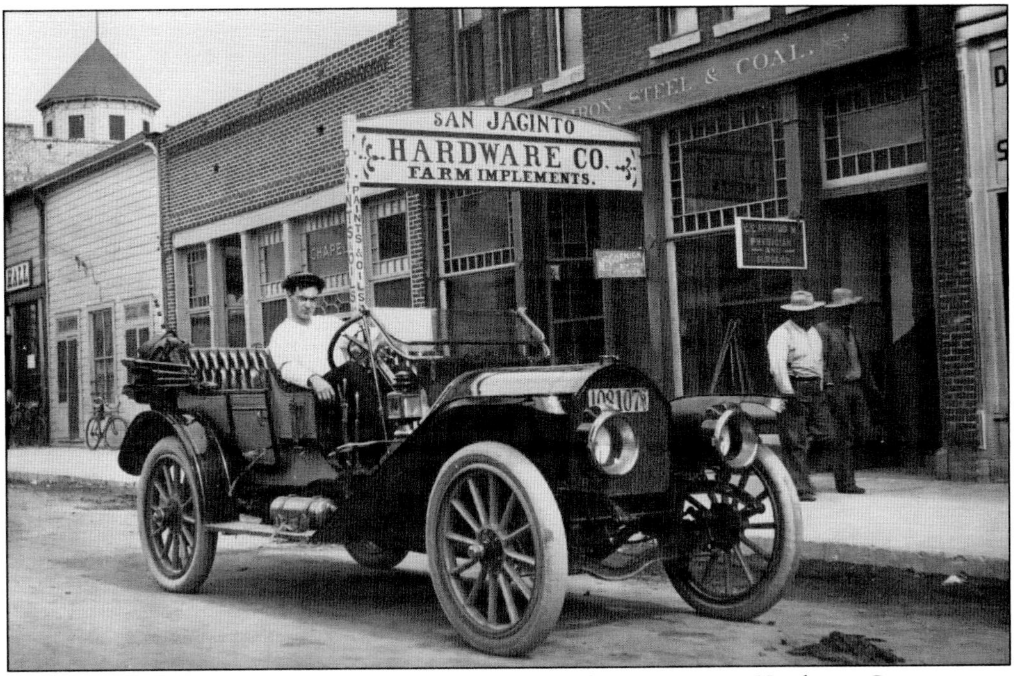

A San Jacinto resident sits in his new car in front of the San Jacinto Hardware Company, on the south side of Main Street, in 1914. The sign above the building's windows indicates that the store sells hardware, iron, steel, and coal. A note of interest is the sign jutting from the wall overhead the two walking men. It reads, "D. E. Arnold, M.D. Physician and Surgeon." (Courtesy San Jacinto Museum.)

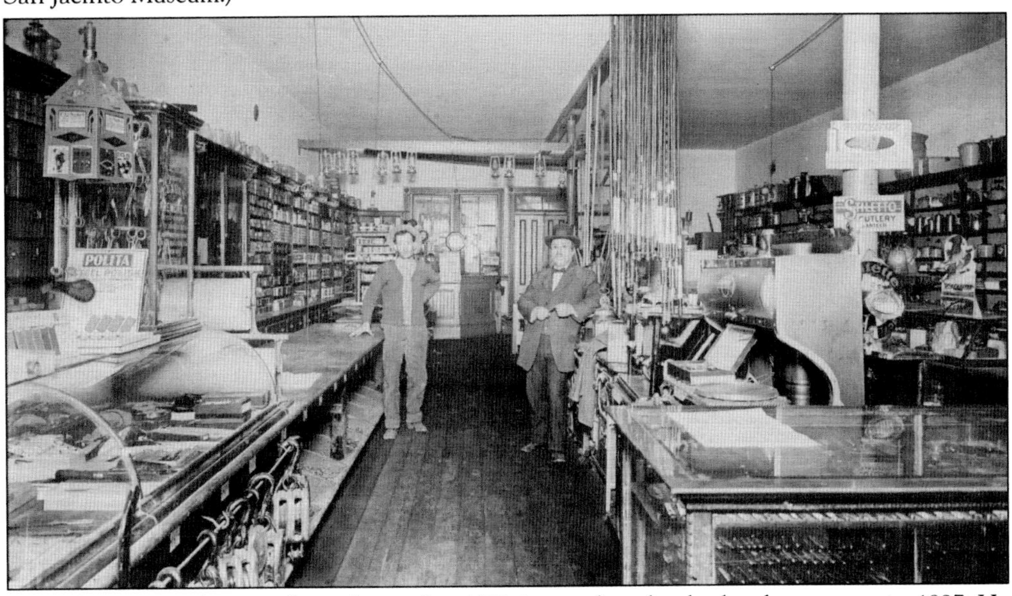

John Shaver, standing on the right in this 1911 image, bought the hardware store in 1897. He came to San Jacinto in 1891, started a lumber mill, and helped to found the San Jacinto Bank. He was elected Riverside County supervisor from 1895 to 1918 and again from 1922 to 1934, serving a total of 36 years. Shaver Street, south of Seventh Street, was named in his honor. (Courtesy San Jacinto Museum.)

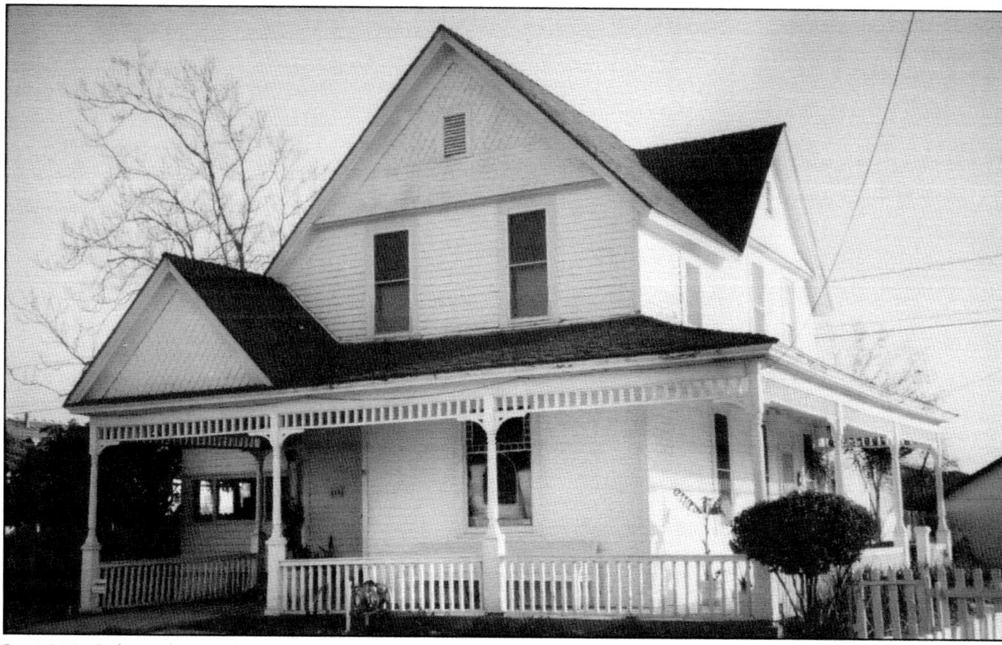

In 1912, John Shaver had this Victorian-style residence built on east Main Street at the corner of Alessandro Boulevard. During the 1980s, the house was used in the television movies *Lassie* and *The Summer of Swans*. William and Evelyne Burke owned the home from 1963 until 1974. Previous owners once told the couple that the house was haunted. The friendly ghost, Arbie, reportedly rocked in a chair while watching television and played tricks on people by pulling their hair and knocking on wood. (Courtesy Ken Holtzclaw.)

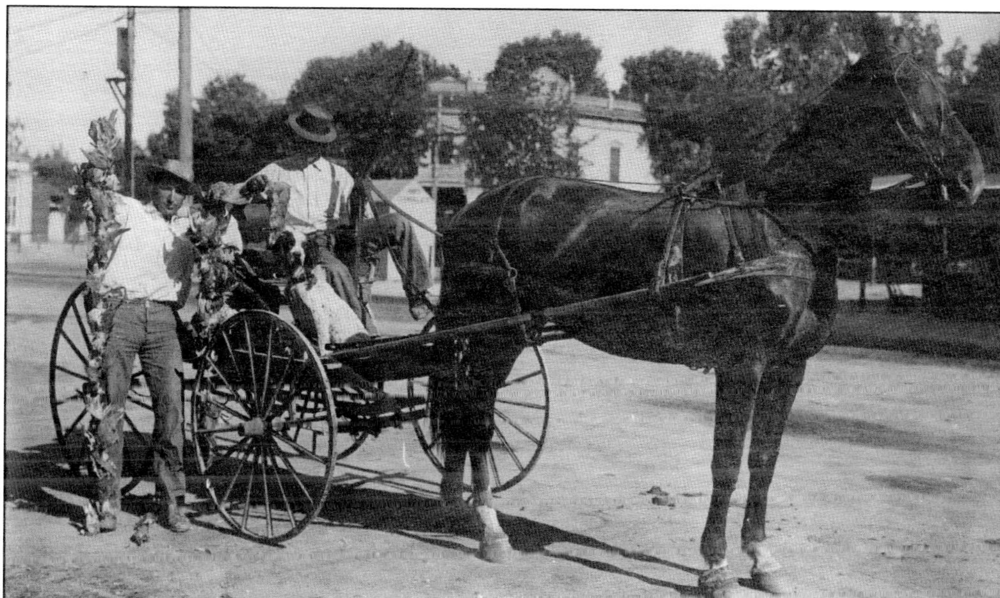

Judge Frazier Sallee of San Jacinto rests in a buggy after arriving from a hunt in the surrounding area around 1900. He holds a small rabbit in his right hand and a shotgun in his lap. Hunting was a desired sport during these years. Brother Joe Sallee stands next to the buggy holding a string of wild birds. (Courtesy Evelyn Sallee Bowline.)

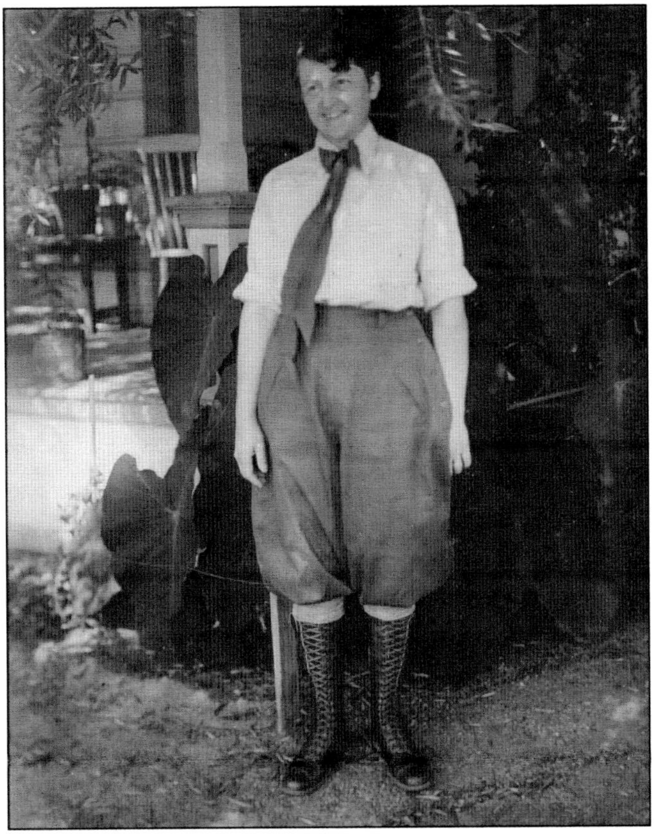

Mary Sallee, the wife of Judge Frazier Sallee, illustrates the style of ladies' outdoor apparel in the early 1900s. Elements of interest in Mary's outfit are the high multiple-laced boots and the knickers. Mary was a founding member of the San Jacinto Museum. (Courtesy San Jacinto Museum.)

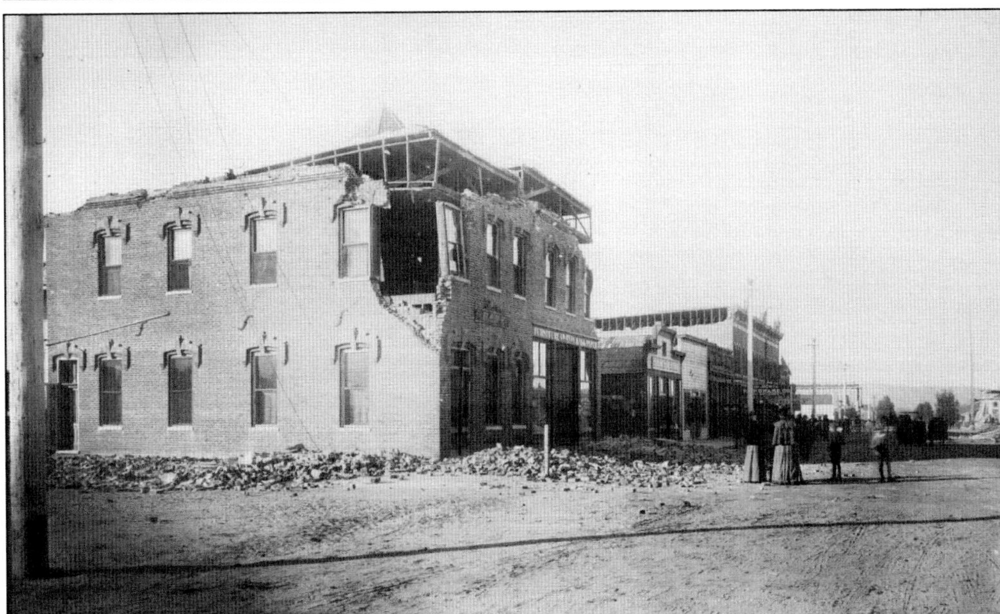

This eastward view shows Main Street and Sheriff Avenue soon after the 1899 earthquake, as witnessed by the rubble of bricks still on the road around the buildings. Structures were all restored, and the businesses returned to normal. (Courtesy Fredie H. Rogers.)

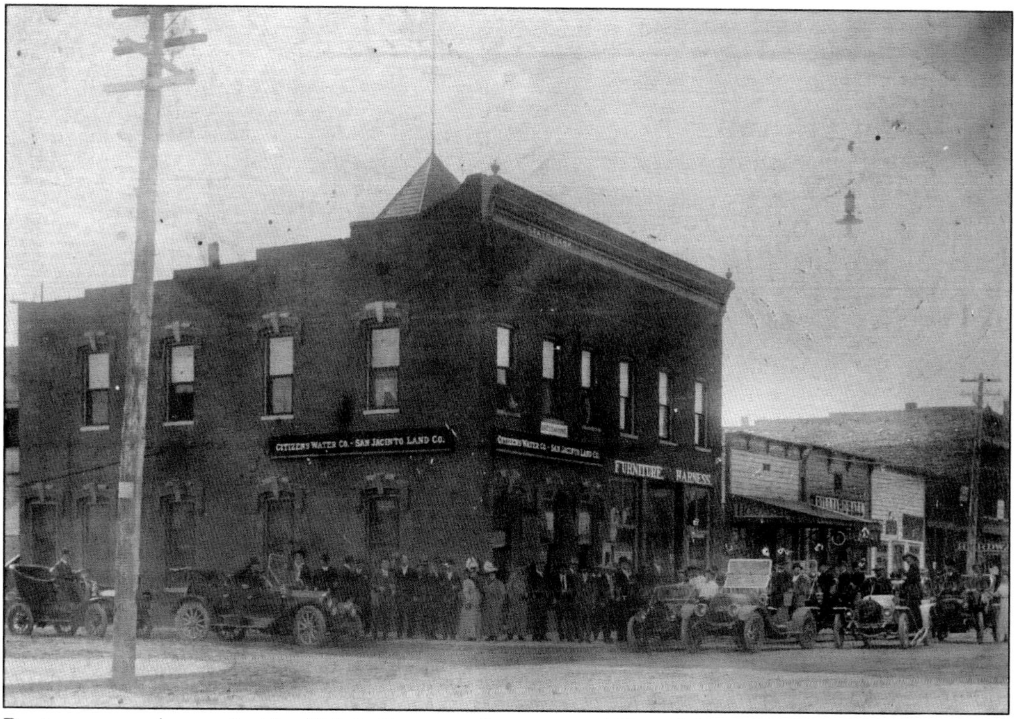

Businesses on the south side of Main Street at the corner of Sheriff Avenue were repaired following damage caused by the 1899 earthquake. In the corner building is the Citizens Water Company–San Jacinto Land Company, a shared space. A furniture and harness store operates out of the right half. The next business bears a sign denoting a billiard hall. (Courtesy San Jacinto Museum.)

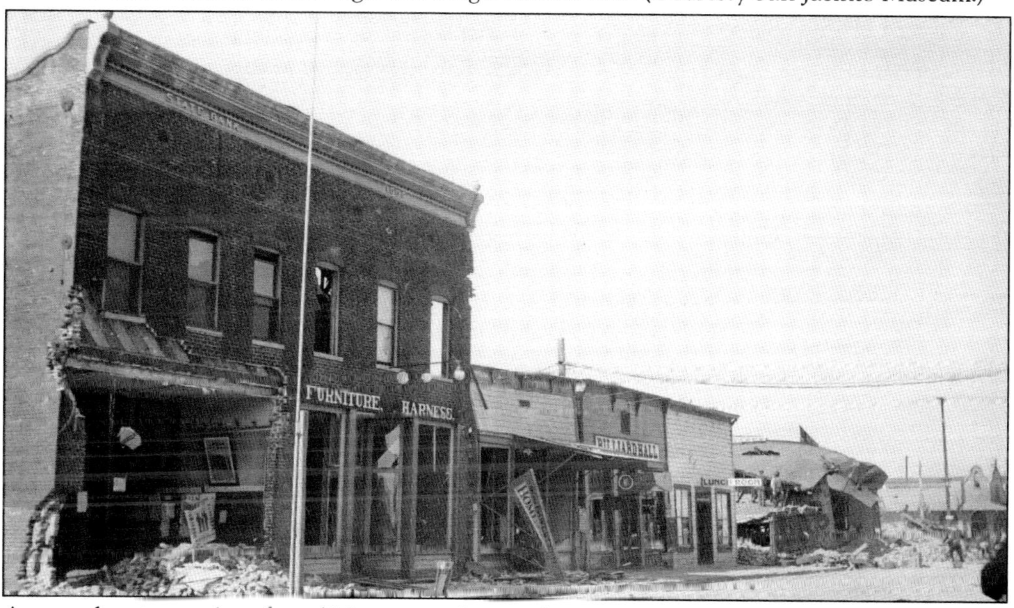

A second major earthquake, of 7.0 magnitude, struck San Jacinto in 1918 and again damaged the same buildings on the corner of Main Street and Sheriff Avenue. Following this earthquake, the buildings were all restored with wood-frame construction and the bricks hauled off. (Courtesy San Jacinto Museum.)

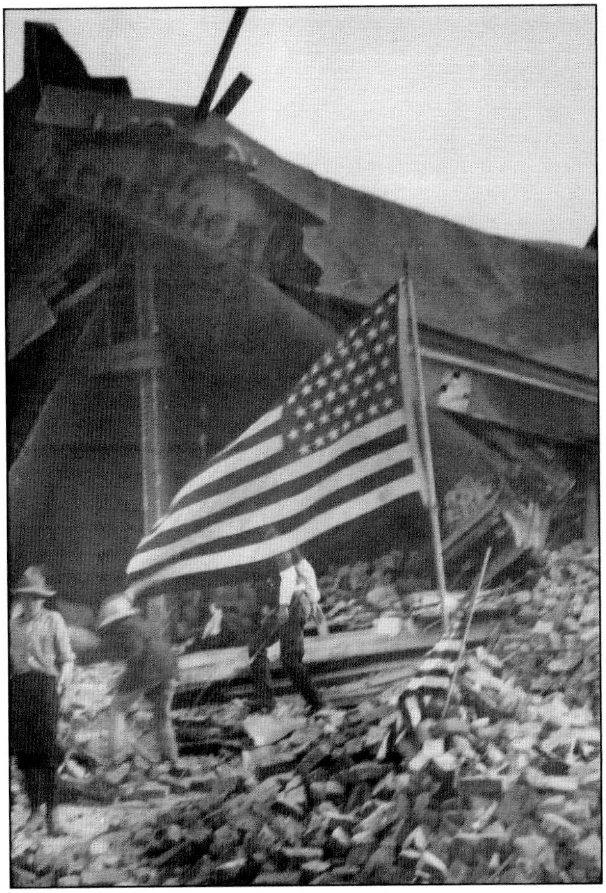

This scene would later be echoed in the flags flying in rubble after the terrorist attack on September 11, 2001. A correlation can be made involving both New York's sense of fortitude and pride and that of San Jacinto. Although the damage in New York was extremely worse, in both instances, the citizens acted courageously with a united spirit. This photograph is identified "Spirit of San Jacinto," April 21, 1918. However, it is interesting to note that the large flag has only 45 stars. This indicates it to be pre-1907 vintage, when Oklahoma became the 46th state. Therefore, either the flag had not been updated when the photograph was taken or the image is of the earlier 1899 earthquake. (Courtesy Charles Van Fleet.)

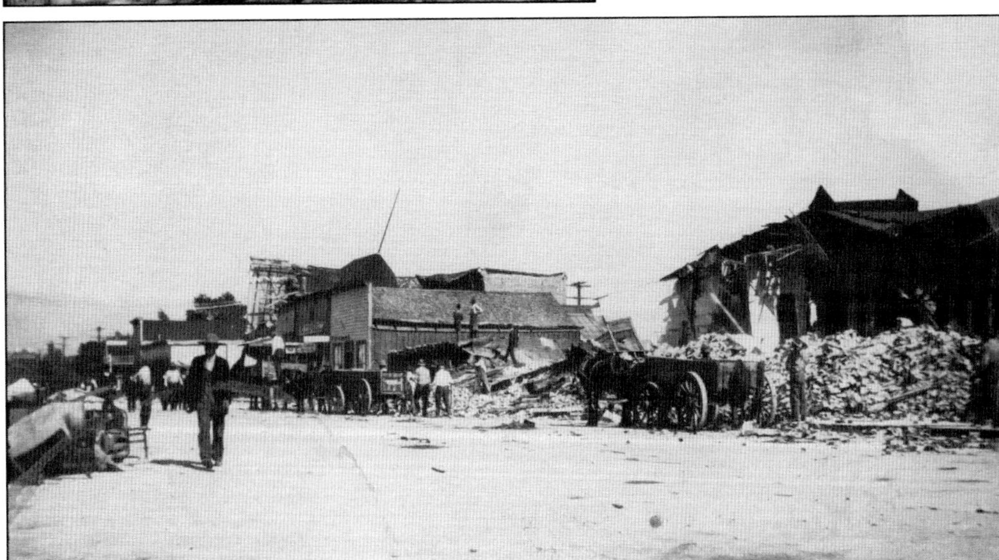

Bricks were not used for construction in San Jacinto after 1918. Loaded with bricks, these wagons express the magnitude of work involved with the cleanup. The brick houses of Francisco and Jose Estudillo both withstood the earthquakes of 1899 and 1918. (Courtesy San Jacinto Museum.)

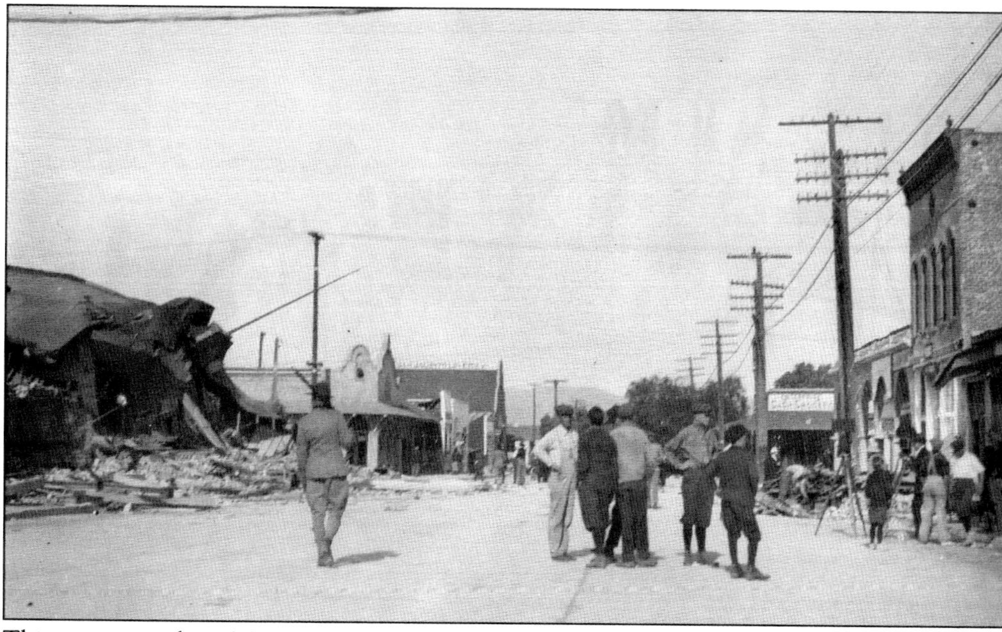

This view east along Main Street reveals the destruction caused by the 1918 earthquake. The National Guard soldier on the left is patrolling to instill a sense of security and to prevent looting. Other soldiers discuss the damage with townspeople. (Courtesy Charles Van Fleet.)

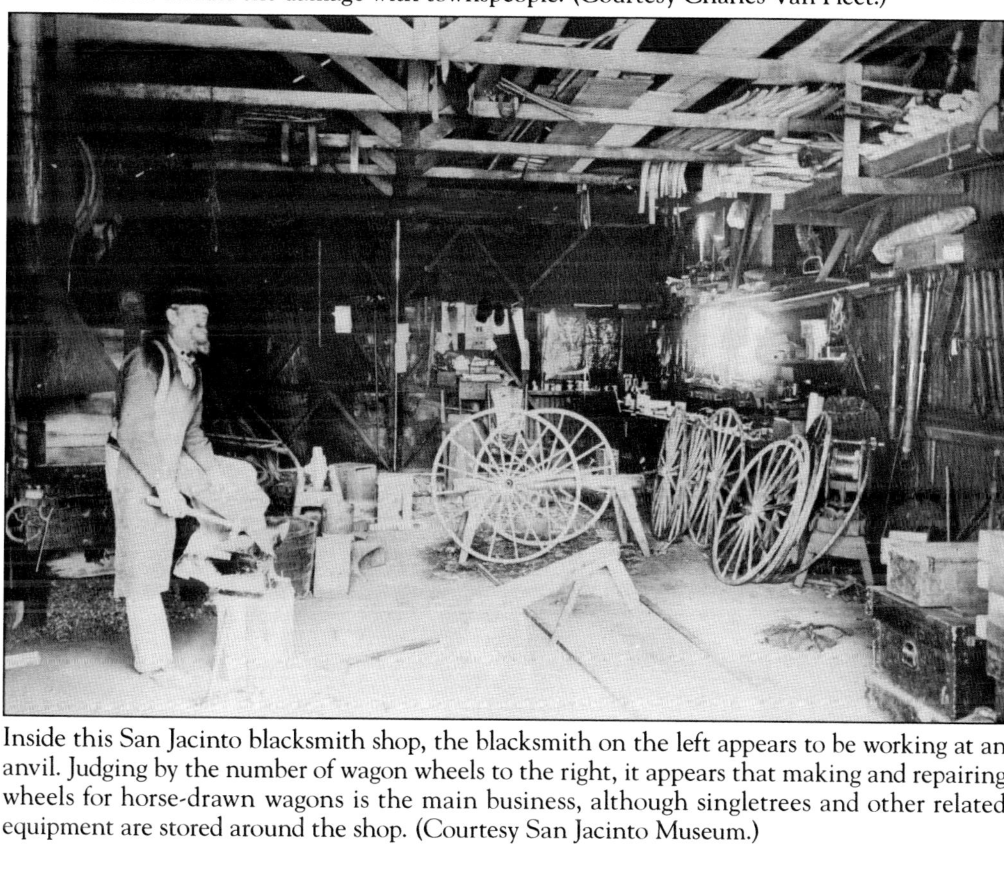

Inside this San Jacinto blacksmith shop, the blacksmith on the left appears to be working at an anvil. Judging by the number of wagon wheels to the right, it appears that making and repairing wheels for horse-drawn wagons is the main business, although singletrees and other related equipment are stored around the shop. (Courtesy San Jacinto Museum.)

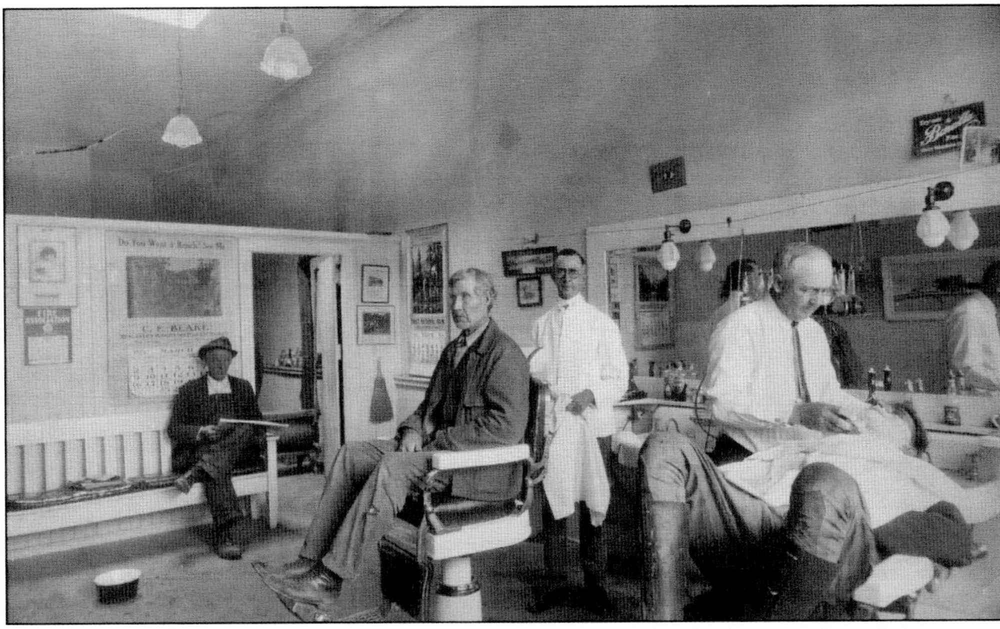

The barber on the right gives a client a shave, while the other barber stands with his apron, ready to cut hair. Note the calendar above the man sitting on the bench to the left. C. E. Blake is probably a realtor, for the inscription on the calendar notes his name and reads, "Do You Need a Ranch? See Me." This San Jacinto barbershop was operated by barbers Clyde and Charlie Starbuck, pictured here. (Courtesy San Jacinto Museum.)

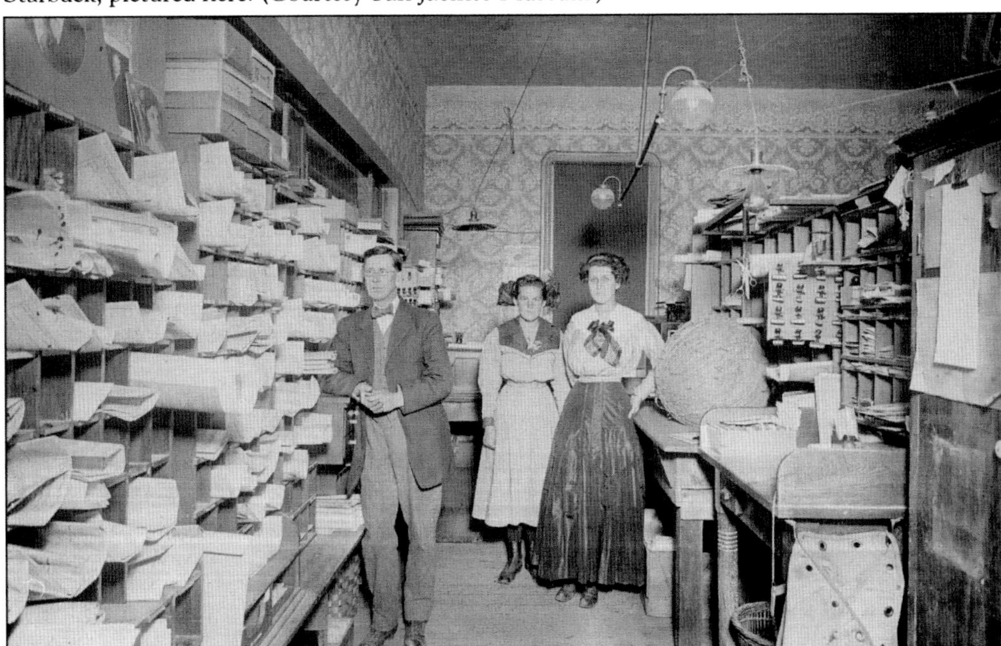

Ellis T. Tanner poses at the mailboxes of the San Jacinto Post Office while two of the women clerks stand in the center behind him. This photograph was taken sometime in the 1920s, after the post office had been firmly established. It was an accomplishment for any community to have a post office such as this. (Courtesy San Jacinto Museum.)

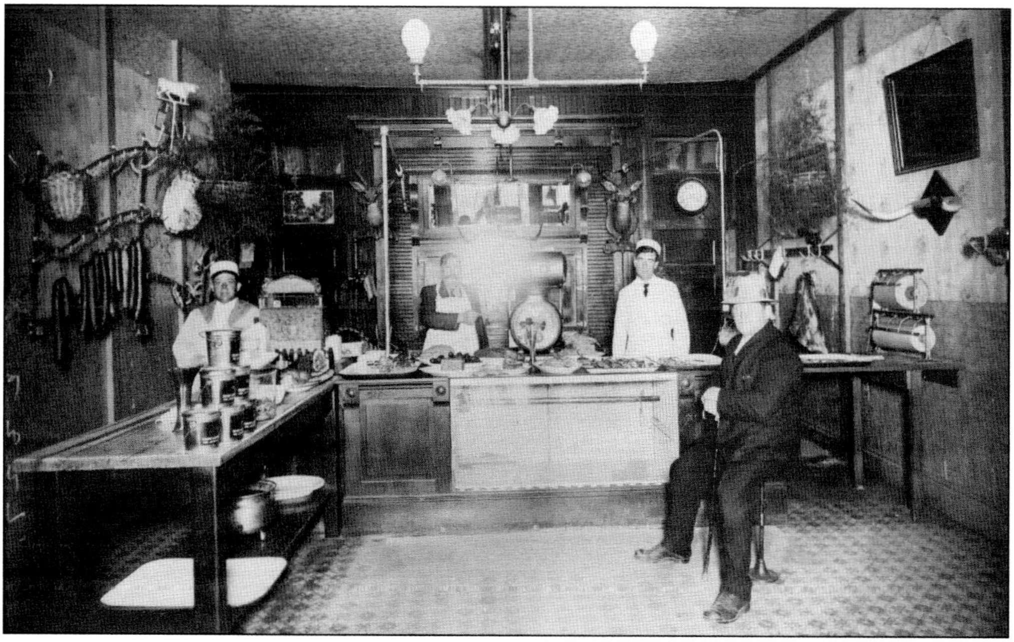

The Hopkins Meat Market is pictured here in 1923. Sitting on the right is William Vosburg Sr., the owner of the landmark Vosburg Hotel. The only other identified person is George O'Loan, the man standing in back of the counter next to Vosburg. Note the rack of sausage hanging on the wall at far left. (Courtesy San Jacinto Museum.)

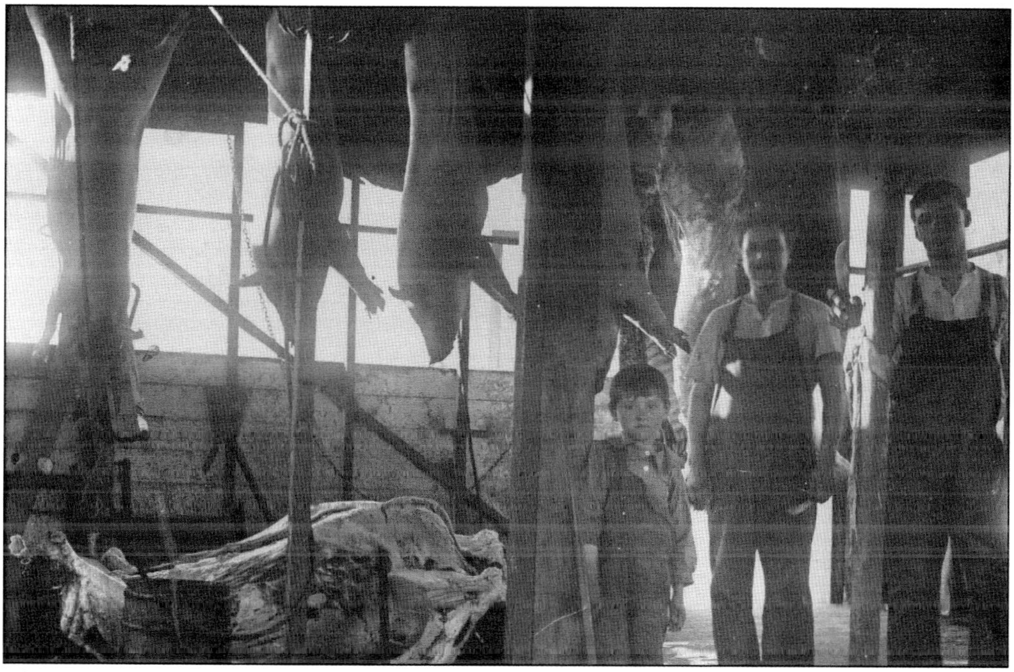

The major meat butchering for the Hopkins Meat Market was accomplished in the back of the shop. Five hog carcasses are hanging from the ceiling, and a beef carcass is on the floor waiting to be cut. The two workers stand by, ready to perform the butchering. George O'Loan is at far right. (Courtesy San Jacinto Museum.)

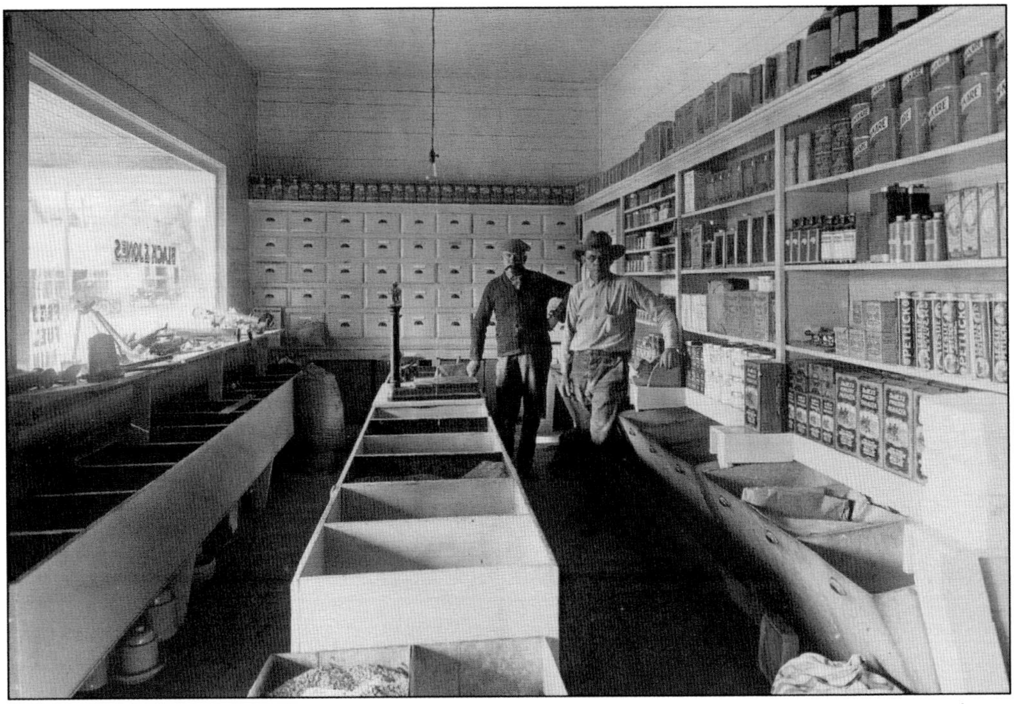

The sign in the window indicates that this business was likely owned by Black and Jones. Judging by the chicken watering containers under the bin at left, the space is believed to have been a veterinarian and feed store. Ben Jones's father is seen at left, with his son standing by his side. Note the large supply of feed containers on the shelves at right and the numerous drawers in the rear of the shop. (Courtesy San Jacinto Museum.)

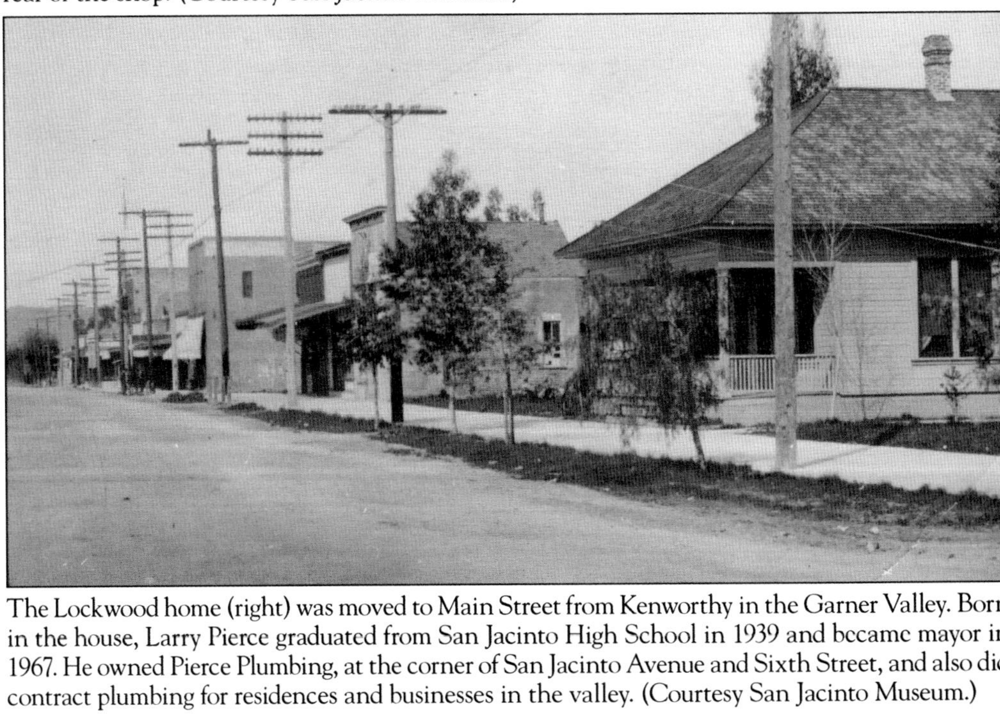

The Lockwood home (right) was moved to Main Street from Kenworthy in the Garner Valley. Born in the house, Larry Pierce graduated from San Jacinto High School in 1939 and became mayor in 1967. He owned Pierce Plumbing, at the corner of San Jacinto Avenue and Sixth Street, and also did contract plumbing for residences and businesses in the valley. (Courtesy San Jacinto Museum.)

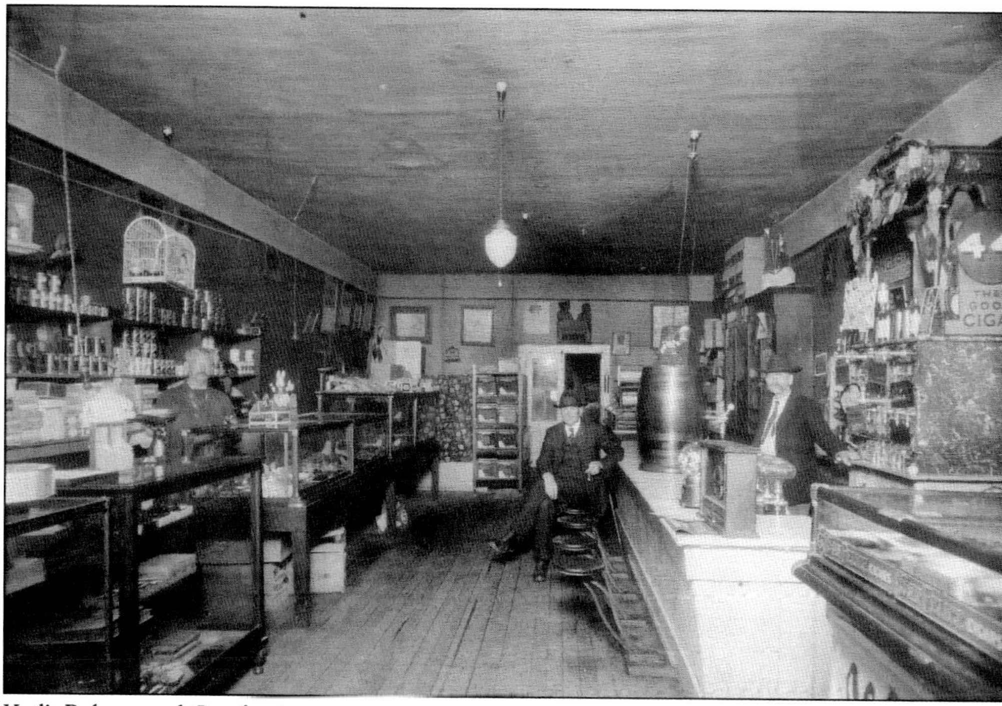

Keil's Bakery and Confectionery was located on the south side of Main Street at the corner of San Jacinto Avenue. The man at the far right has placed his hand on the large soda fountain, which bears the number on its side. Note the immensity of this soda fountain as compared to today. (Courtesy San Jacinto Museum.)

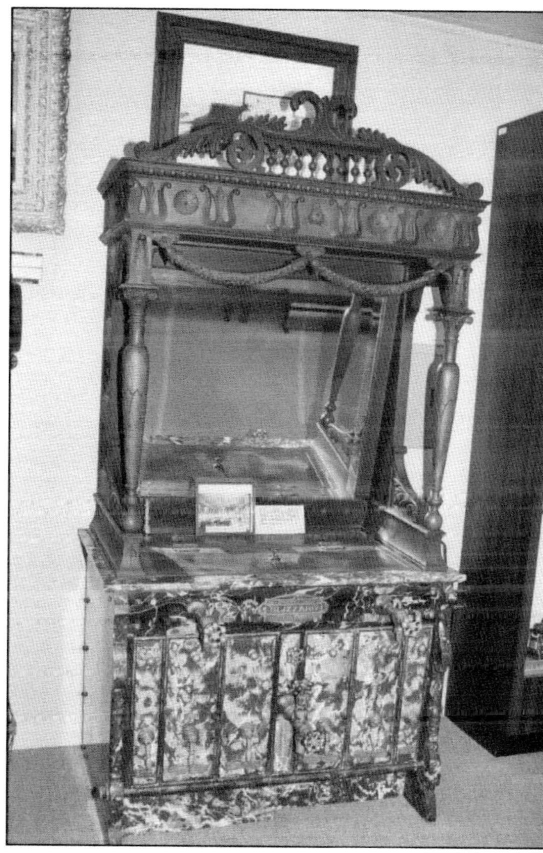

This soda fountain from Keil's Bakery and Confectionery includes a lower half made of marble and weighing 600 pounds, plus six compartments for six different flavors to be selected. It is now on display in the San Jacinto Museum. (Courtesy Mary Collier.)

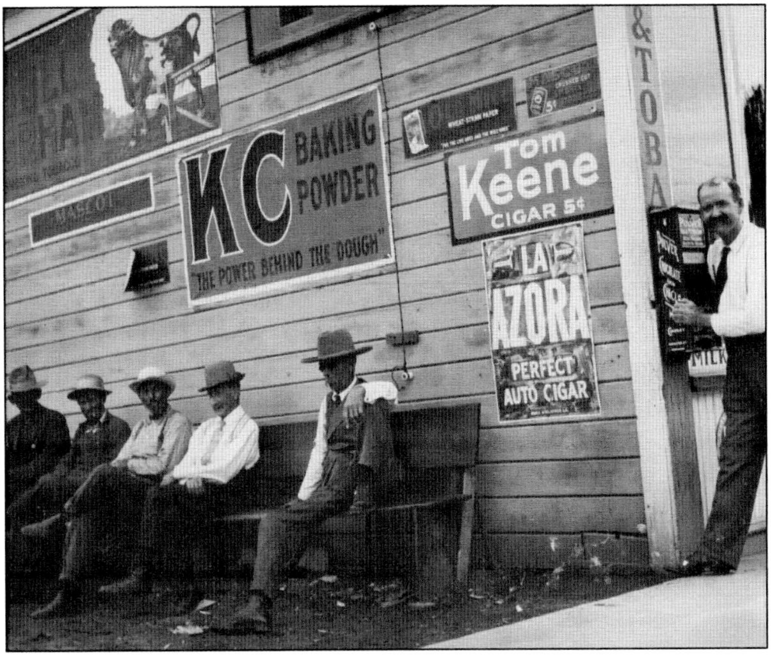

This scene takes place on the east side of Keil's Bakery about 1909. Pictured from left to right are William Wall, a cement mason; John Potter, a well driller; Hartman Van Dusen, a drayman and the first auto bus driver; Gustav Miller, a printer at the *San Jacinto Register*; Thomas Campbell, a Civil War veteran; and Wilson Roork, a bakery employee. (Courtesy Charles Van Fleet.)

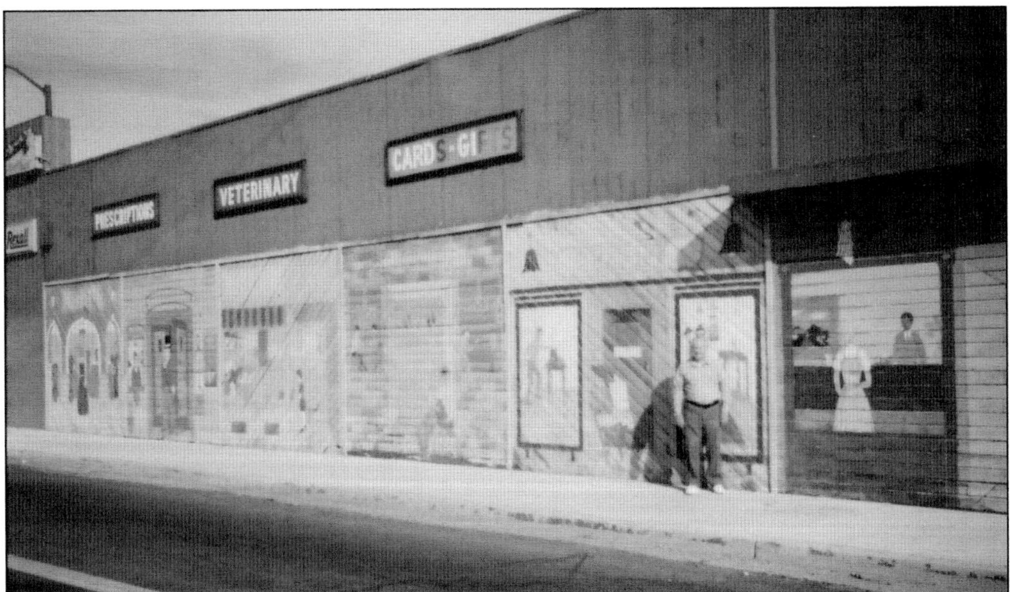

This present-day mural decorates the east side of the Rexall Drug Store building on San Jacinto Avenue at the corner of Main Street. Author Ken Holtzclaw stands to the right. Several buildings in the city now have murals painted on the side rather than advertisements. (Courtesy Jack Warneke.)

Three

HOTELS AND RESORTS

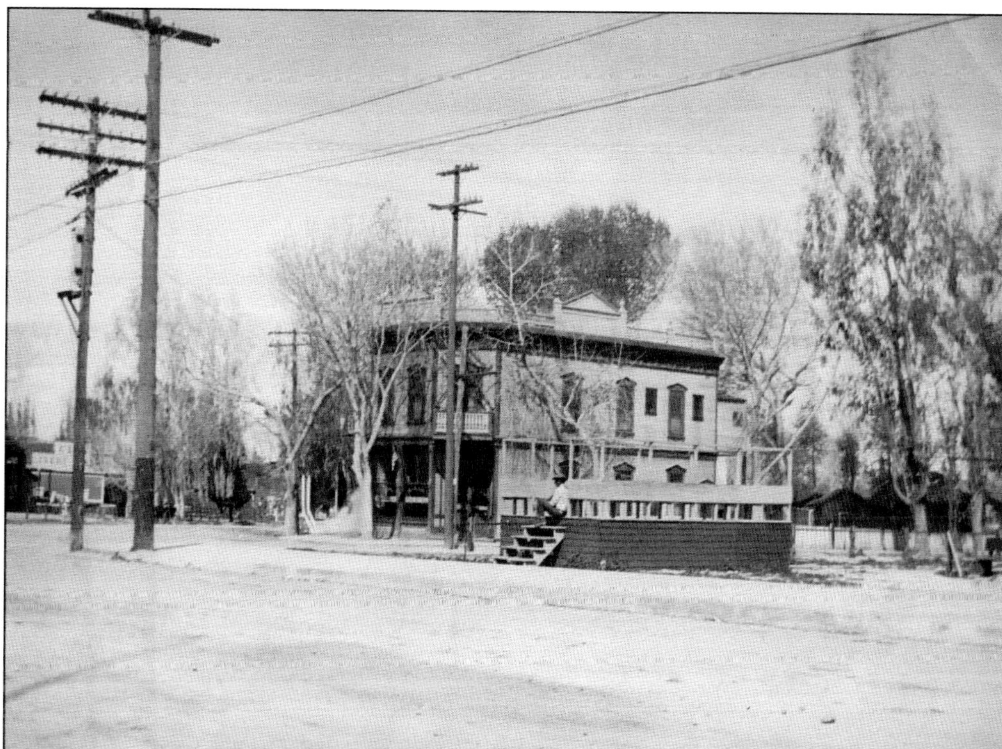

In 1888, Thomas and Jane Farmer emigrated from England with their four children and opened the Farmer House, pictured here. The Farmer House was later incorporated into the Vosburg Hotel in 1907. The Farmer House and Vosburg Hotel served the city for nearly 100 years before the most recent renovation. (Courtesy San Jacinto Museum.)

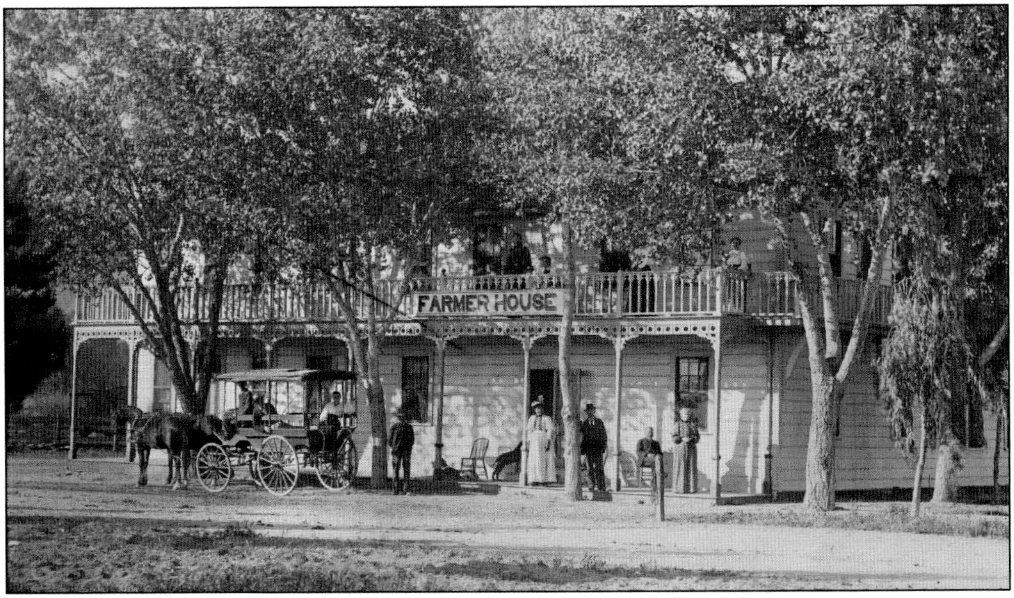

The Farmer House is pictured around 1900, after its exterior had been changed and a veranda added on the second floor. In 1904, William G. Vosburg arrived in San Jacinto and became involved in several business ventures. He married Annie Farmer, the daughter of Thomas and Jane, in 1907. (Courtesy San Jacinto Museum.)

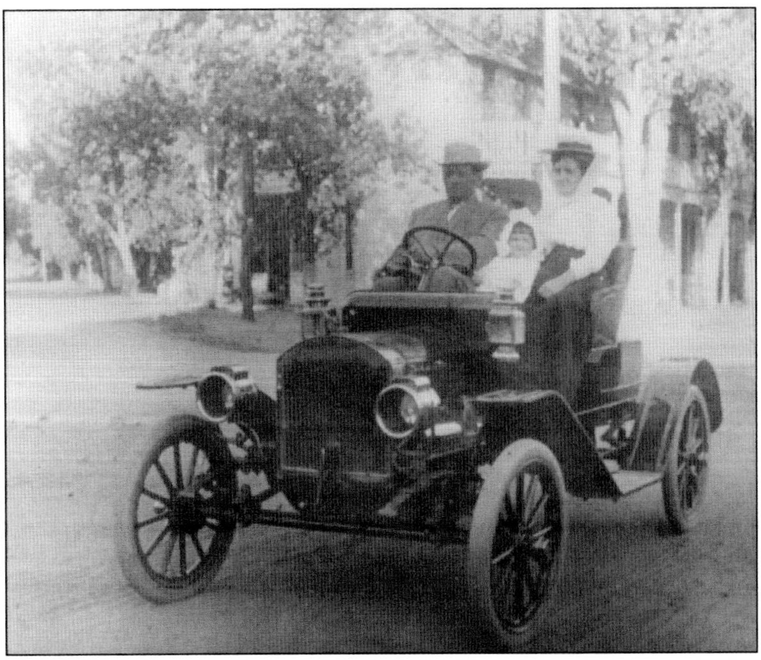
William and Annie Vosburg and their daughter Ruth sit in the family automobile on Central (Ramona) Boulevard at the corner of Third Street, next to the Vosburg Hotel, in 1910. William and Annie had purchased the Farmer House from Annie's parents in 1907, changing the name to the Vosburg Hotel. They managed the business until the 1930s. (Courtesy Betty Jo Dunham.)

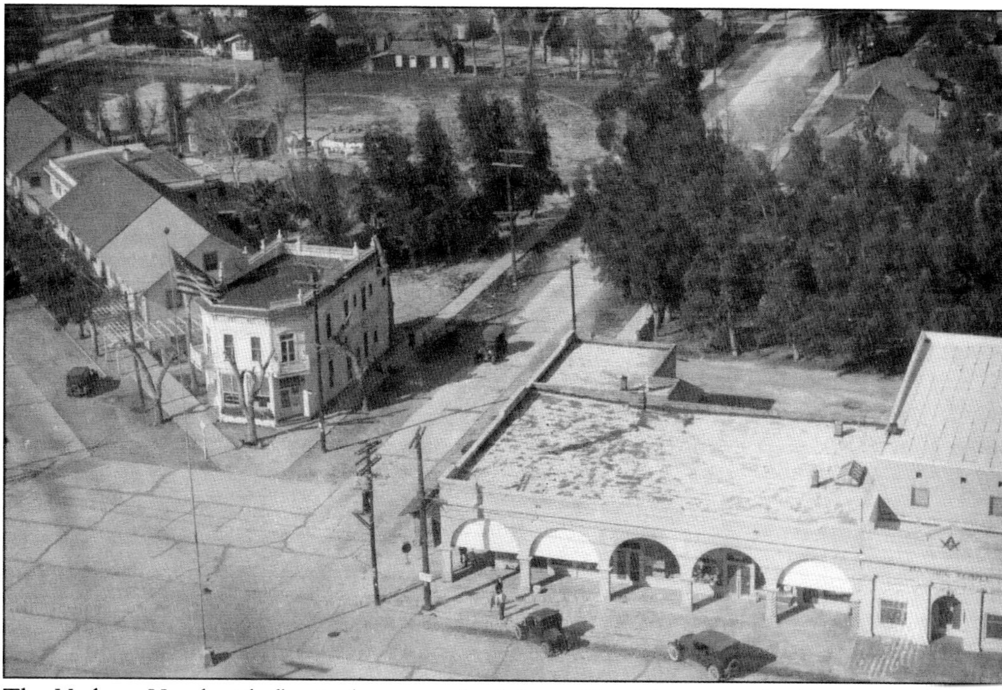

The Vosburg Hotel with flag is shown on the left in 1923. The corner building was once used as the water company and later the city library before being incorporated into the hotel. In the upper right, the Methodist church stands at the corner of San Jacinto Avenue and Second Street. Main Street businesses are on the right. (Courtesy Charles Van Fleet.)

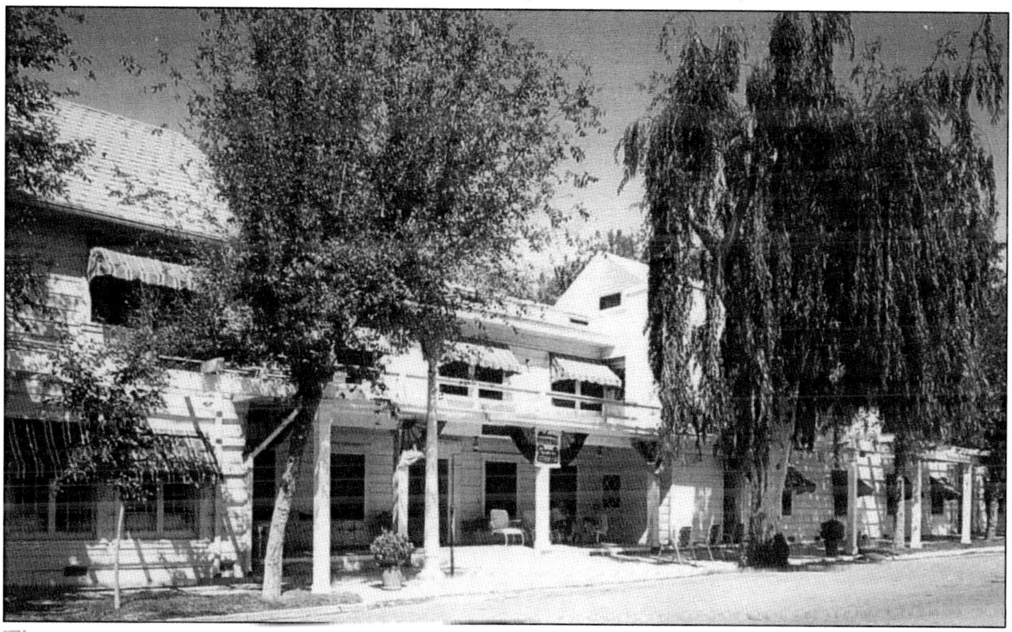

The main entrance to the Vosburg Hotel, along Ramona Boulevard, is decked with hanging banners advertising the Ramona Pageant at the Ramona Bowl. William R. (the son of William G.) and Jane Vosburg managed the hotel from the late 1930s until 1971. The hotel had 52 rooms, a large dining room, and a library lounge. (Courtesy San Jacinto Museum.)

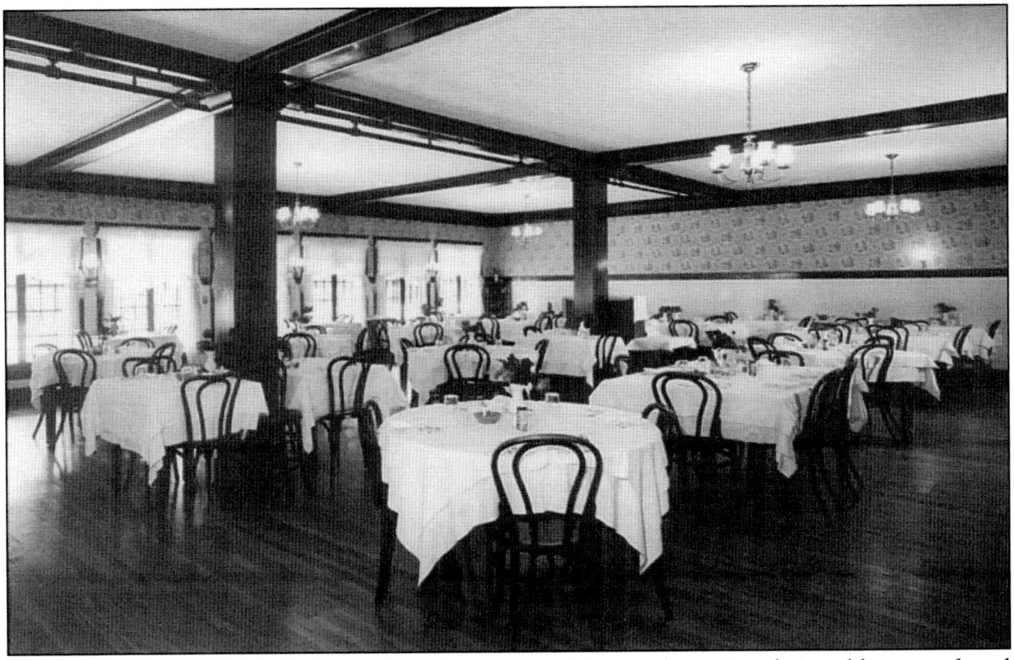

The main dining room was located in the center of the Vosburg Hotel. In addition to hotel guests, the dining room attracted customers from surrounding towns, as it had a reputation for fine food. Eva Dunham served as a waitress here for many years. The 52-room Vosburg Hotel was sold to Willie Ryan in 1971. He continued to operate both the lodging and restaurant until 1985, when they were sold to developers and closed. The building is now being restored. (Courtesy San Jacinto Museum.)

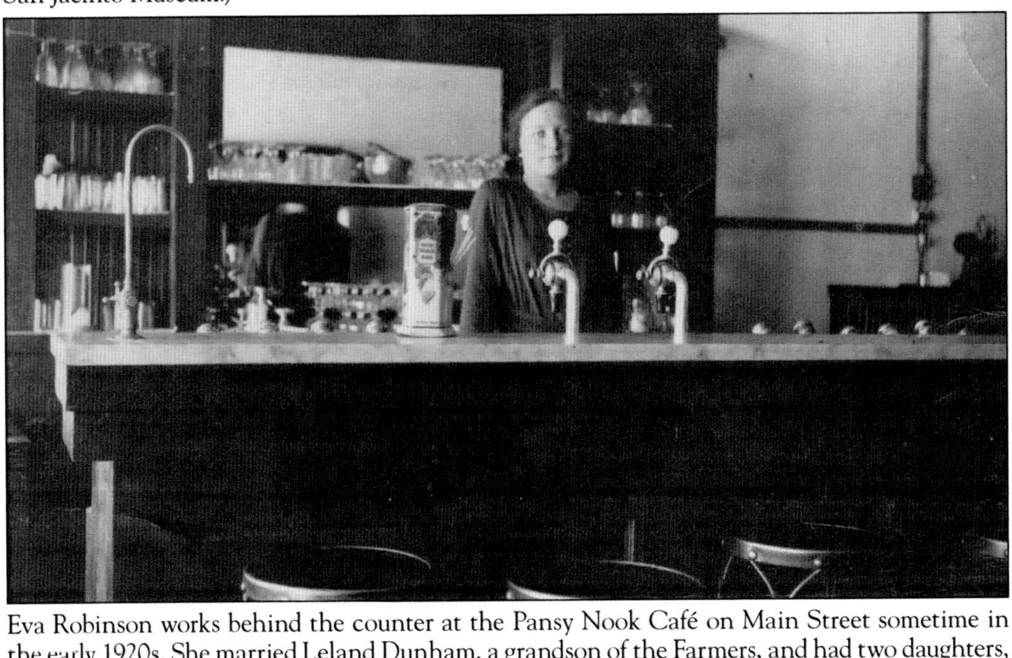

Eva Robinson works behind the counter at the Pansy Nook Café on Main Street sometime in the early 1920s. She married Leland Dunham, a grandson of the Farmers, and had two daughters, Betty Jo and Barbara. Eva later worked as a waitress at the Vosburg, formerly the Farmer House. (Courtesy Betty Jo Dunham.)

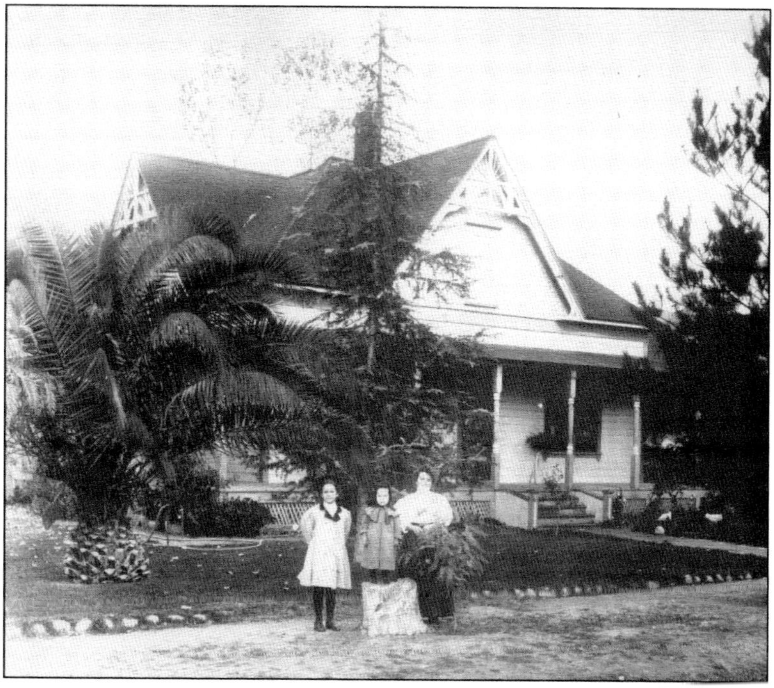

The J. E. and Emma Jane Dunham home stood at the corner of Estudillo and Second Street, just one block from the Vosburg Hotel. Standing in front of the house are Emma Jane Dunham and her daughter Florence, with a neighbor girl on the left. Emma Jane is the grandmother of Betty Jo Dunham and Barbara Dunham Walsh. (Courtesy Betty Jo Dunham.)

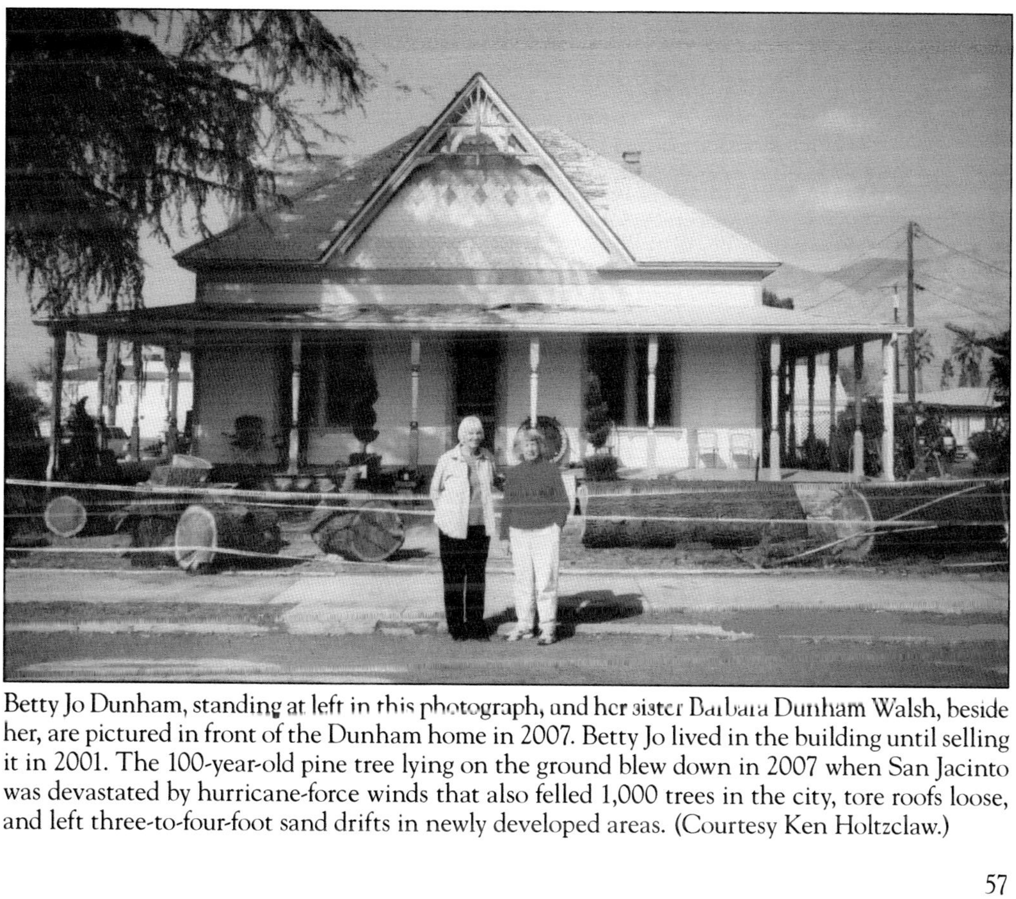

Betty Jo Dunham, standing at left in this photograph, and her sister Barbara Dunham Walsh, beside her, are pictured in front of the Dunham home in 2007. Betty Jo lived in the building until selling it in 2001. The 100-year-old pine tree lying on the ground blew down in 2007 when San Jacinto was devastated by hurricane-force winds that also felled 1,000 trees in the city, tore roofs loose, and left three-to-four-foot sand drifts in newly developed areas. (Courtesy Ken Holtzclaw.)

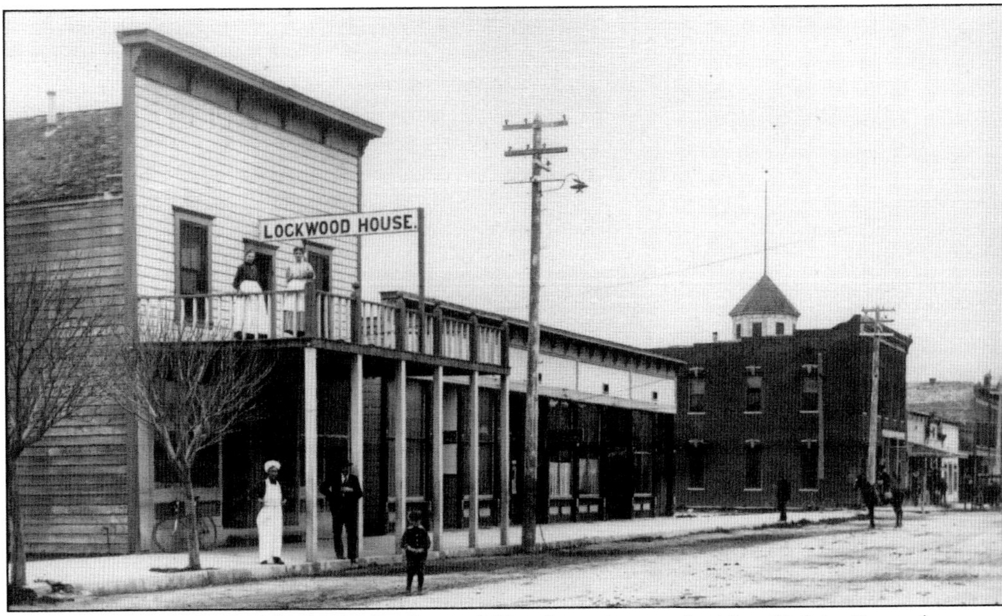

In 1883, Tom Lockwood built the Lockwood Hotel on the south side of Main Street between Sheriff and Jordan Avenues. The 15-room hotel is seen here in 1907. The cook, known as Ming, stands on the curb and Charles Lockwood in the street. Lorinda Lockwood appears on the balcony. (Courtesy San Jacinto Museum.)

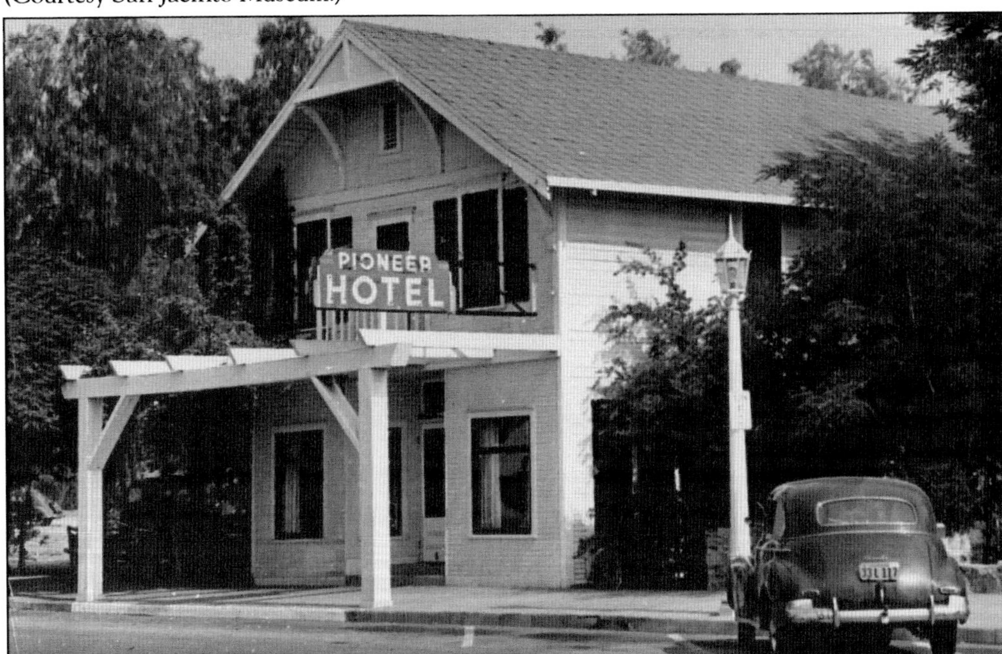

Tom Lockwood's granddaughter Lela and her husband, Tom Williamson, took over operation of the hotel in 1938, at which time they remodeled it and changed the name to the Pioneer. Kenneth Kreigh did the rock wall from the Hogan gift shop to the hotel in the 1930s. He also did the rock work for the museum building across Main Street. The Williamsons sold the Pioneer to the Leightons in 1948. (Courtesy San Jacinto Museum.)

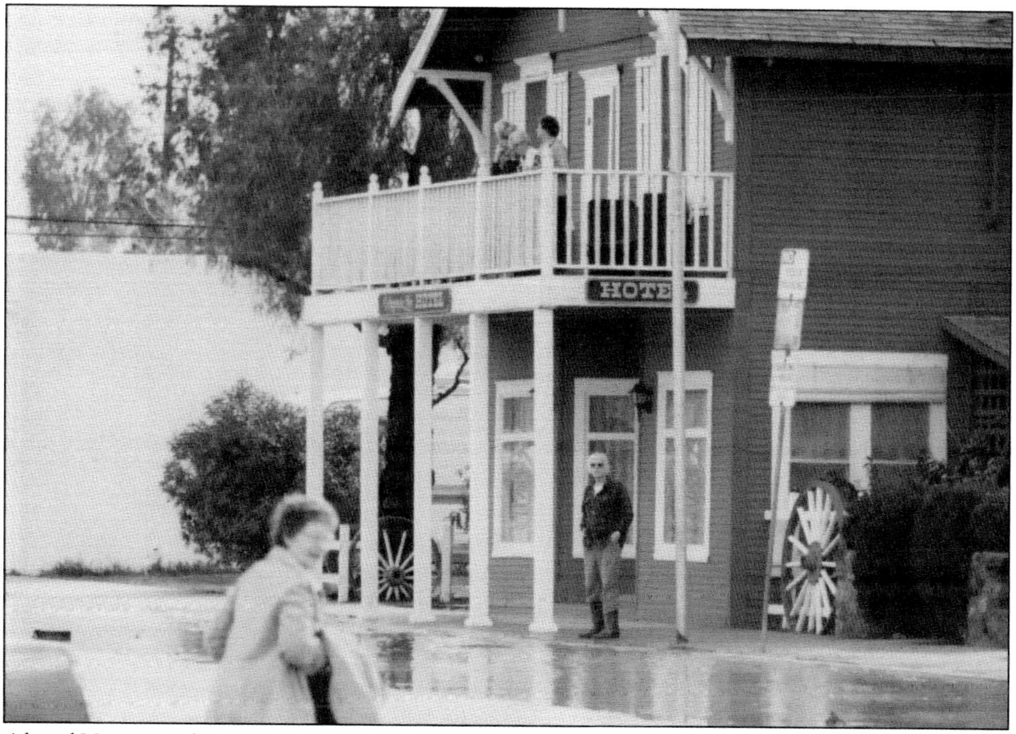

Al and Virginia Thompsen purchased the Pioneer in 1976 and changed the name to the Virginia Lee Hotel. In February 1980, heavy rains broke the river levee east of town, causing water to flow directly down Main Street and Idyllwild Drive, flooding most of the city to depths of two to four feet. In this photograph, Al Thompsen observes the water level as it recedes down Main Street as well as a resident crossing the street. Virginia, in the center, and others view the flooding from the balcony. Now owned by the City of San Jacinto, the hotel building is used for administrative offices. (Courtesy San Jacinto Museum.)

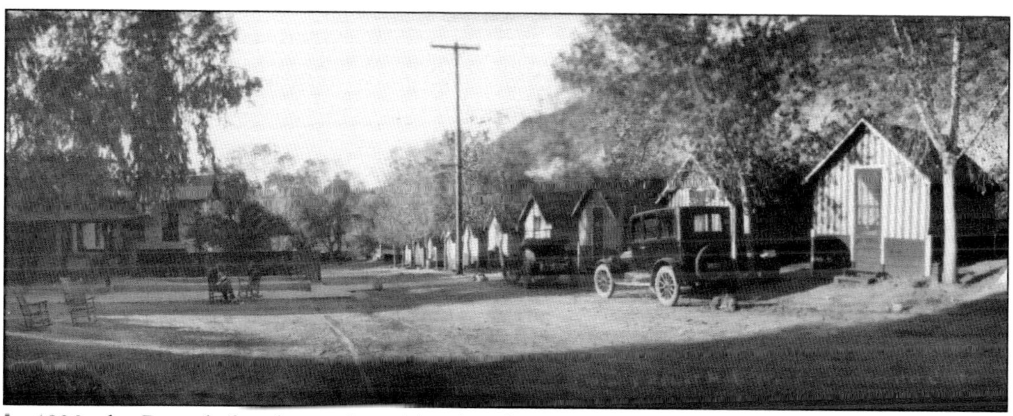

In 1890, the Branch family purchased land with natural hot springs north of town and called the site Relief Hot Springs. When the Gilmans bought the property in 1913, they changed the name to Gilman Relief Hot Springs. *Relief* was later dropped from the name. Shown here are the bungalows at Gilman Hot Springs. (Courtesy San Jacinto Museum.)

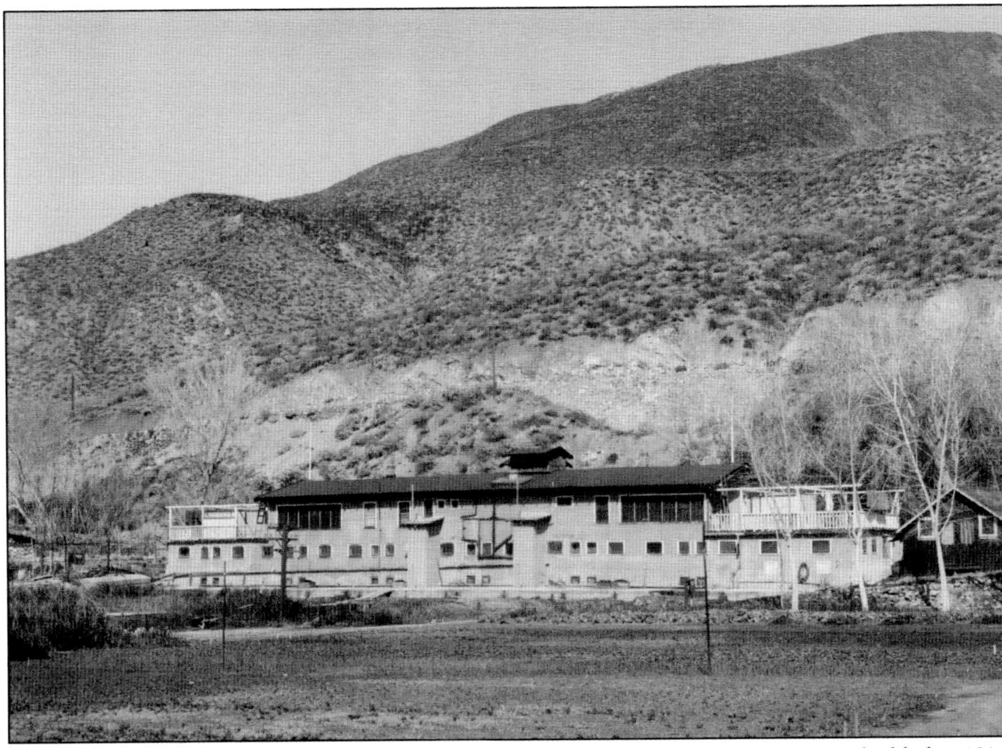

The original bathhouse at Gilman Hot Springs was built in 1913, with a swimming pool added in 1914. The bathhouse is pictured in the 1930s, which at that time contained an Olympic-sized swimming pool. Many came to enjoy the popular resort's hot springs. (Courtesy San Jacinto Museum.)

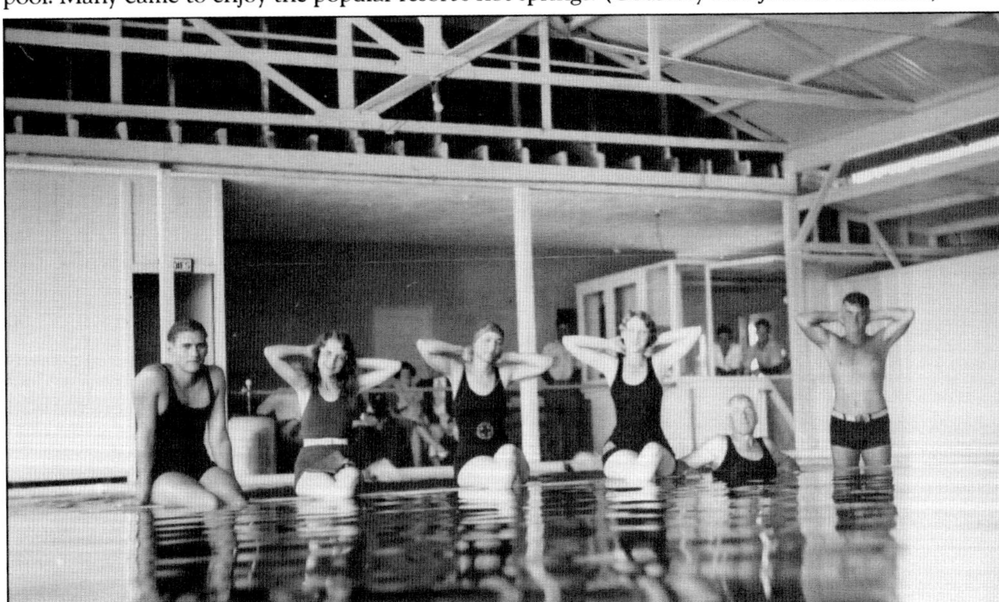

The Gilman Hot Springs indoor swimming pool is seen during the 1930s. On the far right is Earl Gilman Jr., the president of the Gilman Corporation. His son Earl Gilman III became manager of the business sometime later. (Courtesy San Jacinto Museum.)

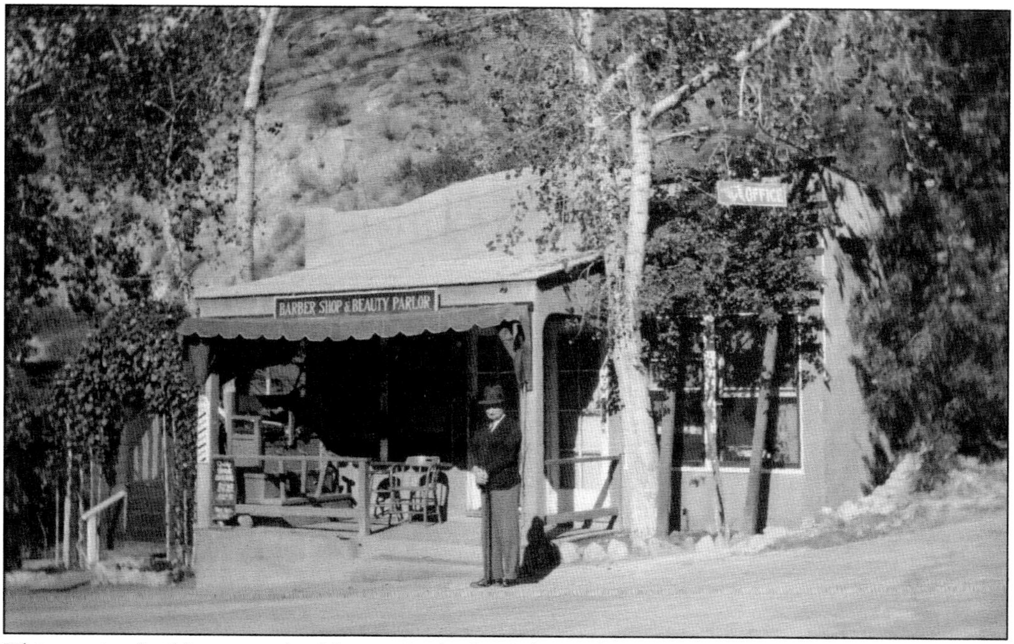

This quaint building, perched beneath the backdrop of one of the area's rural mountainsides at Gilman Hot Springs, housed both a community barbershop and beauty parlor. Gilman Hot Springs also had its own post office, garage, and service station to accommodate travelers to the facility. (Courtesy San Jacinto Museum.)

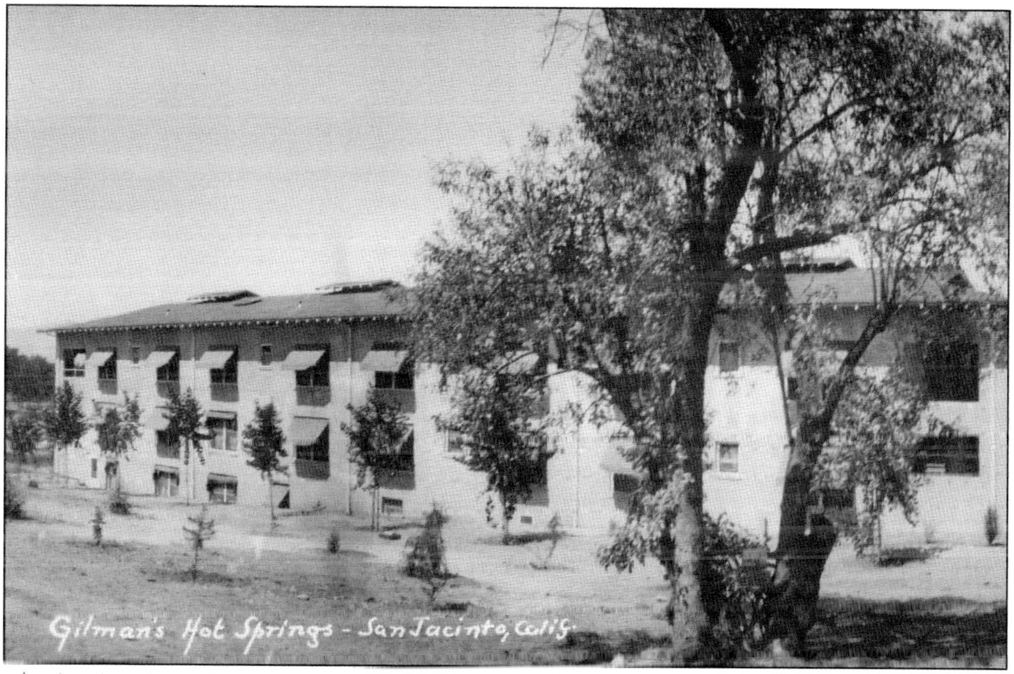

The first hotel at Gilman Hot Springs burned in 1918; rebuilt, it withstood the 1918 earthquake. A 50-room annex was added in 1921. In the 1920s, two daily trains brought visitors to San Jacinto. A representative from the hotel met each train and delivered guests to the resort. This 200-room structure housed travelers in the 1940s. (Courtesy San Jacinto Museum.)

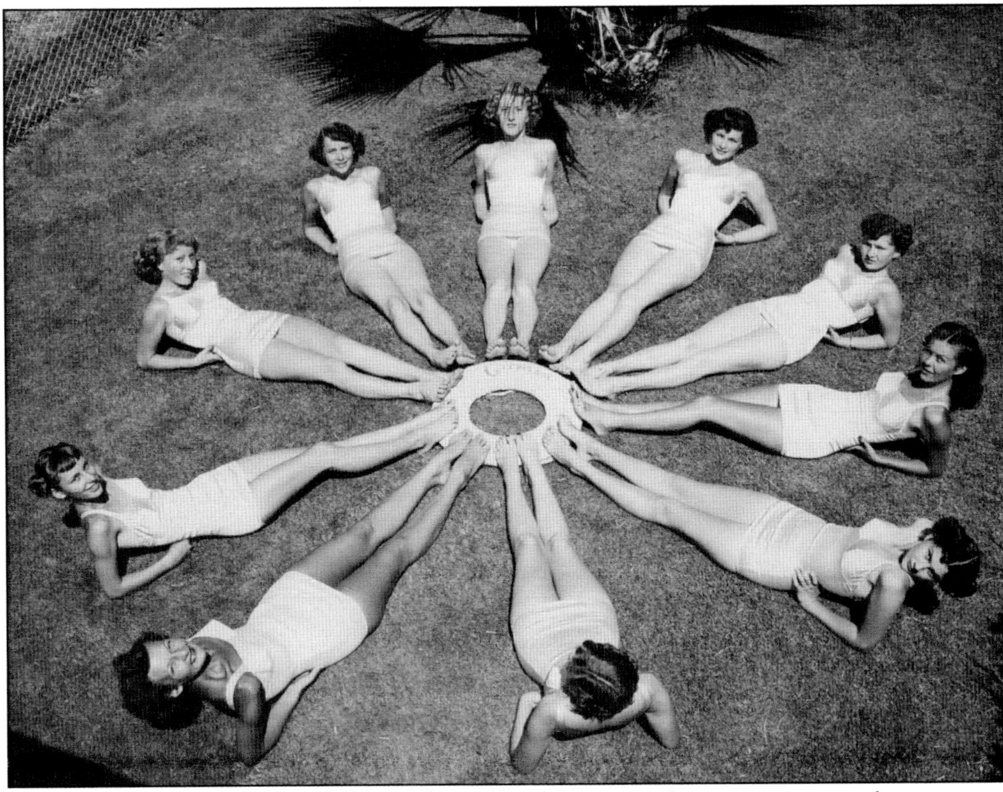

One of the many special events held at Gilman Hot Springs was a beauty pageant to select queens of the cities of San Jacinto and nearby Hemet. Girls of the 1950 beauty pageant pose near the outdoor swimming pool. Pictured clockwise from bottom left to bottom right are Shirley Hodus, Sally Hall, Bessie Waggoner, Kathleen Robinson, Harriet Waggoner, Dorothy Scott Searl, unidentified, Rodie Williams Long, Sue Colvin, and unidentified. (Courtesy San Jacinto Museum.)

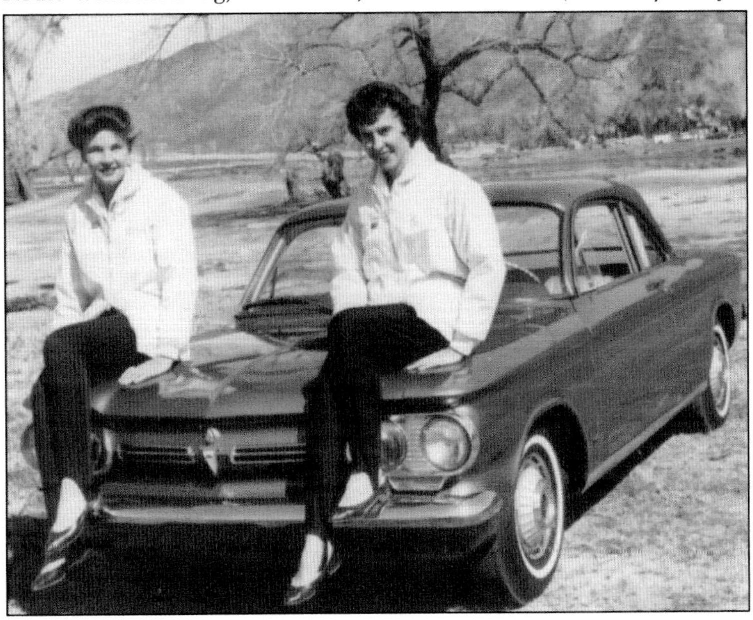

Kathleen Gilman (left), the wife of Earl Gilman, and Pat Sawyer pose on Pat's 1962 Chevrolet Corvair near the golf course at Gilman Hot Springs. The two entered cross-country car races for women in the 1960s. Also a pilot, Sawyer competed in the Powder Puff Derby, in which women pilots raced from the West to East Coasts. Gilman flew as her copilot. (Courtesy San Jacinto Museum.)

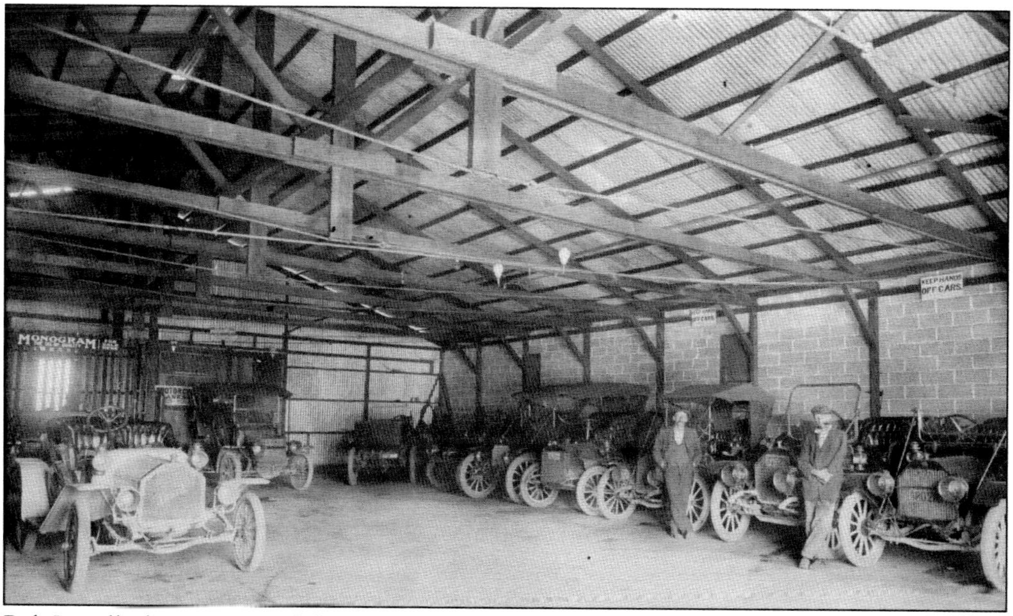

Bob Lawell, the manager of the Gilman Hot Springs Garage, smokes a pipe at the far right of this 1920 photograph. In the 1930s, Bob's daughter Beryl also worked at the garage, where she kept the books and pumped gas. Beryl Penacho Andrews wrote a book on the San Jacinto Valley apricot industry in 2001. (Courtesy San Jacinto Museum.)

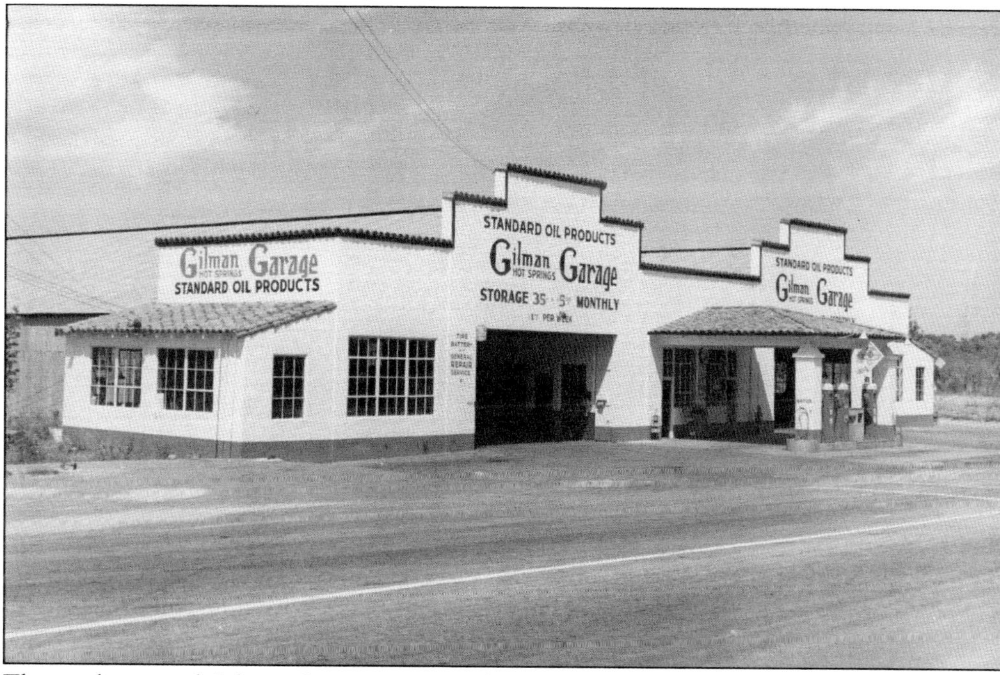

The newly painted Gilman Garage is pictured on the south side of Gilman Road (Highway 79) in 1942. The sign indicates the availability of monthly storage at $5. The family sold the resort and its grounds to the Golden Era of the Church of Scientology in 1978; the site is now closed to the public. Golden Era razed the Massacre Canyon Inn, Gilman Garage, and the golf course to develop land for the church's use. (Courtesy San Jacinto Museum.)

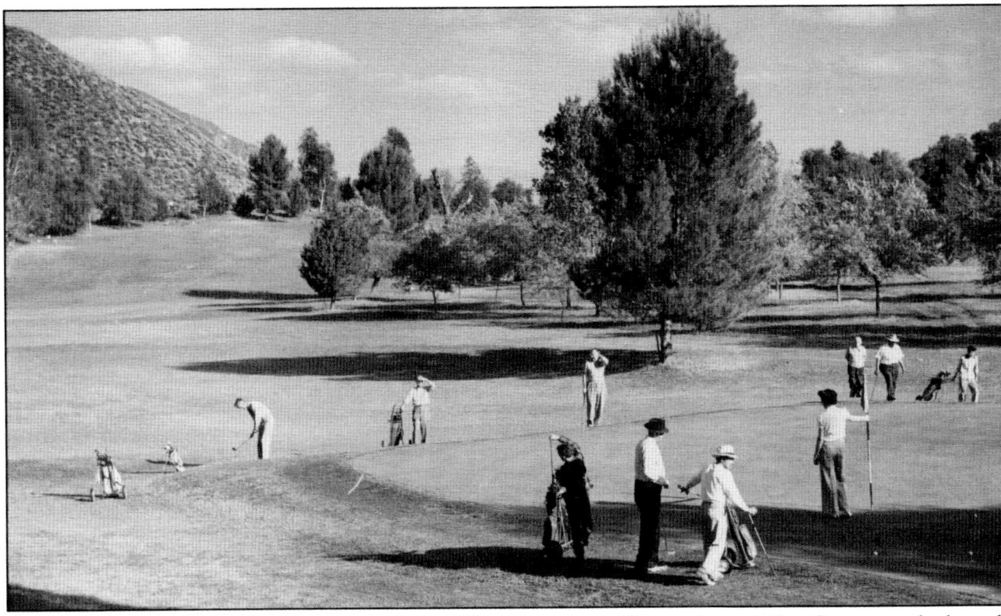

Part of the 27-hole golf course at Gilman Hot Springs is shown here. The first nine-hole golf course opened in 1930, following the north side of the San Jacinto River west of State Street to Potrero Creek and out of Massacre Canyon. Kathleen Gilman is on the tight edge of the green holding the flag. (Courtesy San Jacinto Museum.)

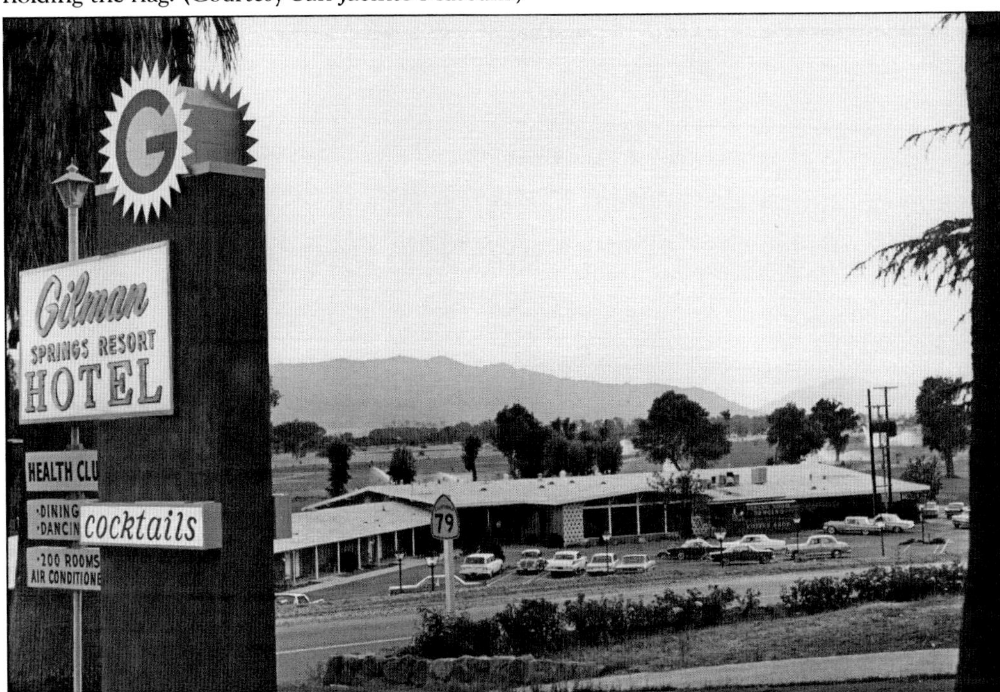

The Massacre Canyon Inn was built for dining and dancing in 1963. It was located on the south side of Gilman Road next to the Gilman Garage. In the 1960s, Earl Gilman added training facilities for the boxers who were training at the camp on State Street and Record Road. (Courtesy San Jacinto Museum.)

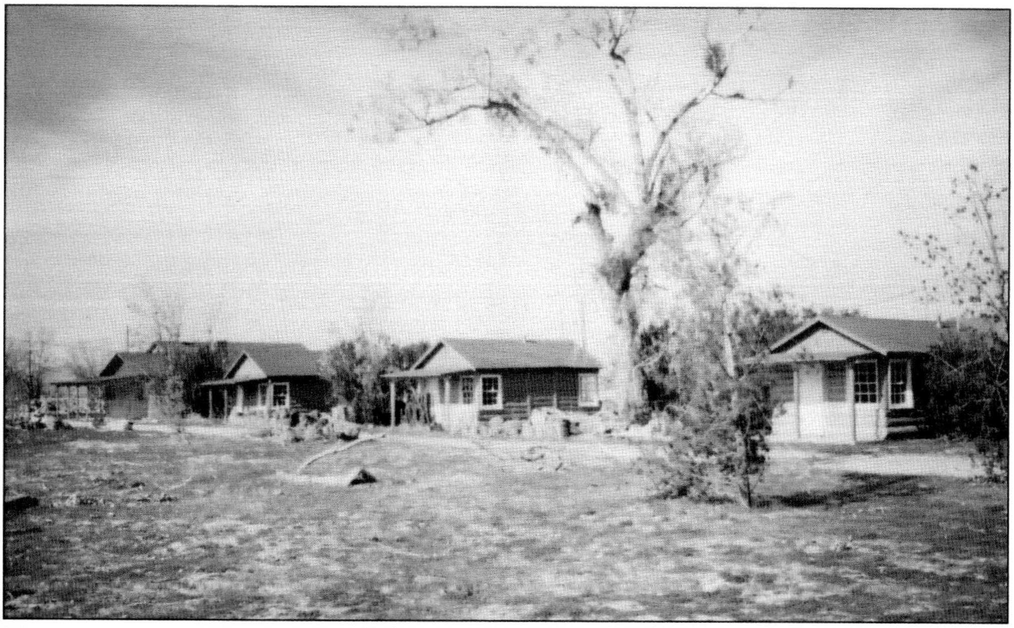

The training camp also contained a boxing ring, visible in the background. From around 1950 until the 1970s, boxers trained here and, starting in the late 1960s, at Gilman Hot Springs. Some of the famous boxers who used the facilities were Muhammad Ali, Ike Chestnut, Evander Holyfield, Sugar Ray Leonard, Ray Mancini, Armando Muniz, Ruben Navarro, Ken Norton, and Jerry Quarry. (Courtesy Jack Warneke.)

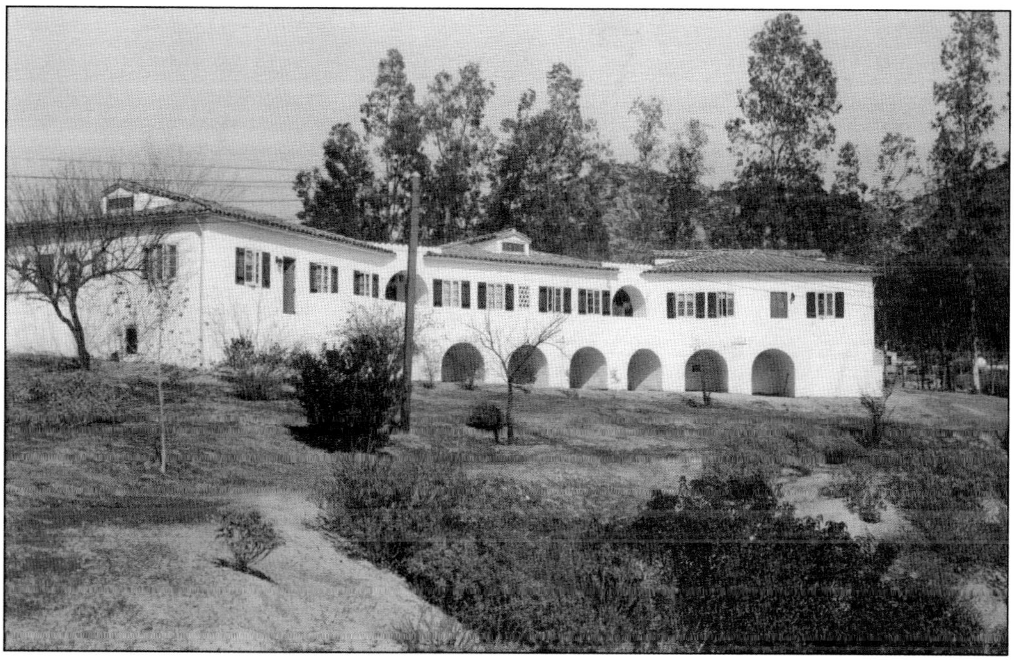

The Eden Hot Springs Hotel, situated north of Gilman Road and about five miles west of Gilman Hot Springs, stands proudly alone on this site. Eden was developed in 1890, and the new hotel was constructed in 1925. When the resort was sold in 1958, the name was changed to Canadian Hot Springs. It closed in the 1970s. (Courtesy San Jacinto Museum.)

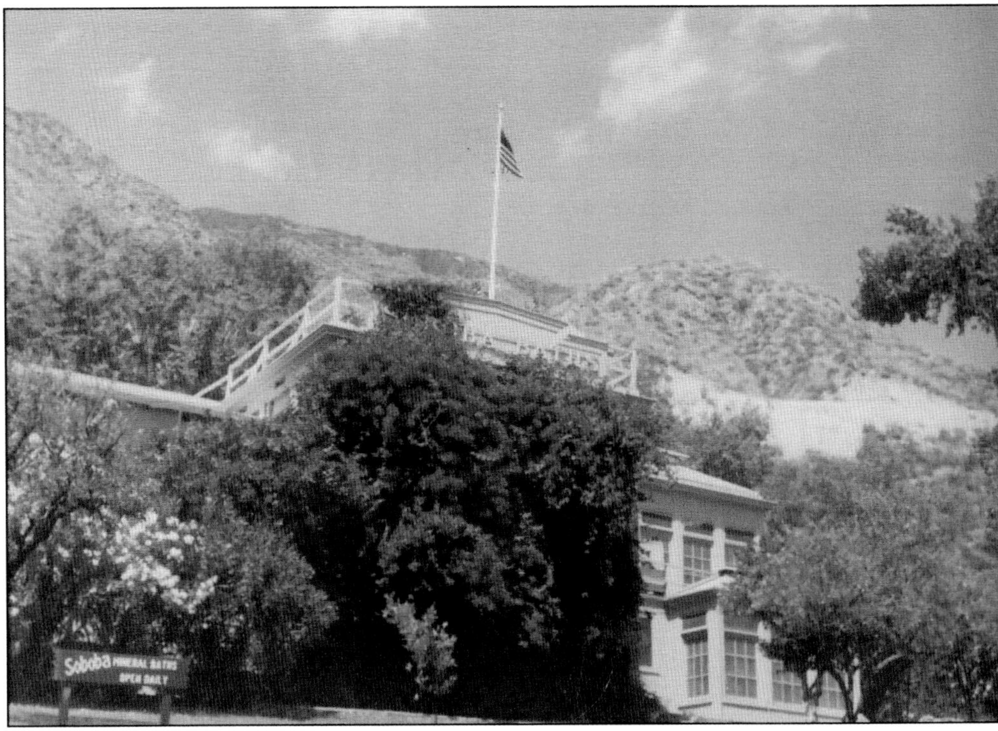

The Soboba Hot Springs Hotel occupied the east end of Main Street along Soboba Road. Col. J. T. Richey owned the site in 1901, selling bottled water from the springs. In 1911, Col. A. B. Bowden purchased the springs, constructed buildings, and opened a resort for the public. The buildings were enlarged to form the Soboba Hot Springs Hotel, managed by the Althouse family from 1919 to 1946. The hotel was closed in the 1970s. (Courtesy San Jacinto Museum.)

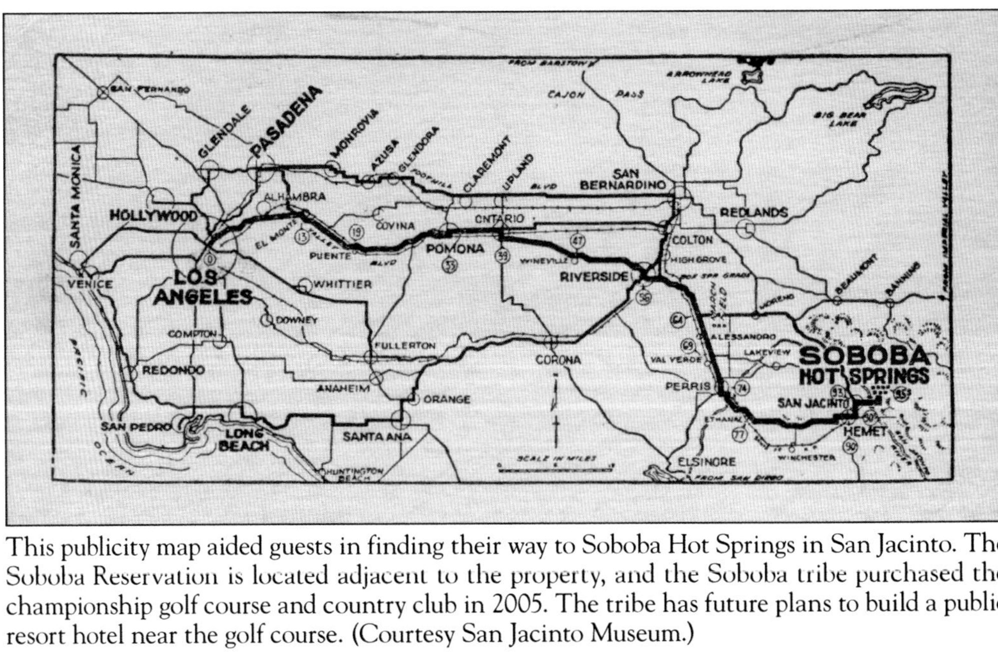

This publicity map aided guests in finding their way to Soboba Hot Springs in San Jacinto. The Soboba Reservation is located adjacent to the property, and the Soboba tribe purchased the championship golf course and country club in 2005. The tribe has future plans to build a public resort hotel near the golf course. (Courtesy San Jacinto Museum.)

Four

20TH-CENTURY SAN JACINTO

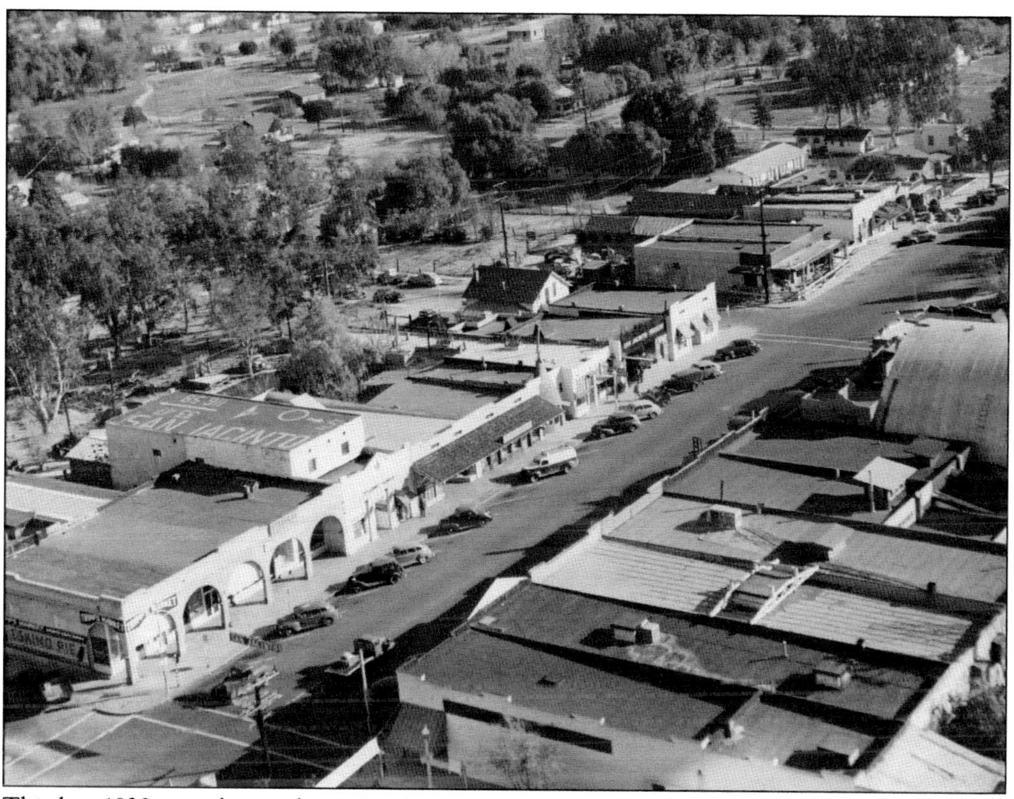

This late-1930s aerial view shows San Jacinto's Main Street, with San Jacinto Avenue along the bottom. Note that the roof of the two-story Masonic temple displays aviation information—the city's latitude of 33 degrees and 17 minutes north, and longitude of 116 degrees and 17 minutes west. The letter O with an arrow designates the southerly direction. These figures helped pilots in navigation before the development of modern radio aids. The oval-roofed structure on the far right is the Soboba Theater. The parklike area to the north of the buildings was the "spit and chew club," where men would hang out to talk while their wives were shopping in the 1930s and 1940s. (Courtesy San Jacinto Museum.)

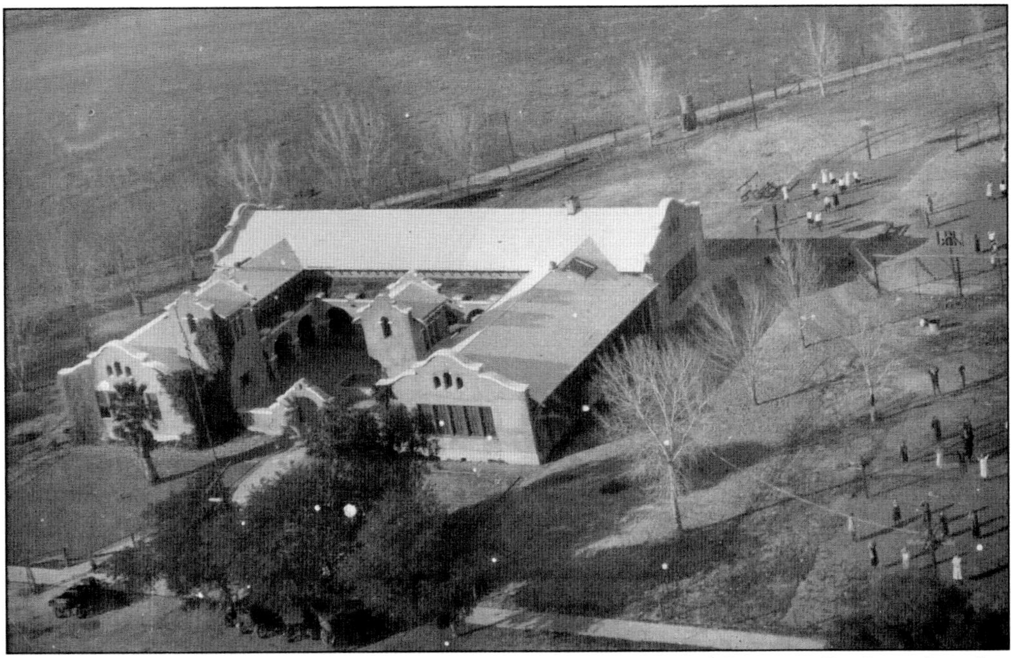

San Jacinto High School, built in 1909, is seen at First Street and Ramona Boulevard in this aerial view. The Edward Hyatt Memorial Tower at the high school was dedicated in 1935. This building is gone today, and Monte Vista Middle School is located near the site. The present-day high school was constructed about a half-mile west, between Idyllwild Drive and Ramona Boulevard, in 1968. (Courtesy San Jacinto Museum.)

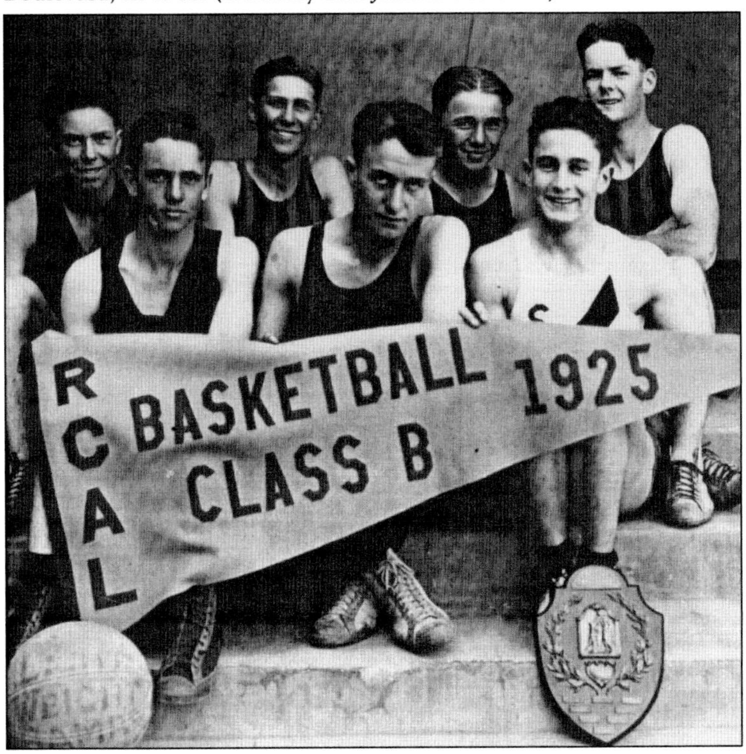

The high school's Class B basketball team proudly poses for a 1925 championship photograph. Pictured from left to right are the following: (first row) Allen Fasley, Armand Viora, and Harry Hofmann; (second row) John Wilson, Newton Bashaw, Eugene Griggs, and an unidentified team member. (Courtesy San Jacinto Museum.)

The San Jacinto Library was located at the corner of San Jacinto Avenue and Central (Ramona) Boulevard in the former San Jacinto Water Company building. In 1931, William Vosburg purchased the facility to incorporate it into the Vosburg Hotel. The library then moved to a building on Main Street. (Courtesy San Jacinto Museum.)

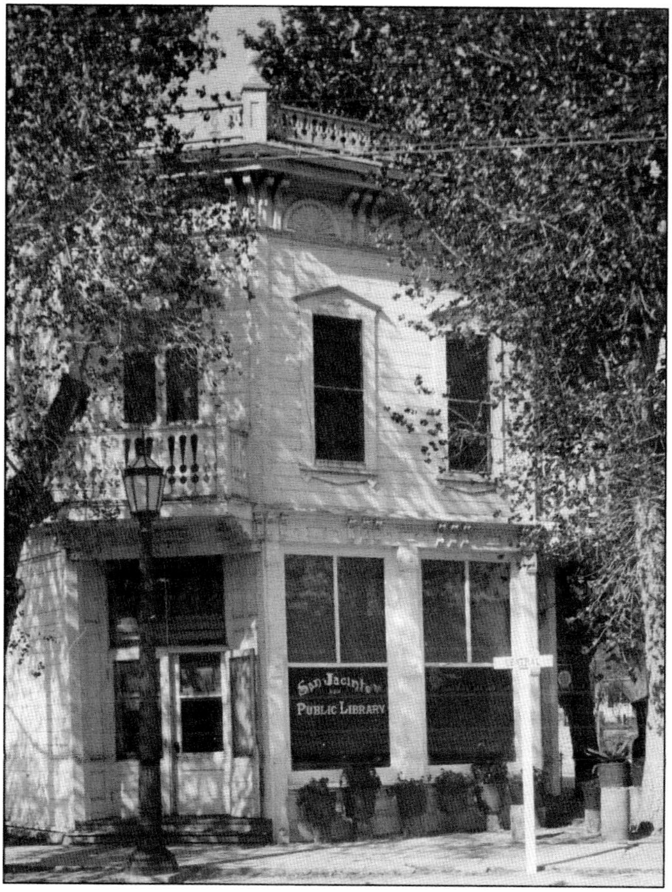

The new San Jacinto Library and Performing Arts Building stands on the San Jacinto High School campus, at the corner of Idyllwild Drive and Tiger Lane. The San Jacinto School District and the Riverside County Library System combined funds to build a joint-use public and student library in 2000, a much better accommodation than the old library on Main Street. (Courtesy Jack Warneke.)

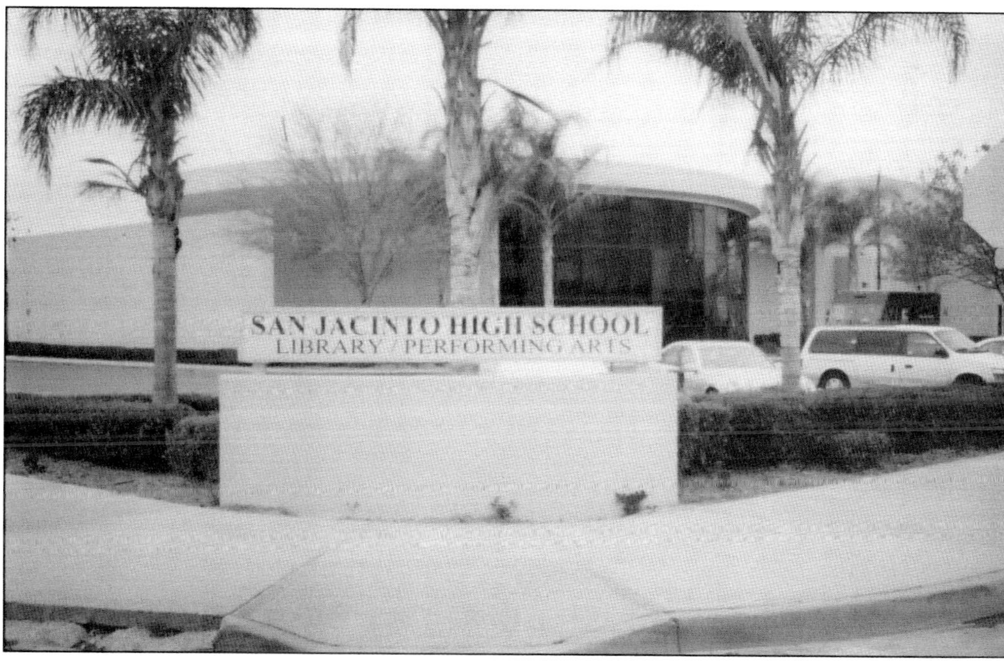

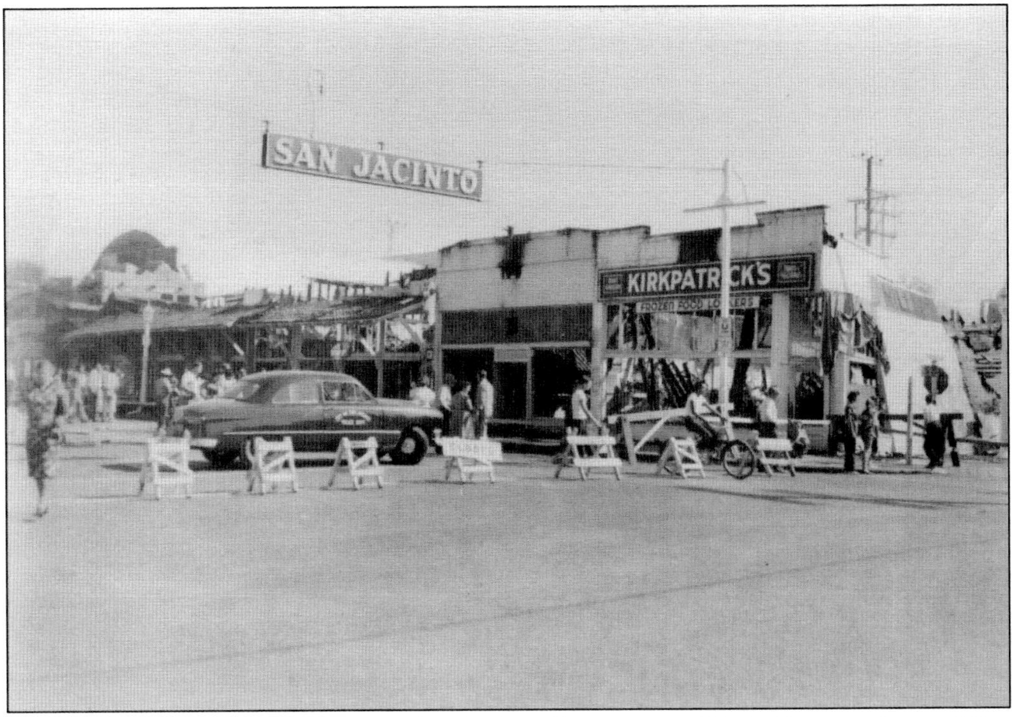

A 1951 fire destroyed nearly the entire block of buildings south of Main Street and east of San Jacinto Avenue. Shown in this photograph is a 1949 Ford police car. The City of San Jacinto owns a restored 1949 Ford for entries in parades and special events. Note the inquisitive bystanders. (Courtesy San Jacinto Museum.)

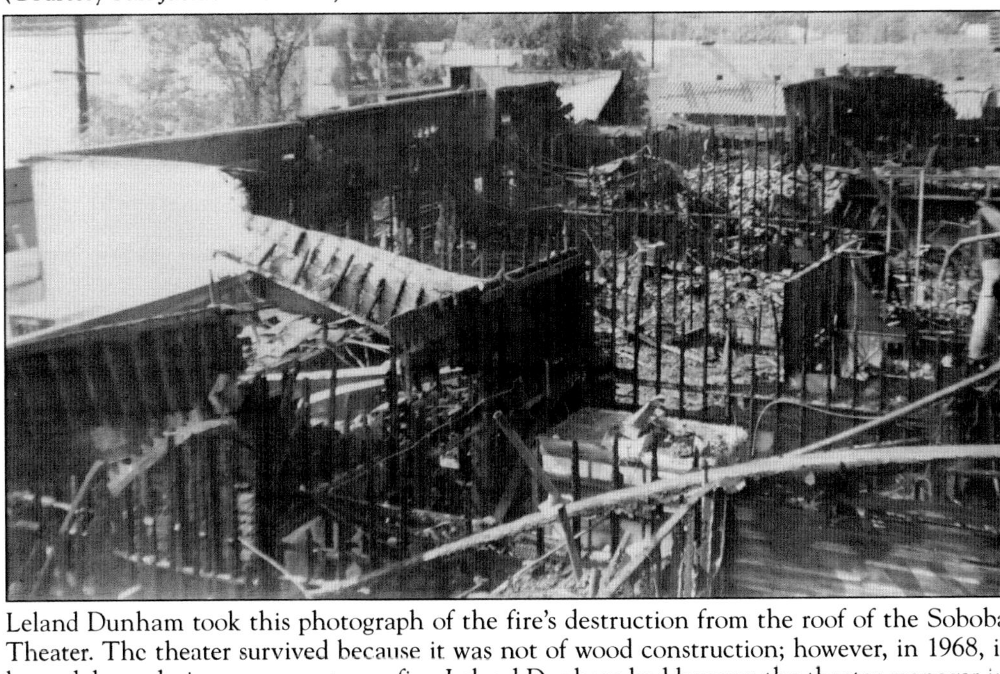

Leland Dunham took this photograph of the fire's destruction from the roof of the Soboba Theater. The theater survived because it was not of wood construction; however, in 1968, it burned down during a more extreme fire. Leland Dunham had become the theater manager in 1942. (Courtesy Betty Jo Dunham.)

Oscar S. Hofmann stands in front of his Hopi Pueblo–style office building in the 1930s. Coming to San Jacinto in the early 1900s, he took a strong interest in the local Native Americans and in Helen Hunt Jackson's book *Ramona*. Hofmann and his business partner, Lester A. Reynolds, designed and built the Soboba Theater, patterned after the Hopi Pueblo style of architecture. (Courtesy Ethel Handcock Harp.)

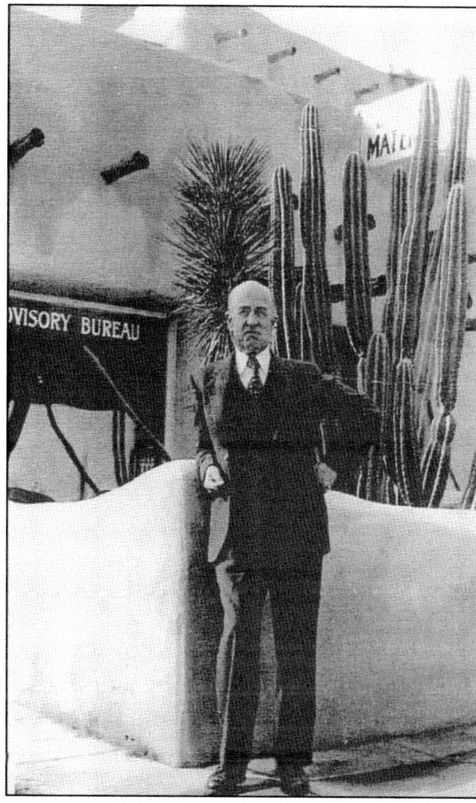

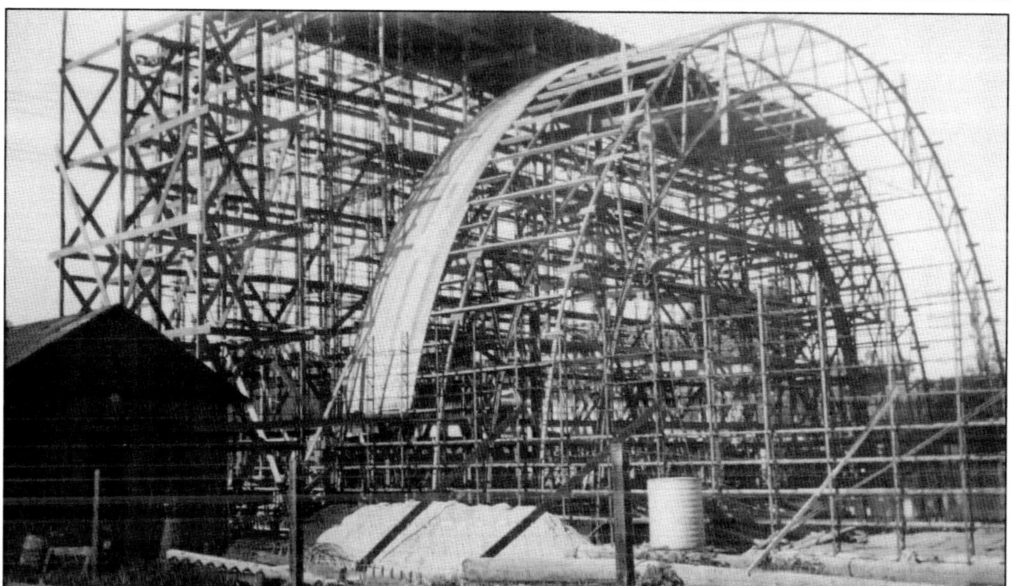

Shown here is the early steel-arch construction of the Soboba Theater, located on the south side of Main Street. Local builder Charles Darling completed the construction of the theater in 1927. Oscar Hofmann hoped the style would make San Jacinto a Pueblo town, thus preserving the Native American culture. The Depression and World War II prevented the wide-scale acceptance. (Courtesy San Jacinto Museum.)

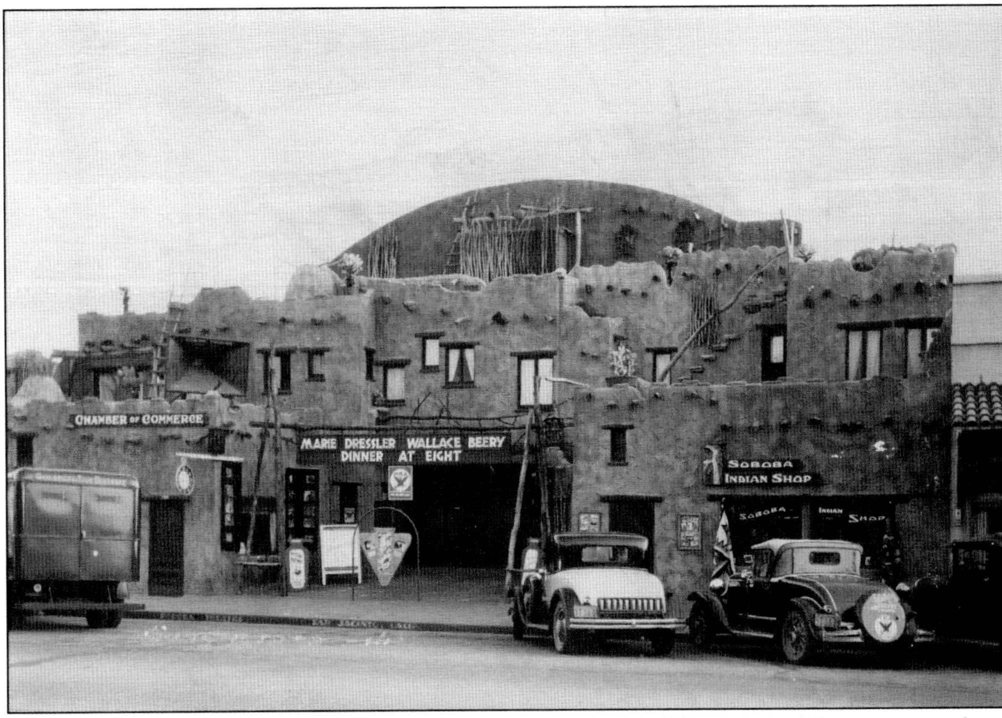

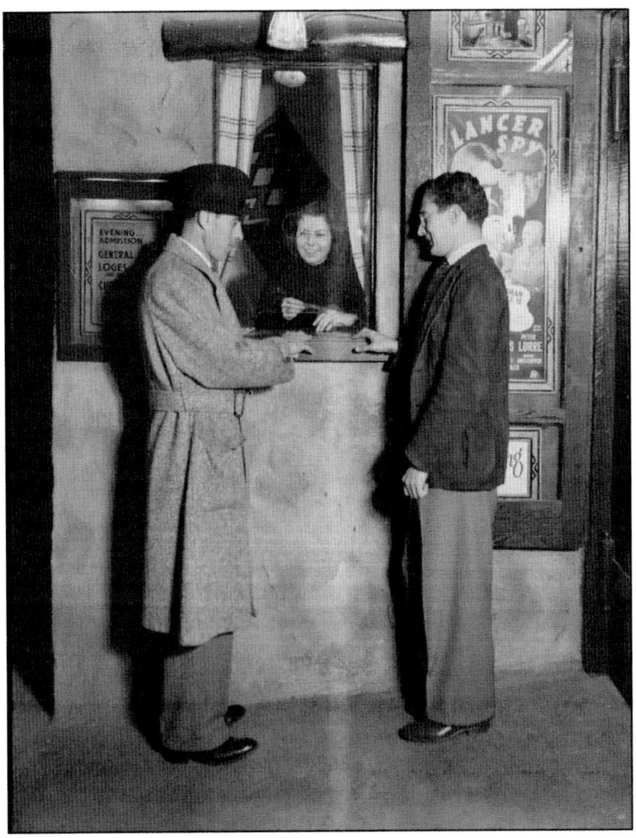

The Soboba Theater opened in September 1927. This front view was taken in the 1930s when the movie *Dinner at Eight* was showing, starring Marie Dressler and Wallace Berry. Oscar Hofmann's dream was for all buildings in San Jacinto to adopt this style, but the concept did not evolve. (Courtesy San Jacinto Museum.)

Oscar Hofmann's son Harry became manager of the Soboba Theater in 1931. Here Harry stands to the right of the ticket booth with his wife, Virginia, inside the booth selling tickets in 1937. The movie playing is *Lancer Spy*, starring Peter Lorre (Major Gruring) and Delores Daria Sunnell (Delores Del Rio). In 1970, Harry, Jeannette, and Judy Hofmann dedicated Hofmann Park, on the west side at the corner of Sixth Street, to the memory of Oscar S. Hofmann. (Courtesy Sam Jacinto Museum.)

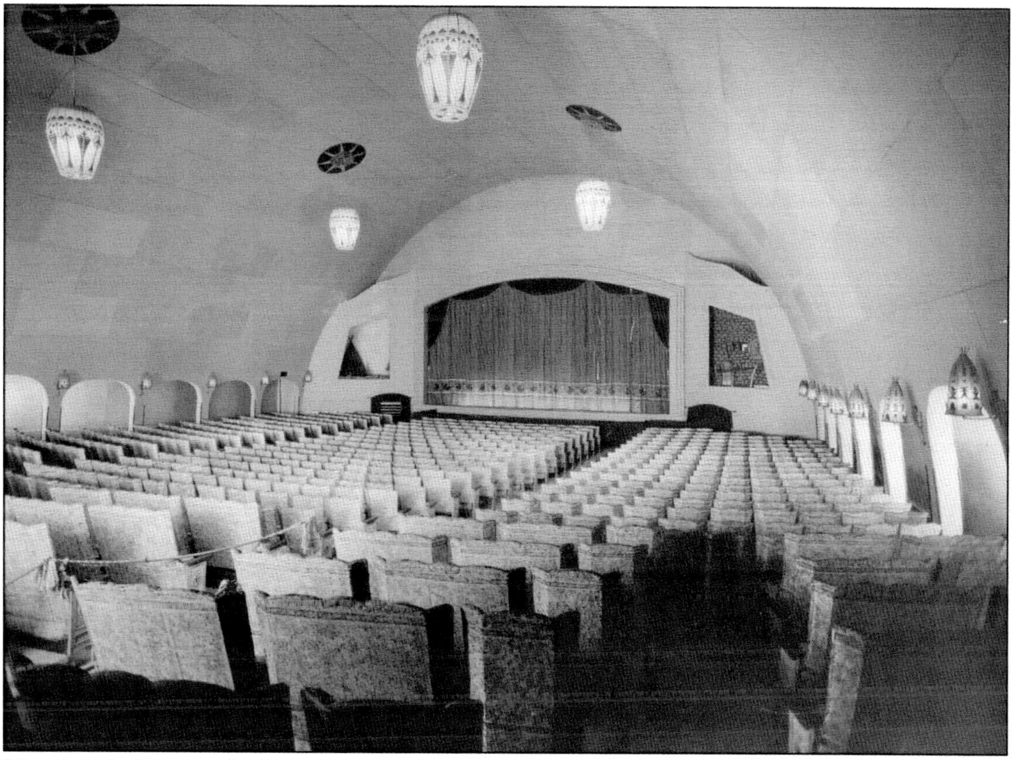

The Soboba Theater had a seating capacity of 750. A new building material at this time, Celotex, was used to cover the dome's interior structure and, by a stroke of luck, made the room acoustically perfect. Another innovation was a second-floor "crying room" for mothers with babies. In 1941, the Soboba Theater was sold to Bill Martin, who also owned the Hemet Theater and the Hemacinto Drive Theater, west of San Jacinto Avenue near Midway, the site of Harmon Airfield in the 1920s and 1930s. (Courtesy San Jacinto Museum.)

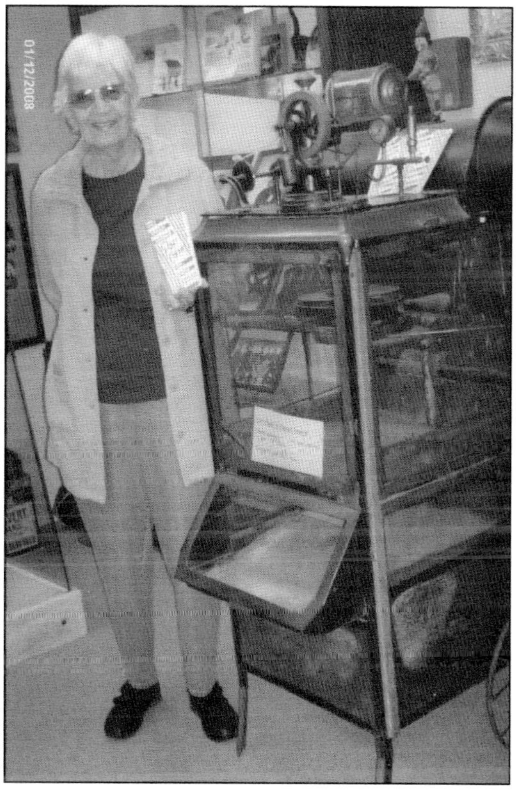

Betty Jo Durham is standing next to an old popcorn machine from the 1920s that is on display at the San Jacinto Museum. Betty Jo and Barbara Dunham, her sister, operated a newer model popcorn machine at the Soboba Theater in the 1940s and shared in the profits. Their father, Leland Dunham, was hired as manager when Bill Martin bought the Soboba Theater in 1941. At the time, the usherettes earned 25¢ per hour. (Courtesy Nancy Warneke.)

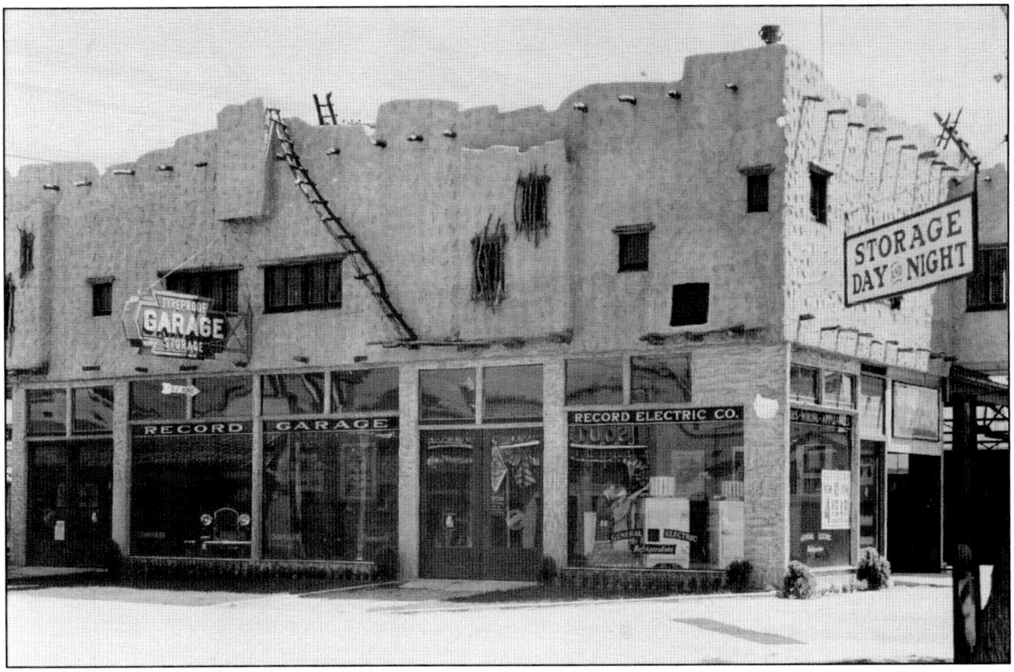

The Record Garage was located on the east side of San Jacinto Avenue and the corner of Fifth Street. Lloyd Record opened his garage in 1918 and, in 1935, changed to the Hopi style of architecture started by Oscar Hofmann. Record was the cousin of Charles Darling, the local contractor who had built the Soboba Theater in 1927. (Courtesy San Jacinto Museum.)

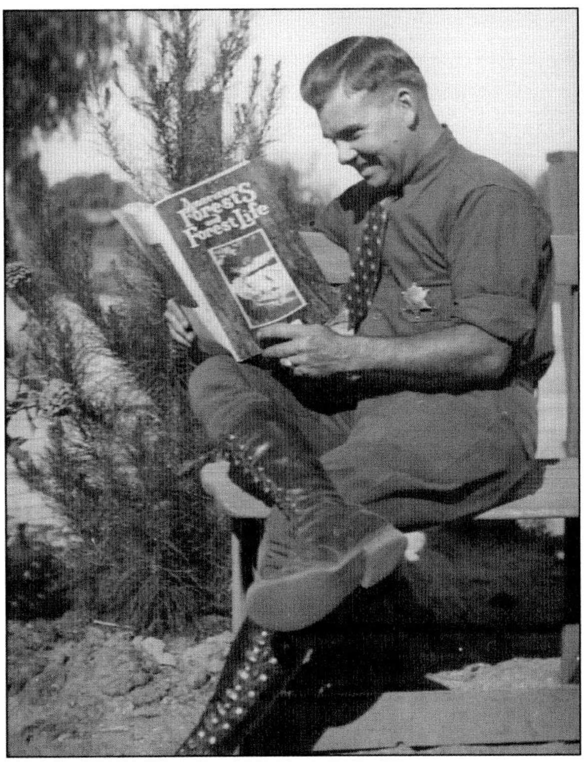

Charles Van Fleet, a 1913 graduate of San Jacinto High School, appears to be engrossed in an issue of *American Forests and Forest Life*. Van Fleet began taking photographs in the early 1900s. As his reputation grew, townspeople would give him old images of the 1800s when they cleaned their attics. When Van Fleet died in 1980, his wife, Marvel, sold his vast collection to Harley Garbani, who in turn donated it to the San Jacinto Museum. (Courtesy San Jacinto Museum.)

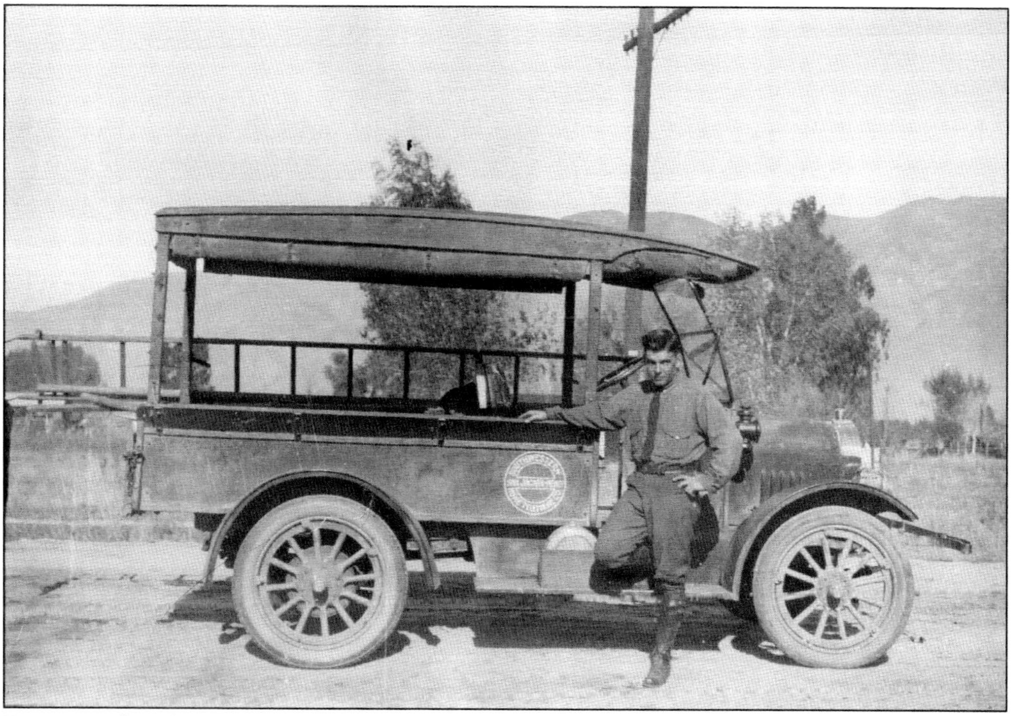

For a period in the 1920s, Charles Van Fleet worked with the telephone company. Here he stands by a utility truck bearing the sign "San Jacinto–Hemet Southwestern Home Telephone Company." The truck looks capable of transporting numerous workmen and a long ladder. (Courtesy Charles Swift collection.)

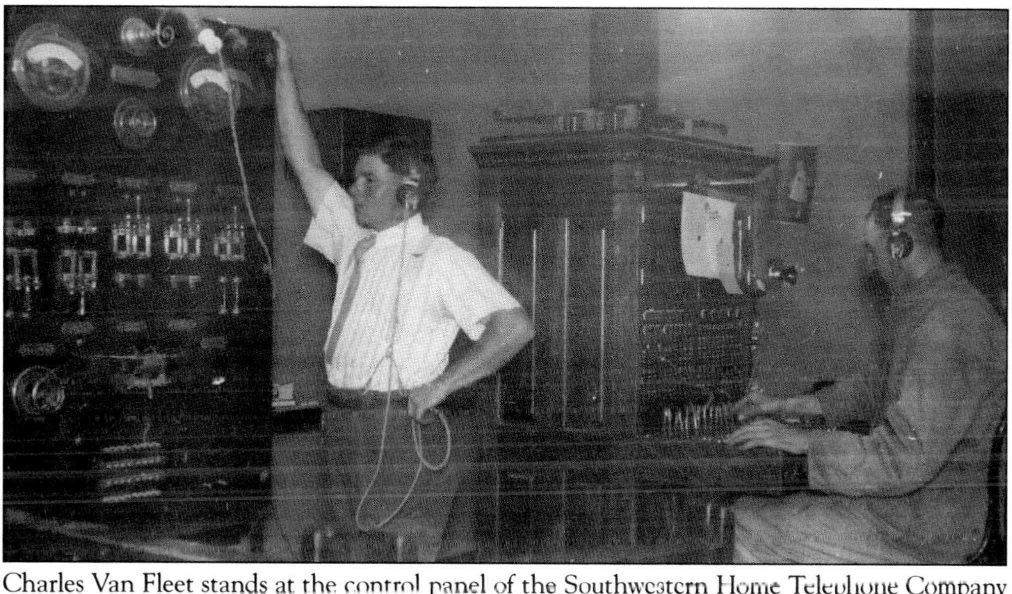

Charles Van Fleet stands at the control panel of the Southwestern Home Telephone Company around 1930. The man on the right is operating the switchboard. When Van Fleet was attending San Jacinto High School, he ran the electric plant in town. When Bill Gray organized the first Boy Scout troop in San Jacinto in 1918, Van Fleet became the adult leader. (Courtesy San Jacinto Museum.)

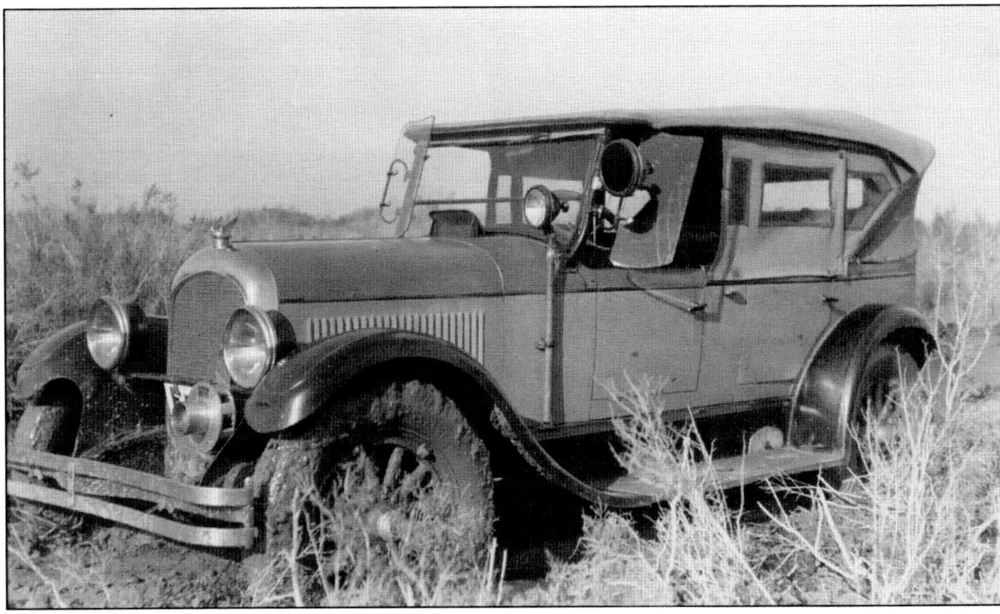

From 1927 to 1929, Charles Van Fleet served as a deputy sheriff; this was the sheriff's car in the late 1920s. Becoming the first fireman for the California Division of Forestry in the early 1930s, Van Fleet ended up making it a 32-year career. The California Forestry fire station is still located at the corner of San Jacinto Avenue and First Street. (Courtesy Charles Van Fleet.)

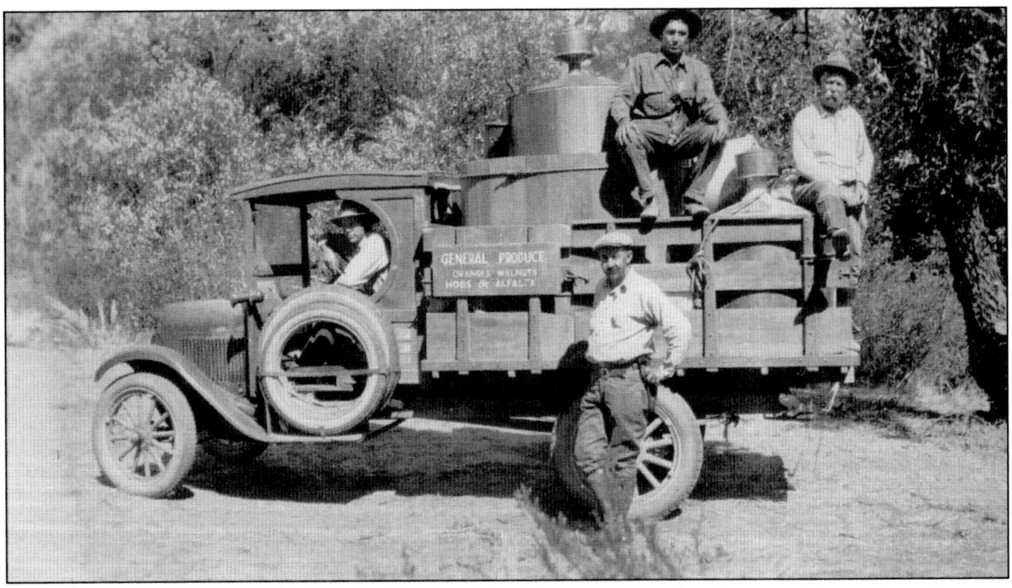

While working as a deputy sheriff, Charles Van Fleet was involved in a raid on a bootlegging operation. He took photographs and wrote up an account of the raid. This image depicts the other deputy sheriffs after the raid. The men borrowed the truck from the General Produce dealer in San Jacinto in order to transport the apprehended equipment from the still. The deputy standing and the one above him both have pistols in holsters and sheriff badges. (Courtesy Charles Van Fleet.)

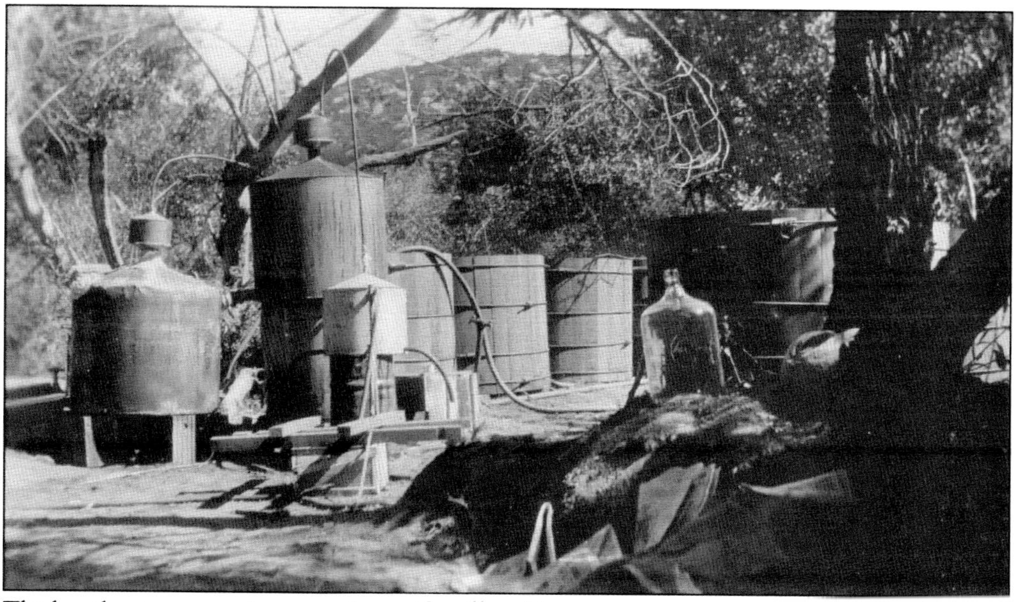

The bootlegging operation, complete with still and fermentation vats, is pictured here. The entire business was located along Portero Creek in Laborda Canyon, which is above Massacre Canyon on the Portero ranch. The bootleggers saw the sheriff unit coming and all escaped capture. (Courtesy Charles Van Fleet.)

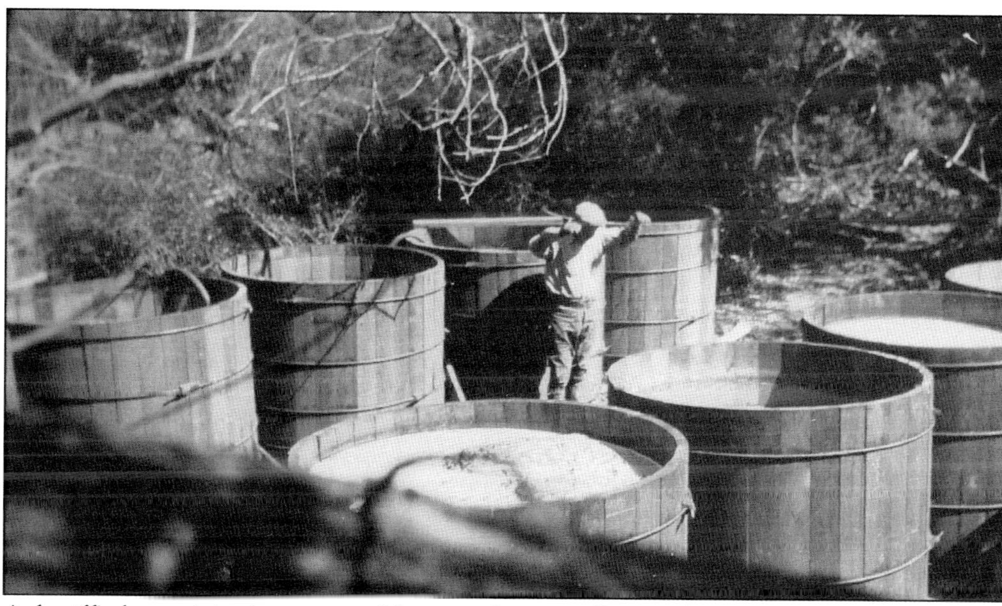

A sheriff's deputy is in the process of draining the vats, allowing the alcohol to run down Portero Creek. Each vat held 500 gallons; the operation included 10 vats for a total of 5,000 gallons. The dismantling took two days, during which the deputies stayed in the bootleggers' shack, which was still well supplied with food. They feasted. (Courtesy Charles Van Fleet.)

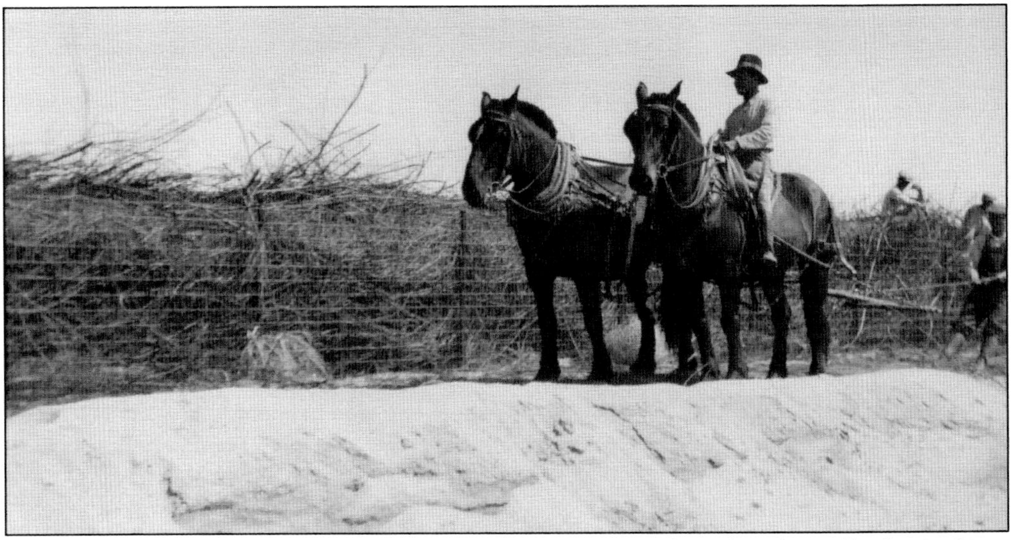

Johnny Rubideaux uses his team of horses to pull apricot pruning branches that will aid in building the levee along the San Jacinto River. The levee was constructed following the devastation of a 1906 flood (not to mention a previous one in 1884). After a fence was built, branches were piled against it and then covered with soil to form a levee. Each year, branches were added. Leland Dunham also worked on the levee. Johnny Rubideaux was a grain hauler from Pico Rancho. (Courtesy Betty Jo Dunham.)

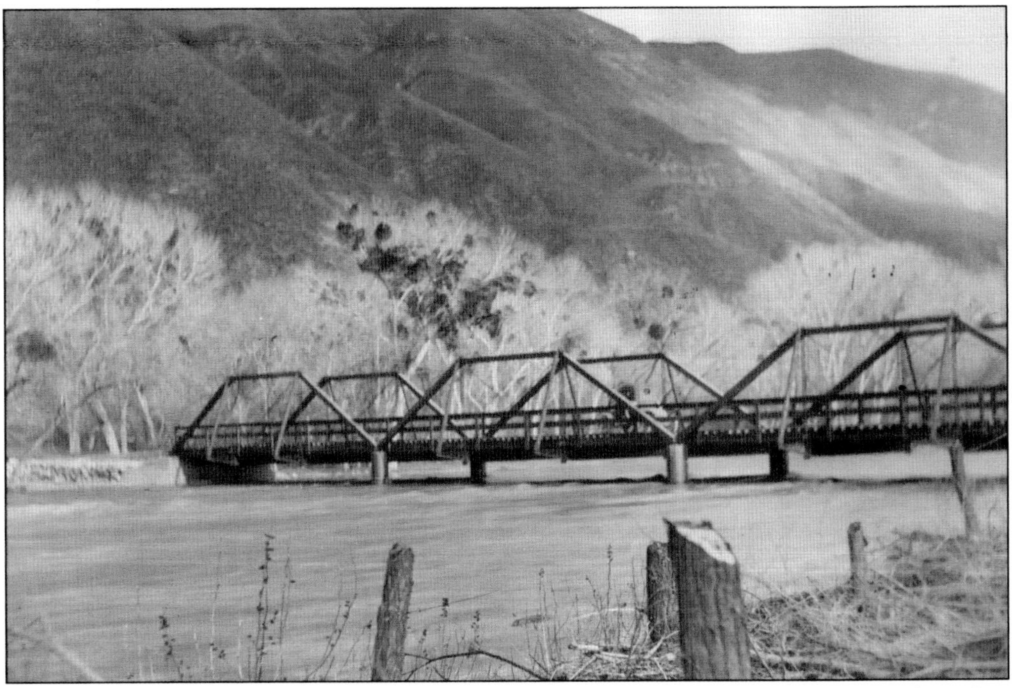

This view of the State Street (Gilman) Bridge, leading across the San Jacinto River from San Jacinto to Gilman Road on the other side of the river, was captured during high water levels in 1917. For years, the span was an important entity that kept both sides of the river in close proximity; however, it was continually threatened with high waters during rainy seasons. (Courtesy Charles Van Fleet.)

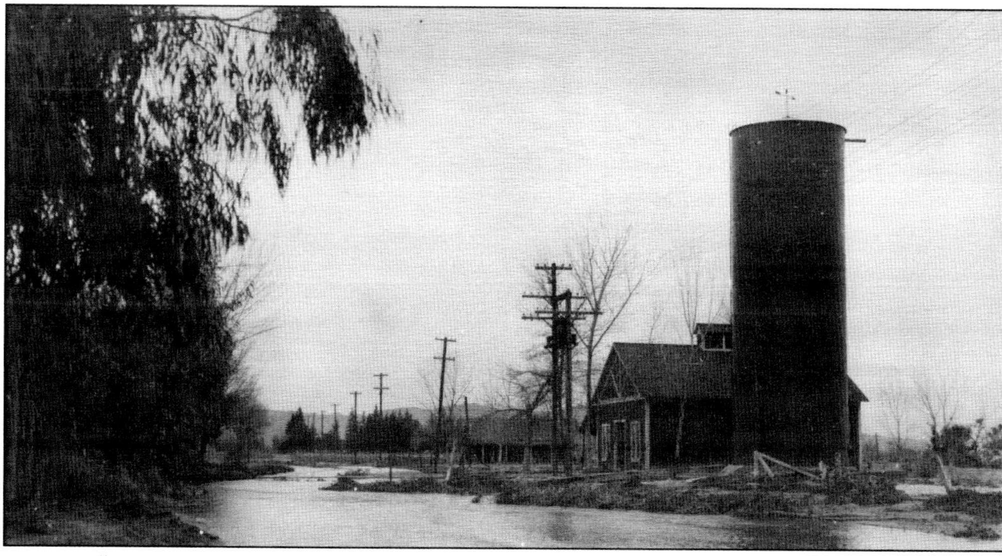

In 1917, floodwaters not only threatened bridges over the San Jacinto River but also the city's pumping plant. As the water level continued to rise, the water storage tank pictured here capsized and floated downstream. Afterward, much renovation of the plant was needed. (Courtesy San Jacinto Museum.)

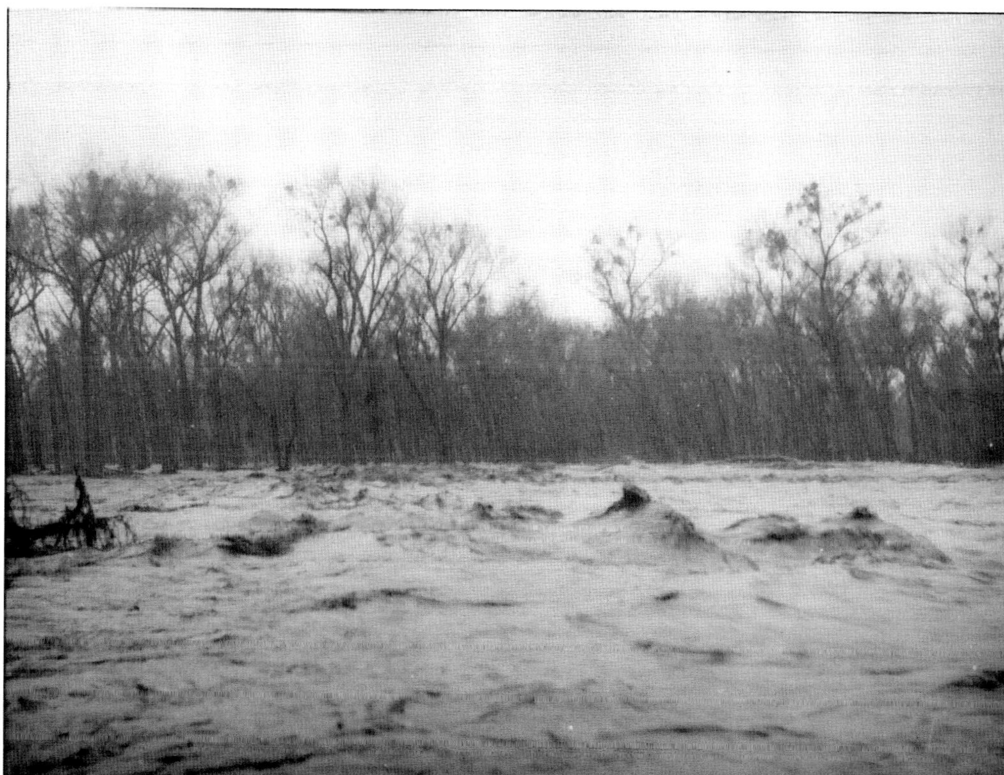

The rapids of the 1917 floodwaters of the San Jacinto River are shown in this photograph. It can certainly be imagined how water of such turbulence could carry away a large pumping tank such as it did during this flood. (Courtesy San Jacinto Museum.)

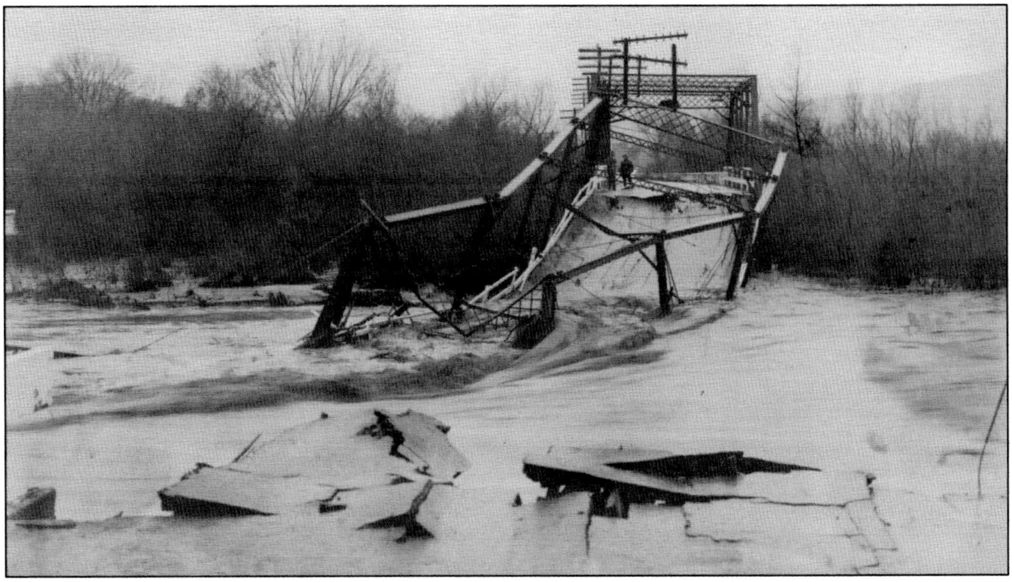

Floodwaters finally took their toll on the State Street (Gilman) Bridge during the flood of 1927, as witnessed in this photograph. The San Jacinto River appeared to be flooding on a 10-year interval, as it did again in 1937. The next major flood, however, did not occur until 1980, when the levee broke east of the city and inundated the entire town with two to four feet of water. (Courtesy San Jacinto Museum.)

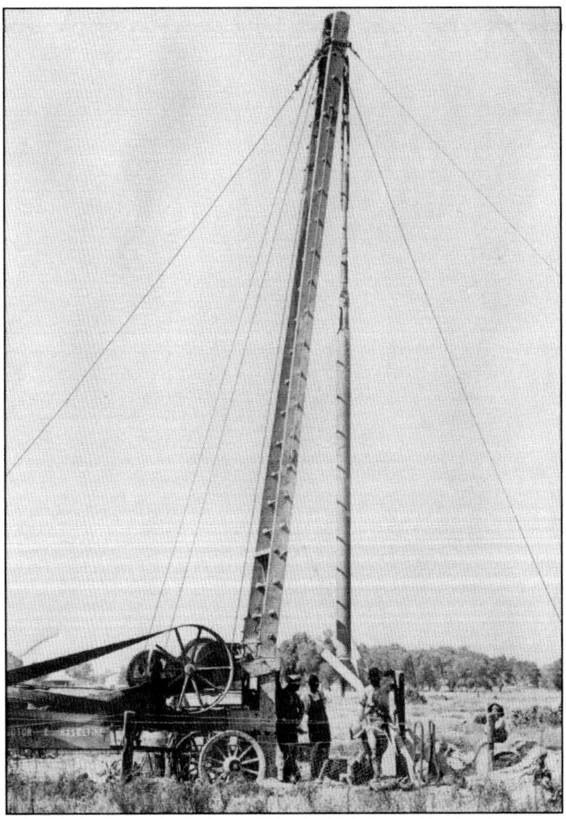

The San Jacinto Oil Company was formed around 1900 and began drilling in several locations around San Jacinto. In this photograph, one of the company's oil rigs is at work drilling in 1901. The firm never found oil but rather lots of water; however, editor Arthur Munn of the *San Jacinto Register* considered water more valuable than oil for the valley. (Courtesy San Jacinto Museum.)

Ed Knapp sits beside an artesian well in San Jacinto about 1900. Many such wells existed in the valley, including the natural hot springs at the three resorts. In 1937, the Metropolitan Water District dug a tunnel through the San Jacinto Mountain Range that cut into an aquifer of the natural water. Subsequently, all of the artesian wells dried up. (Courtesy Charles Van Fleet.)

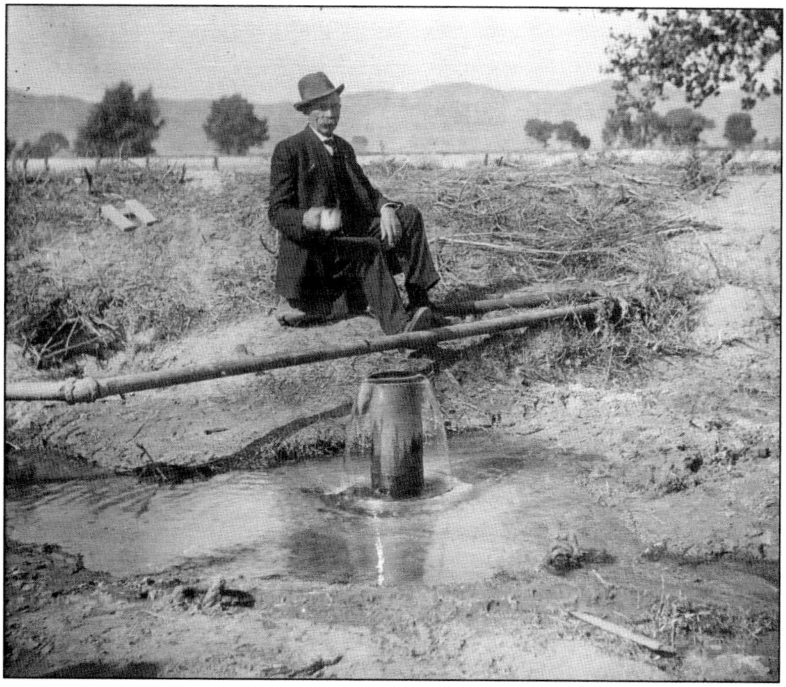

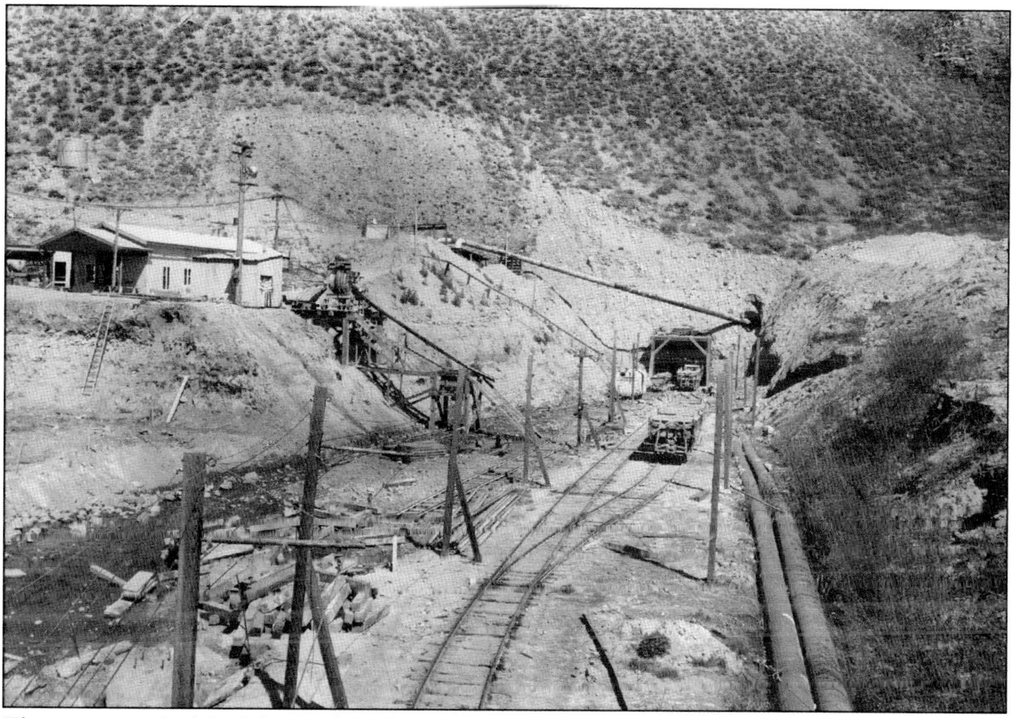

The west portal of the Metropolitan Water District tunnel, shown here, is located along Soboba Road east of State Street. The tunnel emits from the eastern portal, on the other side of the mountain at Cabazon. The water comes from the Colorado River's Parker Dam and is deposited to reservoirs at Lake Mathews for Orange County, Diamond Valley Lake, and Lake Skinner for distribution to San Diego. (Courtesy San Jacinto Museum.)

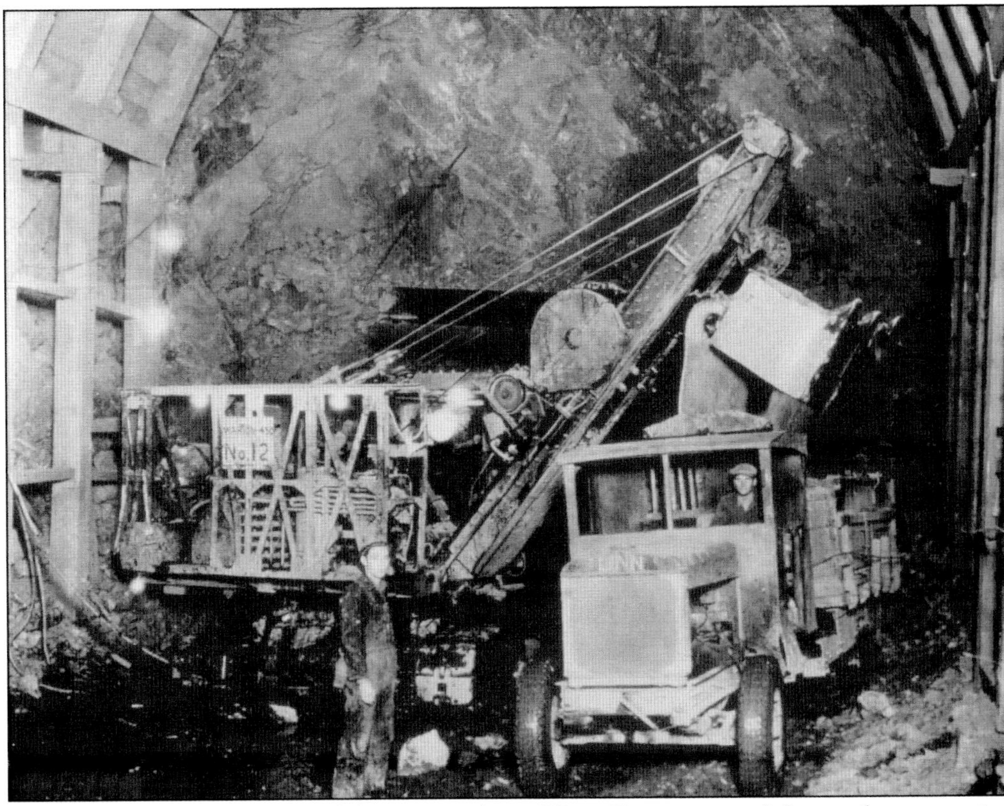

This view shows the interior of the Metropolitan Water District tunnel during the excavation process. The tunnel was completed in 1937, at which time water soon started flowing through via the influx of water from the California Aqueduct. By 1947, the Soboba Indians had lost their natural water supply, as their wells dried up. (Courtesy San Jacinto Museum.)

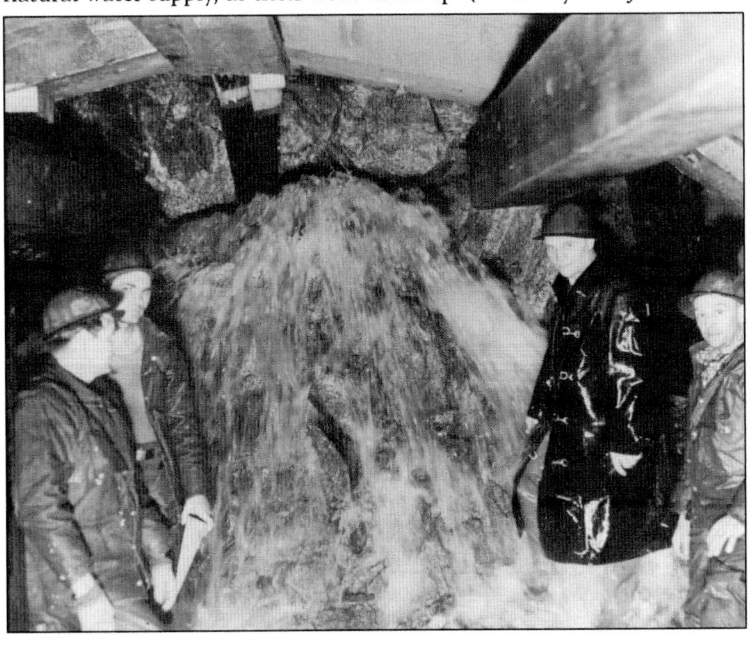

Water flows into the new tunnel from the disrupted aquifer. The water was the source of the San Jacinto artesian and Soboba wells. Not surprisingly, the Metropolitan Water District still gets more water out of the tunnel than the organization put into it. (Courtesy San Jacinto Museum.)

The eastern portal of the Metropolitan Water District tunnel is seen here at Cabazon. Drilling of the tunnel was started from both sides of the mountain until meeting in the center, exactly lined up. Once a year, the water supply is cut off so the tunnel can be inspected. (Courtesy San Jacinto Museum.)

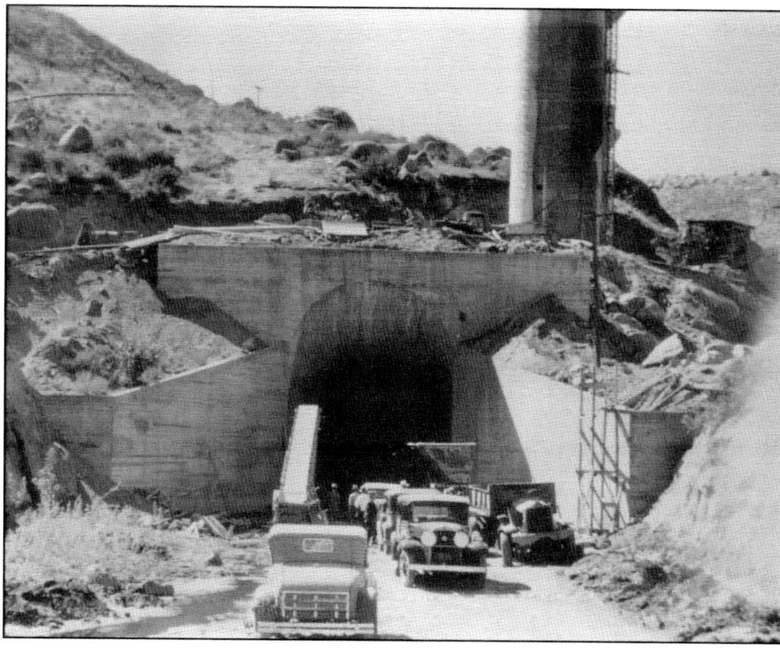

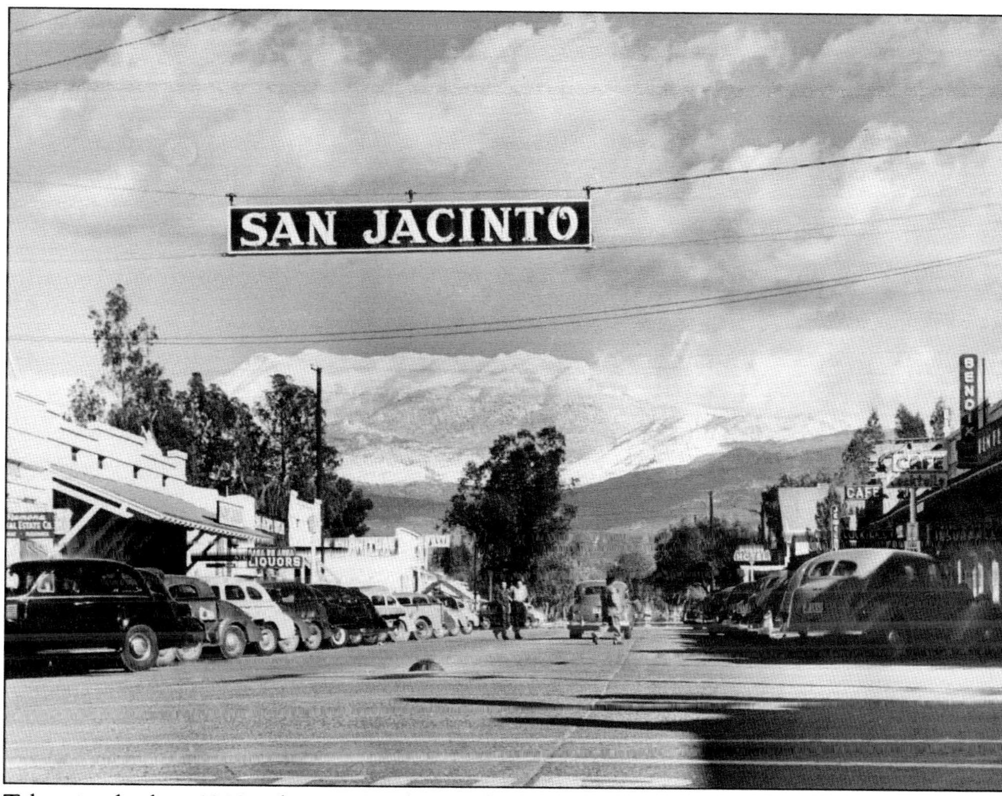

Taken in the late 1940s, this eastward view shows Main Street in San Jacinto. Snow is visible on Mount San Jacinto, which has an elevation of 10,804 feet. During the winter, snow can drop down to about 3,000 feet. (Courtesy San Jacinto Museum.)

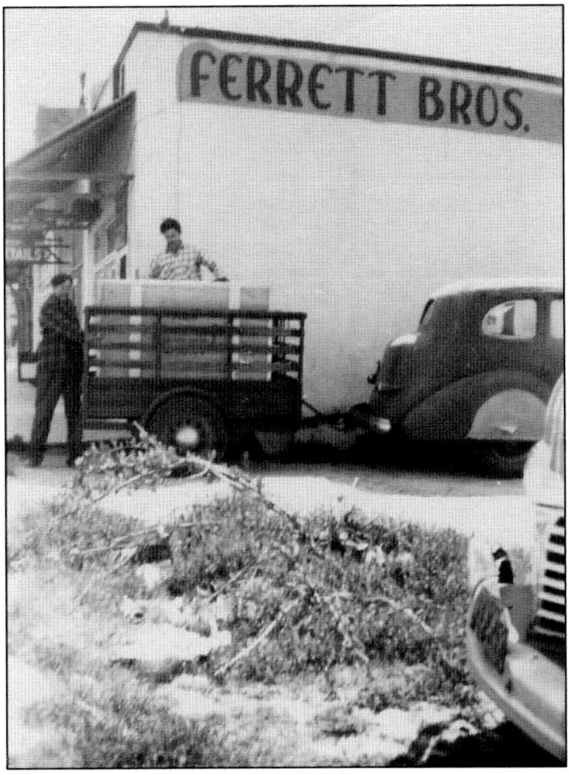

Fred Ferrett (left) and his brother Charles unload an organ at their music store at 130 West Main Street in the 1950s. Their father, John Ferret, moved to De Anza Drive in 1928 and established a plumbing store on East Main Street and a shop on De Anza. Charlie and Fred opened the Pioneer TV and Music Store in the 1950s and became the first in the San Jacinto Valley to sell television sets. (Courtesy Mildred Ferrett Dummer.)

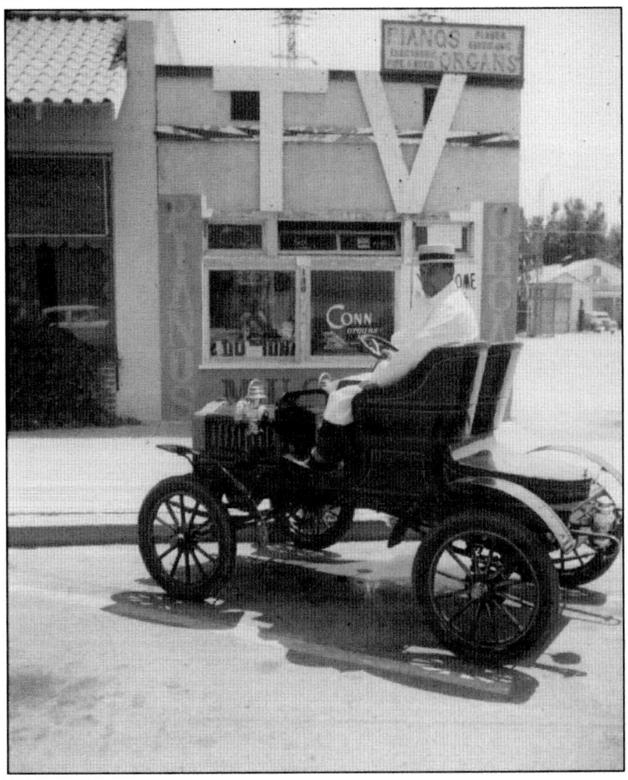

In front of the Main Street Pioneer TV and Music Store, Fred Ferrett sits in a 1905 Buick that his brother Charles restored. The store was removed in the 1970s to build a bank parking lot at the corner of Main and San Jacinto Avenue. The brothers sold and repaired pianos, organs, Zenith televisions, and musical instruments. (Courtesy Mildred Ferrett Dummer.)

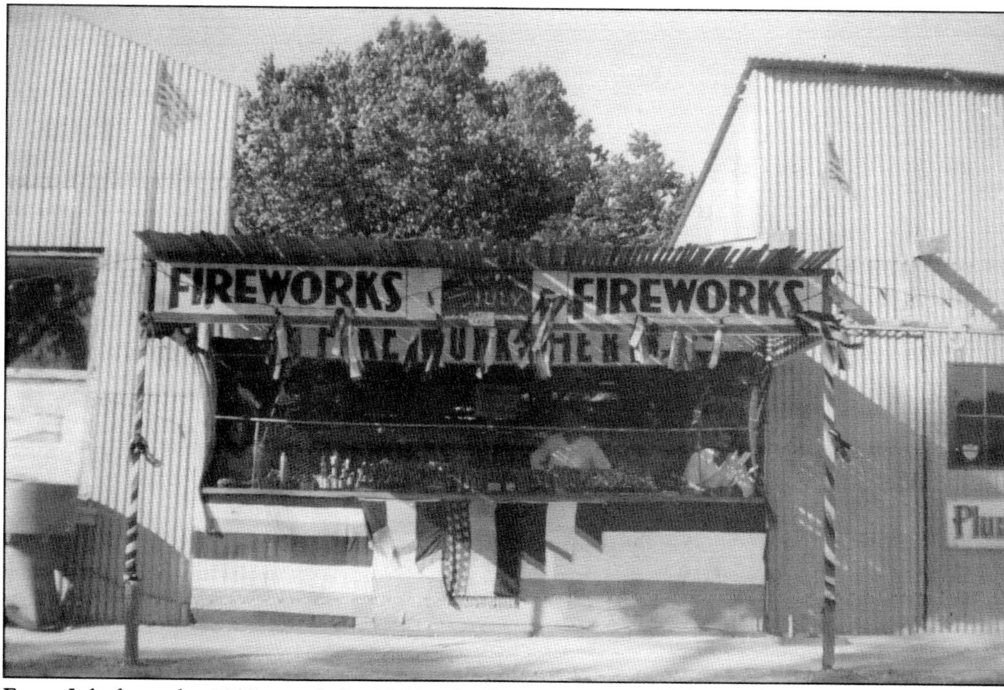

Every July from the 1930s until the 1960s, the Ferrett family sold fireworks for the Fourth of July. When the brothers had to move the music store from Main Street, they shifted to the family buildings on De Anza Drive. (Courtesy Mildred Ferrett Dummer.)

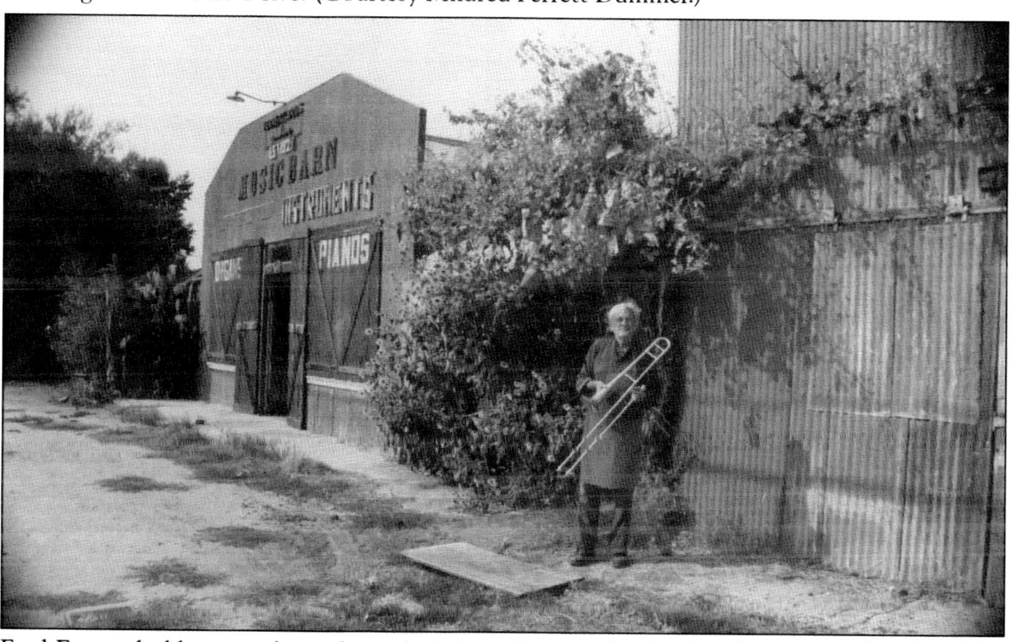

Fred Ferrett holds a trombone from the Music Barn in the 1990s. The sign at the top of the building reads, "Ferret Brothers. Est. 1929. Music Barn. Instruments, Pianos, and Organs." Both parents, John and Edna, had musical backgrounds. In addition to playing piano and writing music and poetry, Edna had her own band, Edna and the Ranch Boys, which played for dances in the valley. (Courtesy Mildred Ferrett Dummer.)

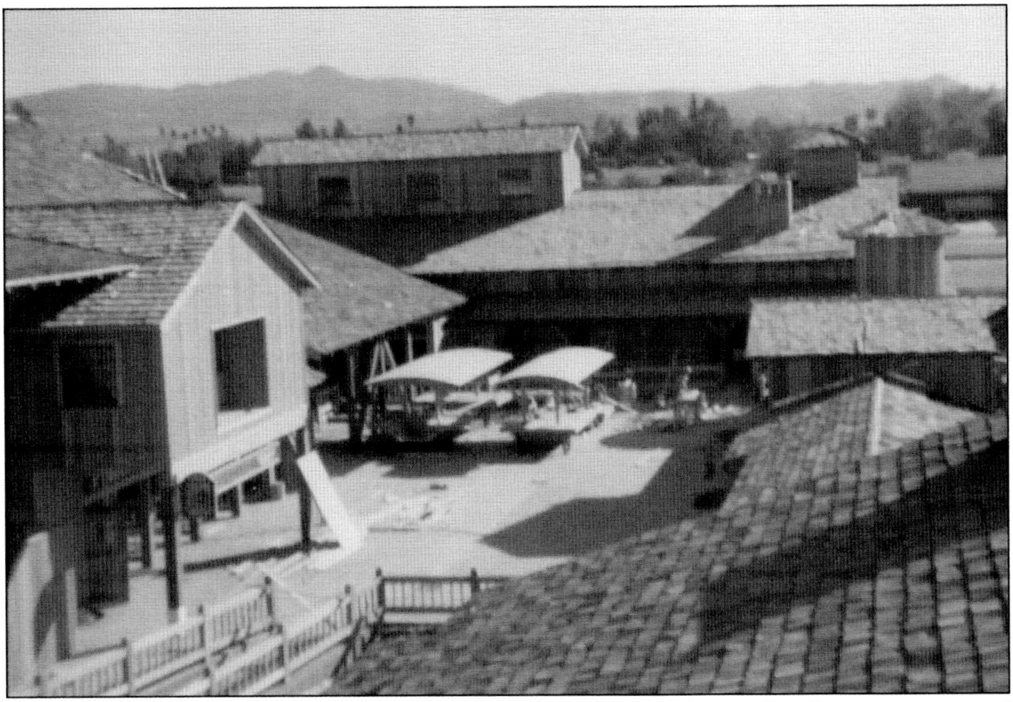

The first shopping center located away from downtown Main Street in San Jacinto was named Farmers Corner. Occupying the northeast corner of Menlo and San Jacinto Avenues, it is a quaint, little all-wood structure. The center opened in the 1970s and served the community well. (Courtesy Betty Jo Dunham.)

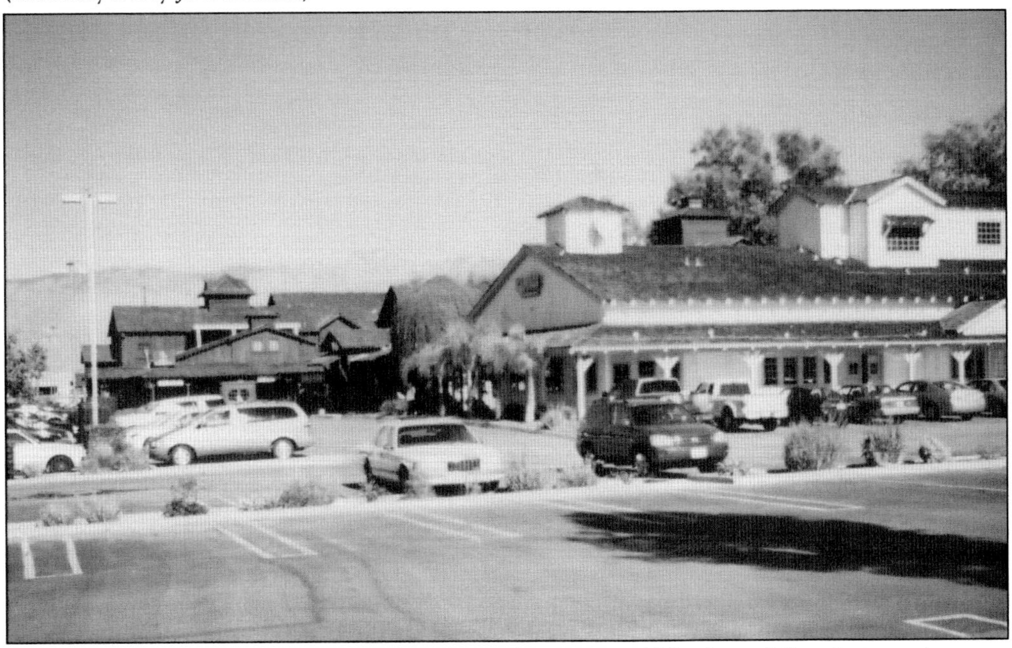

This view of Farmers Corner was taken from the corner of Menlo and San Jacinto Avenues looking north. The restaurant at the left is Mister T's and the one at the right is the Acapulco Restaurant. (Courtesy Jack Warneke.)

Five

AGRICULTURE

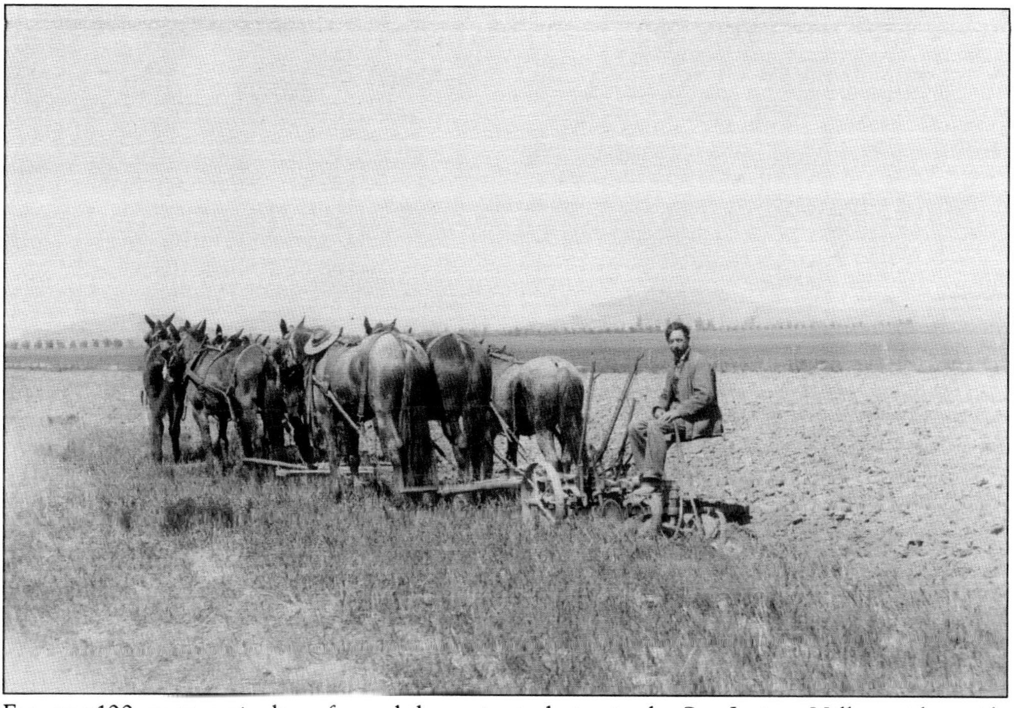

For over 100 years, agriculture formed the major industry in the San Jacinto Valley, with a wide range of crops grown. The first step in growing most crops was land preparation. Here a team of six horses pulls a two-furrow moldboard plow in preparation for planting grain, alfalfa, or vegetable crops in 1912. (Courtesy San Jacinto Museum.)

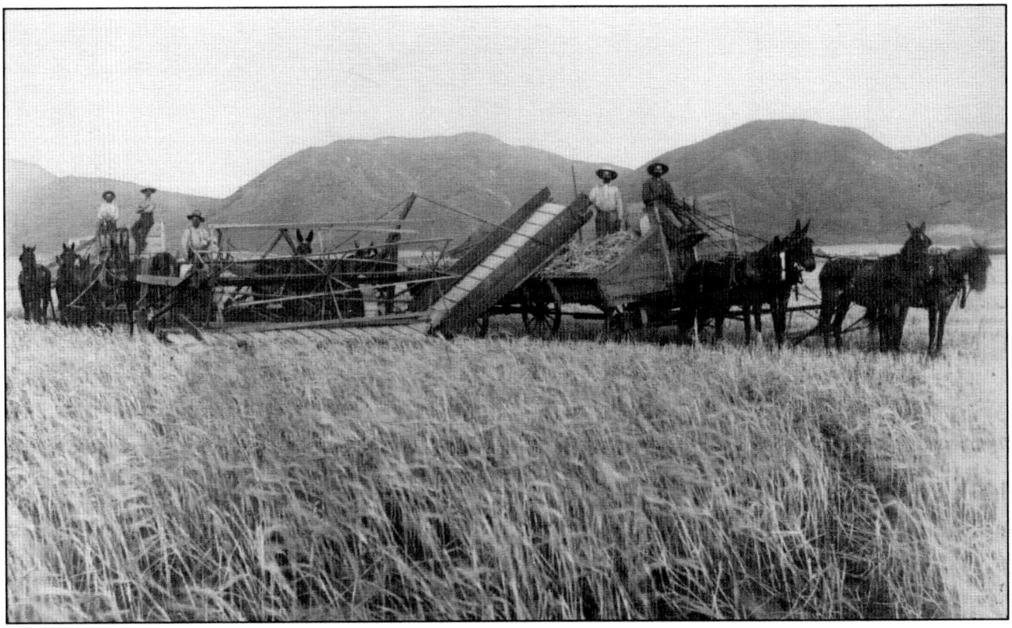

This early grain reaper was used to cut wheat or barley and to convey the plant onto a wagon. Upon completion of this process, the loaded wagons would be hauled to a nearby location where the cut plants could be threshed to remove the grain from the straw. (Courtesy San Jacinto Museum.)

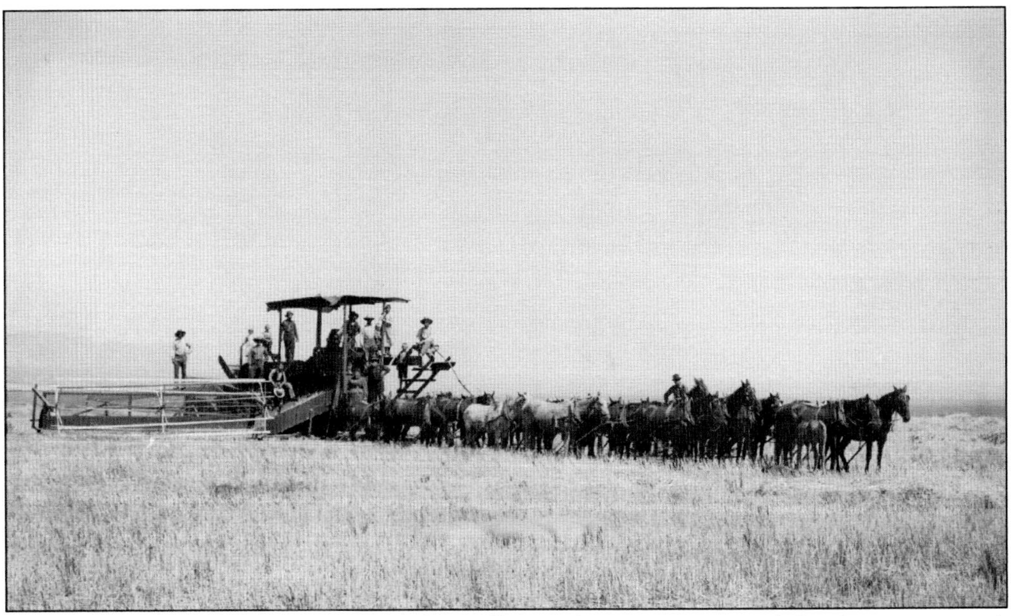

A team of at least 20 horses was required to pull a combination reaper and thresher, as pictured. The first combines were developed in California, where the large, open fields could accommodate the massive equipment. The grain could now be cut and threshed directly in the field. (Courtesy San Jacinto Museum.)

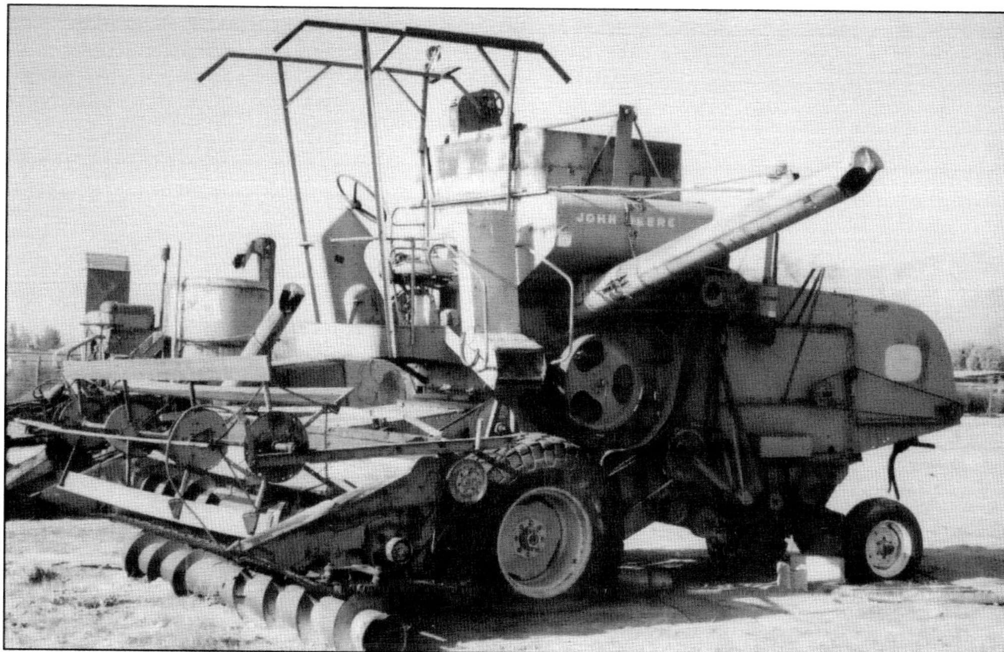

After horse-drawn combines came the advent of self-propelled combines. The first ones were very large and propelled by steam engines. The John Deere combine shown here was used at Al and Pricilla Pastor's Spice Ranch around 1960. The ranch grew various herbs and spices like dill and basil along East Main Street and south of the Ramona Expressway until the 1980s. (Courtesy Ken Holtzclaw.)

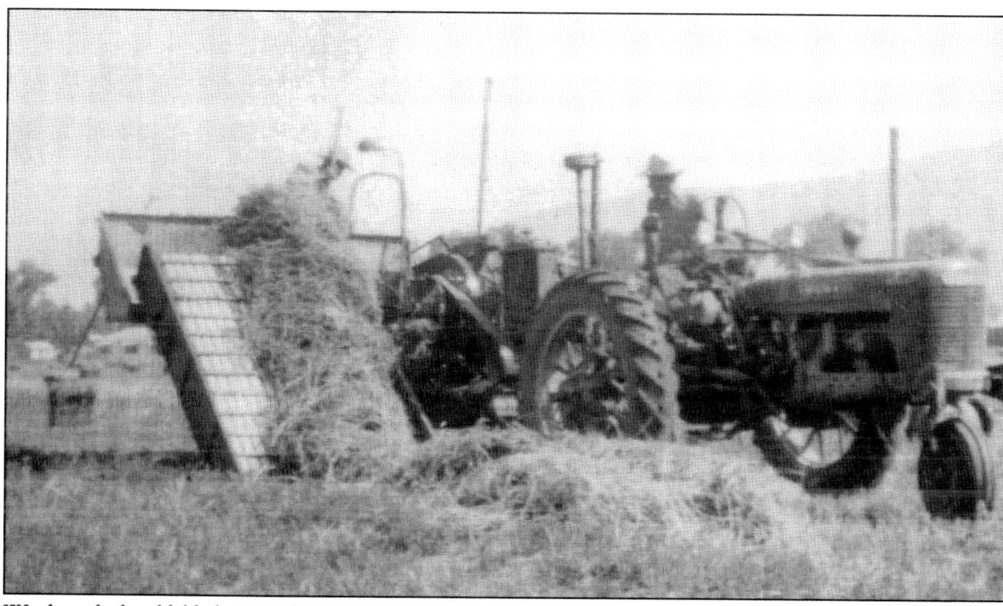

Workers bale alfalfa hay with an International Farmall tractor driven by Kenneth Quandt on the Quandt ranch in the 1940s. This early model did not automatically tie the bales. Two people, one on each side, rode on the back to poke wires through the bales and tie them while they were compressed in the machine. The man at the top is guiding the alfalfa into the baler compressor. (Courtesy Marjory Quandt Goodwin.)

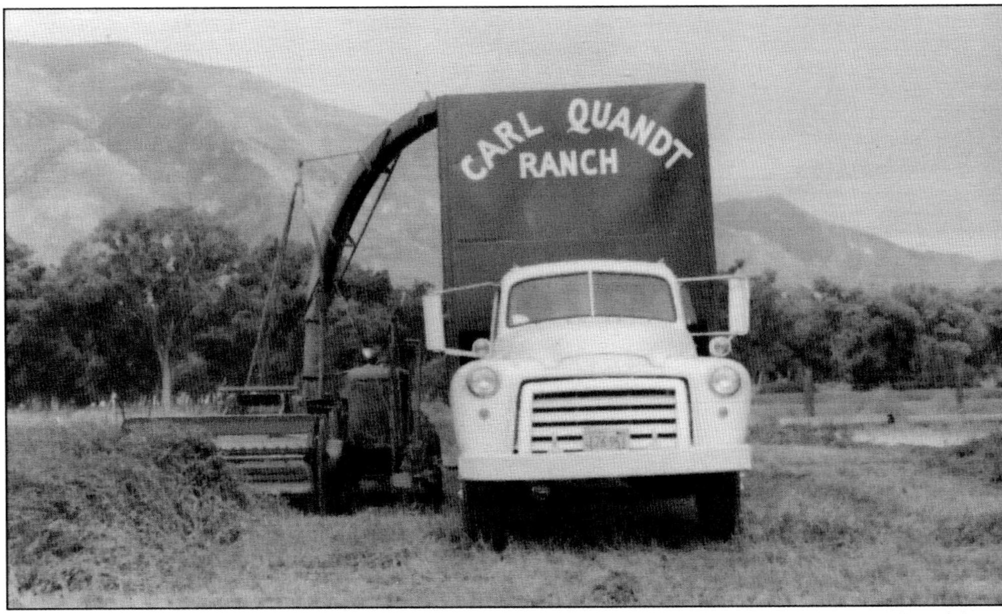

Later in the 1950s, the alfalfa was cut into windrows, chopped while still green, and then blown into a truck, as seen here. The load of green chop was delivered directly to neighboring dairies for feeding the milk cows. Any excess was covered with plastic to make silage. (Courtesy Marjory Quandt Goodwin.)

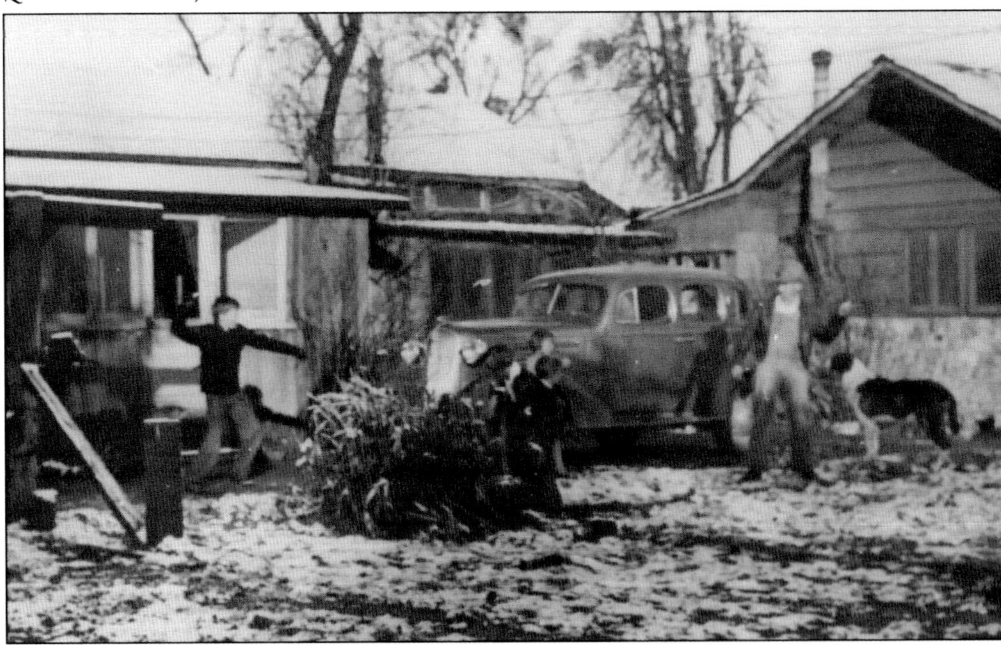

The Woodhead ranch was the home of the Carl Quandt family. The Quandt children are, from left to right, Kenneth, Ella Mae, Sonny, and Marjory. They are engaged in a snowball fight with their uncle Louis Quandt sometime in the late 1930s. Carl leased the ranch from C. B. Woodhead in 1937 and bought the land after the house burned down in 1946. The 600-acre ranch extended north of Idyllwild Drive to the San Jacinto River and east of State Street. (Courtesy Marjory Quandt Goodwin.)

Carl Quandt stands beside the bed of his truck, which is filled with lugs of onions. He is showing his own grown onions to be used for seeding the next crop. Carl also grew his own seed potatoes, cutting the potatoes in sections by hand for planting. Each section had to have at least one eye for sprouting. (Courtesy Marjory Quandt Goodwin.)

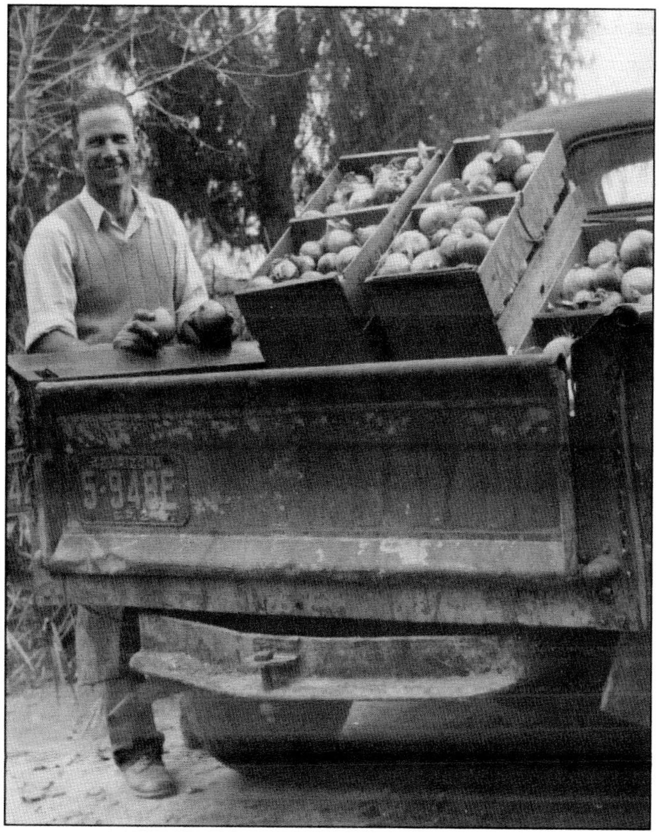

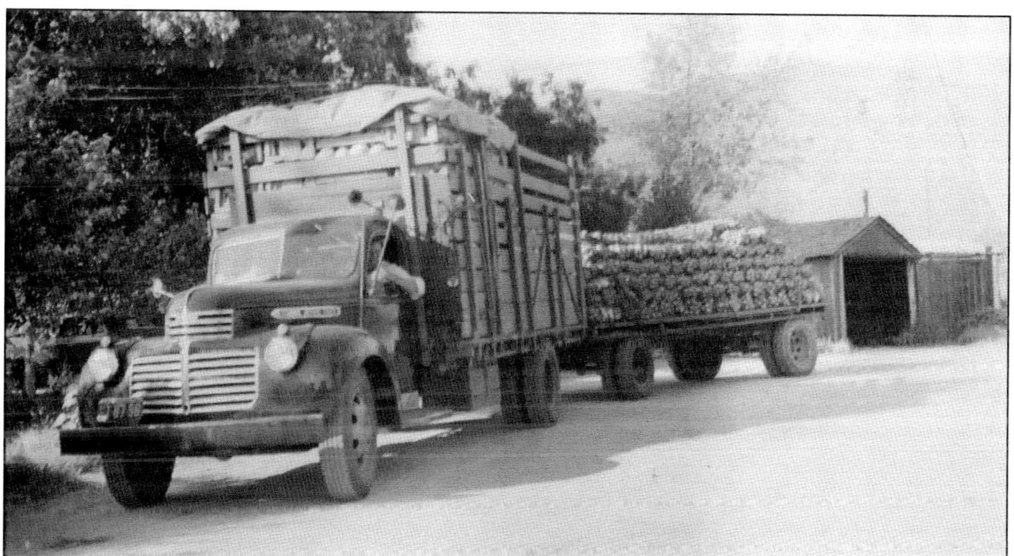

His truck loaded with cabbage, Carl Quandt pulls a trailer filled with sacks of onions. He sold and delivered produce to the U.S. Marine base at Camp Pendleton and to the U.S. Navy station in San Diego. Carl also grew sugar beets during World War II. (Courtesy Marjory Quandt Goodwin.)

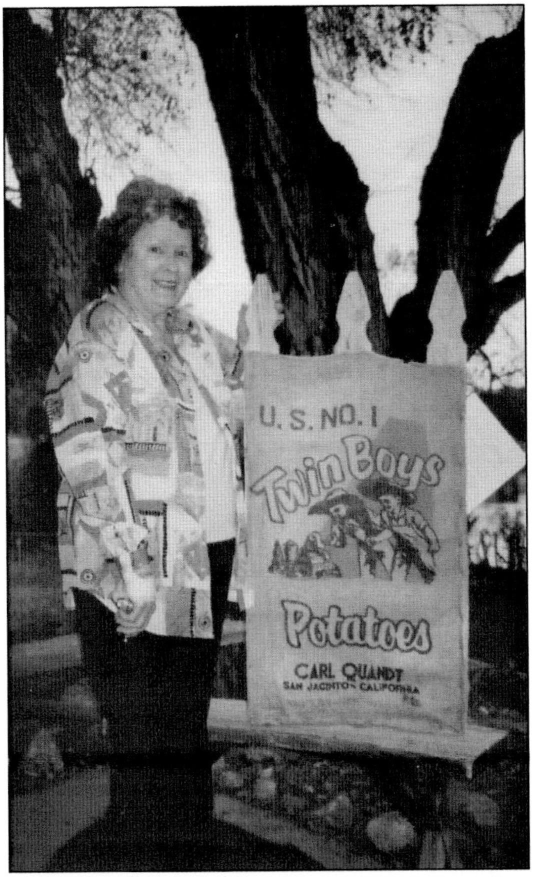

Marjory Quandt Goodwin holds a burlap sack of one of the family's potato brands. Each sack held 100 pounds of potatoes. Marjory and her husband, Dan Goodwin, still live on the Quandt ranch property near the San Jacinto River. The remainder of the ranch has been disposed of. (Courtesy Jack Warneke.)

In 1965, Carl Quandt donated land for the construction of Mount San Jacinto College along the east side of State Street. This photograph was taken near the entrance of the college campus. Carl also developed Country Lake Mobile Home Park and other housing developments on the ranch land. The most recent is the opening of a shopping center at the northeast corner of State Street and the Ramona Expressway. The tall palm tree at the corner of the shopping center came from the Quandt home site to the north. (Courtesy Jack Warneke.)

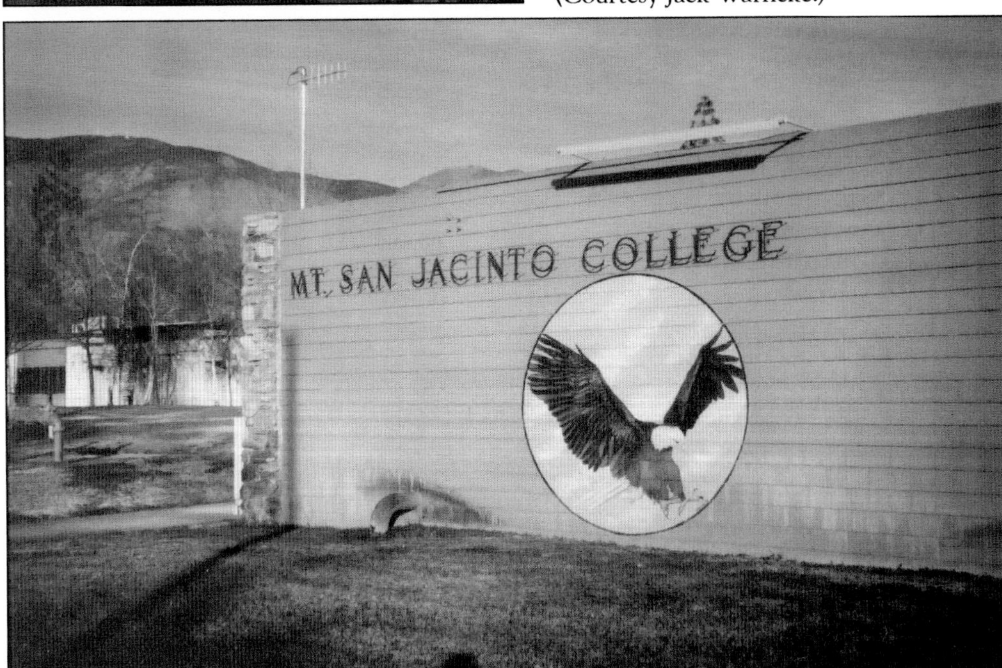

Wilbur J. "Webb" Corwin shows Janice Minor how the walnut rake operates during a Little Lake School field trip to the Corwin ranch in 1956. The Corwin ranch, situated on north Hemet Street south of Mountain Avenue, contained 200 acres in walnuts along with apricots. William N. Corwin was a charter member of the California Walnut Growers Association, organized in 1916. His son Webb was named state director in 1959. (Courtesy Bill Corwin.)

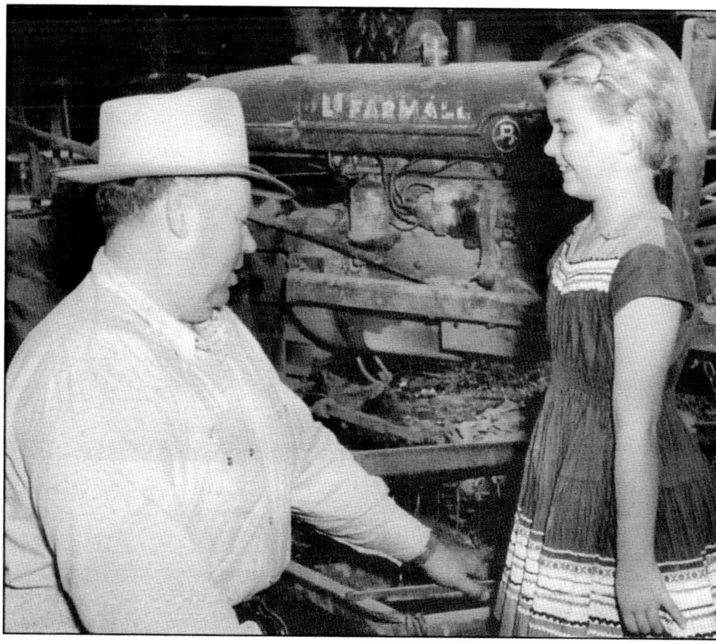

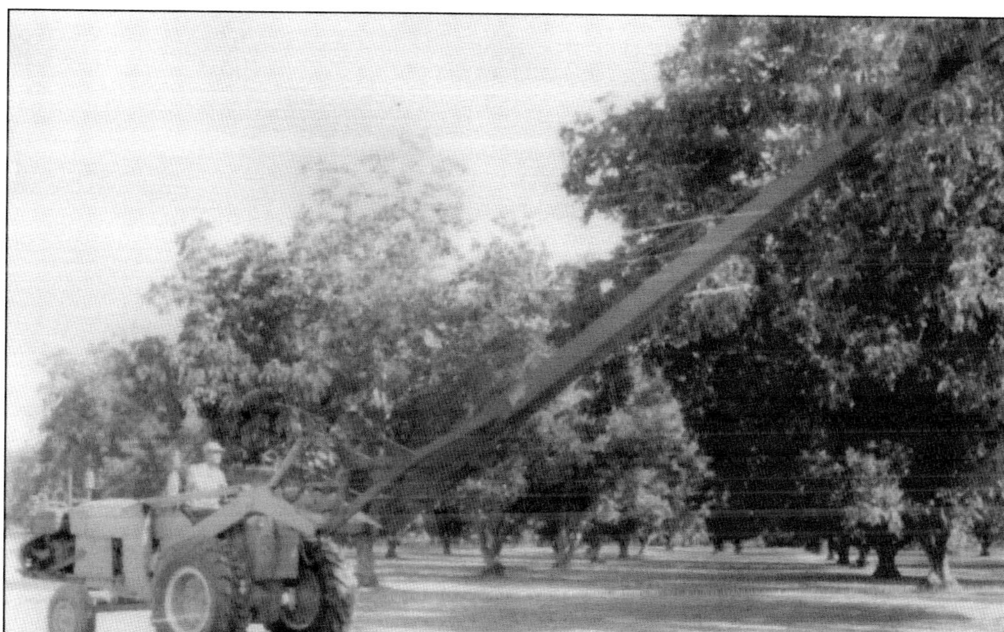

A pneumatic walnut shaker was used on the Corwin ranch in the 1950s. During a picking operation, a metal extension was connected to a limb of the walnut tree. A hydraulic mechanism then induced the arm to vibrate the tree limb, causing the walnuts to dislodge and fall to the ground. (Courtesy Bill Corwin.)

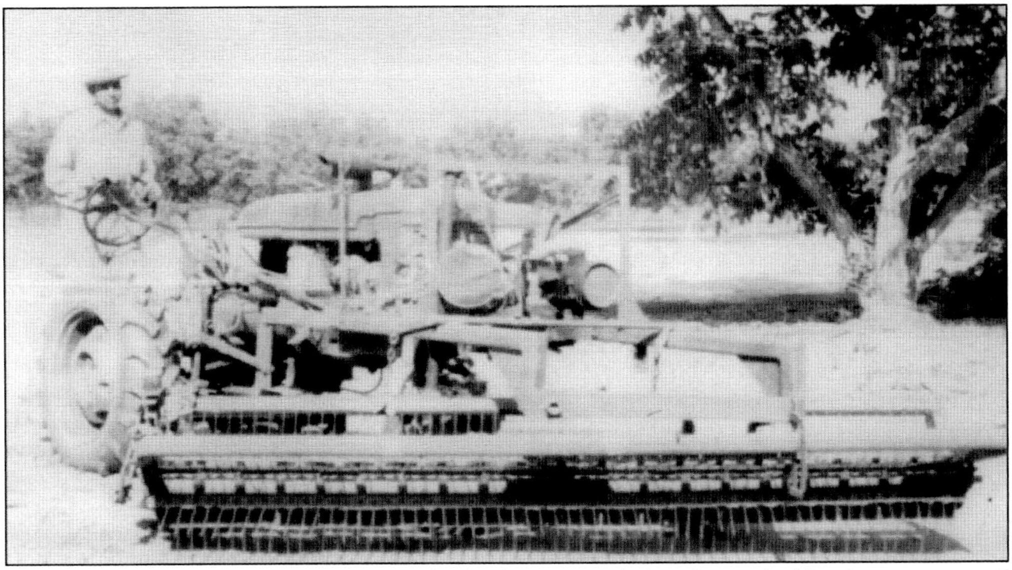

After the walnuts fell from the tree, they had to be retrieved. A walnut rake like the one pictured was used on the Corwin ranch to facilitate this process. The rake brought walnuts away from the tree and into a windrow for pickup. Prior to the 1950s, the walnuts were picked up by tedious hand labor. (Courtesy Bill Corwin.)

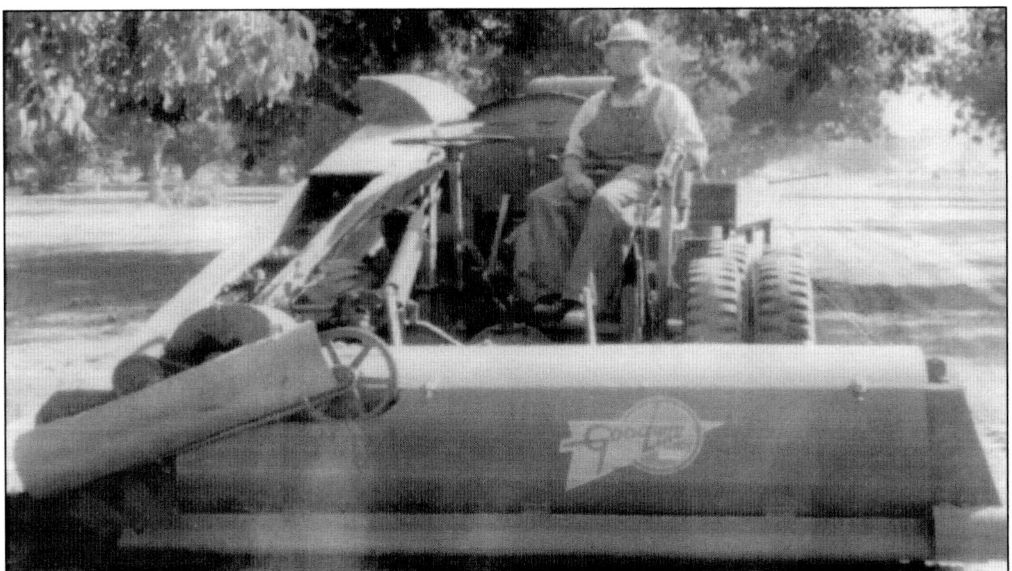

A walnut picker machine developed in the 1950s is seen picking up walnuts on the Corwin ranch. As the walnuts were gathered, they were conveyed into a hopper on the machine that could then be transferred to a truck for delivery to a nearby processing plant. (Courtesy Bill Corwin.)

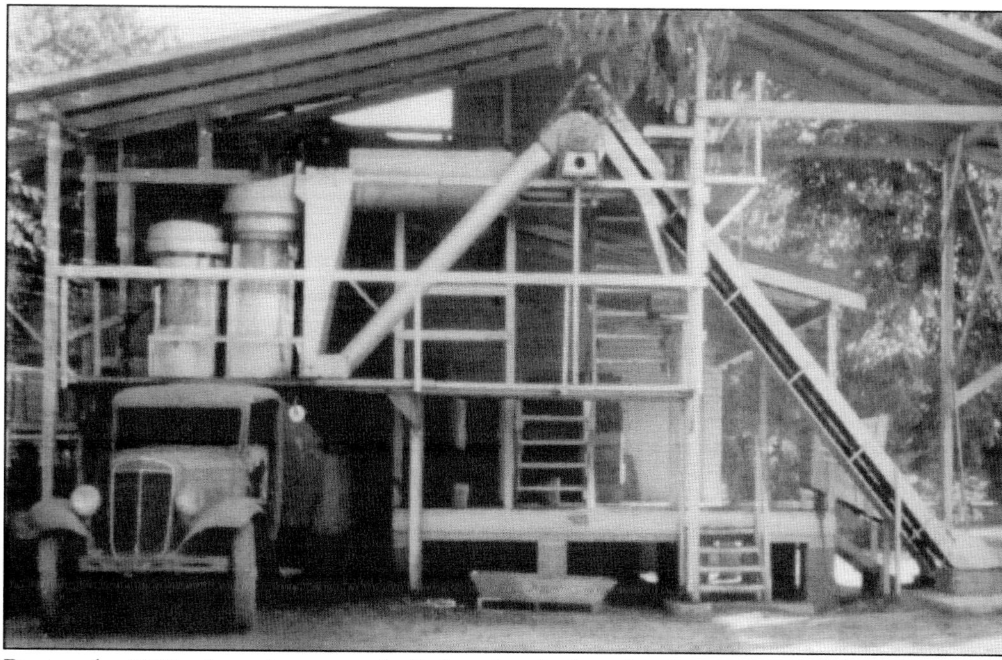

During the 1950s, the walnuts were hulled in this shed on the Corwin ranch. The walnuts were sorted on a conveyor belt. A dehydrator in the shed then brought the walnuts to the desired moisture content before shipping. The Corwin ranch shipped walnuts to various places. (Courtesy Bill Corwin.)

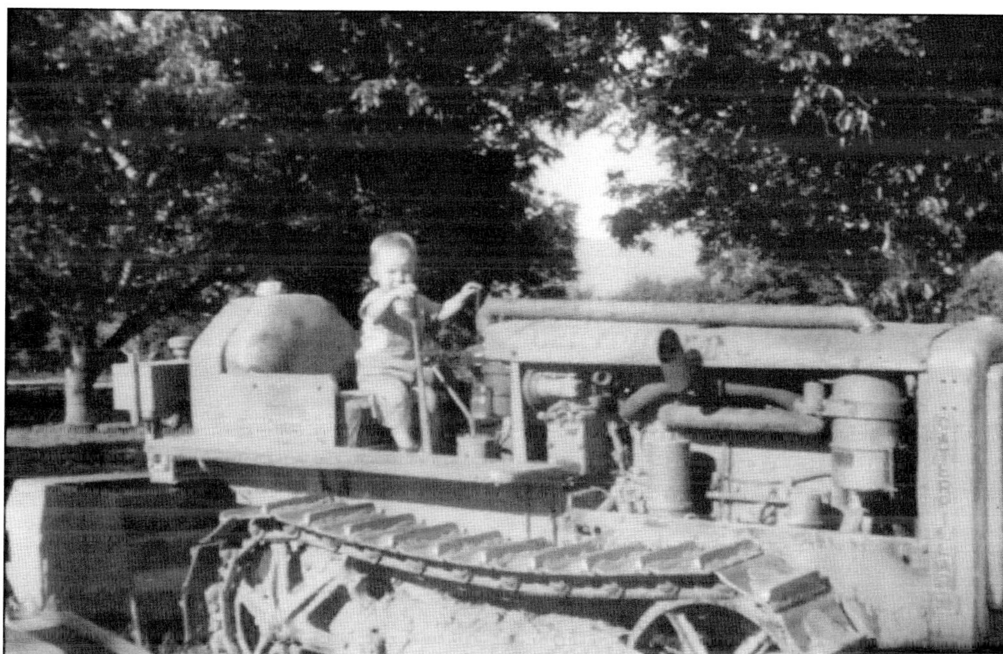

William W. "Bill" Corwin sits at the controls of a Caterpillar tractor while a youngster in 1946. Webb Corwin was featured in a Caterpillar advertisement by Johnson Tractor of Riverside in the 1950s. This tractor was used extensively on the Corwin ranch. (Courtesy Bill Corwin.)

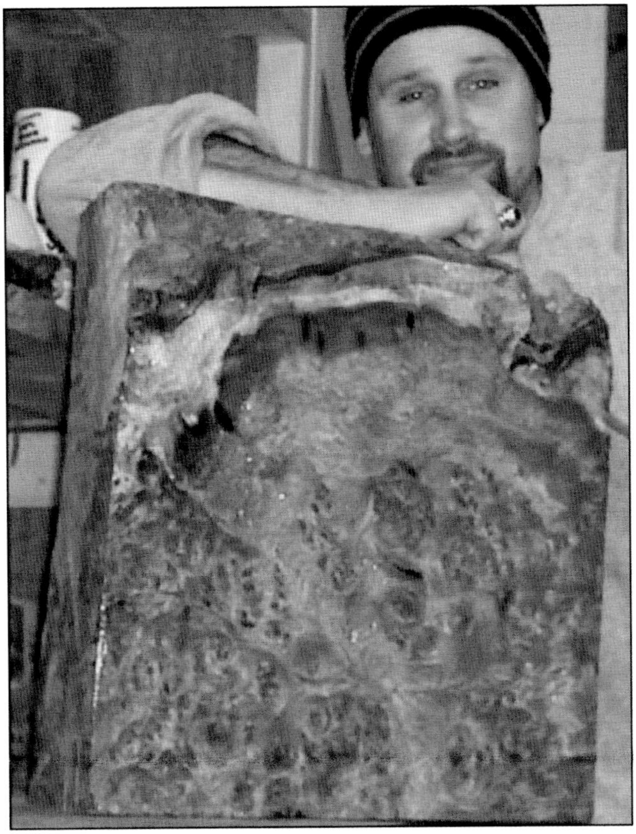

Many walnut stumps, or burls, were removed with the termination of walnut groves in the 1960s. A burl is a result of a dome-shaped growth around the trunk, the growth where the scion wood, a selected walnut variety, is grafted onto a walnut rootstock. The rootstock is a walnut variety that is hardy and disease resistant but not a good producer. The harvested burl, like the one presented, is sliced to make burl-wood veneer. Each burl can bring more than $1,000. (Courtesy Ken Holtzclaw.)

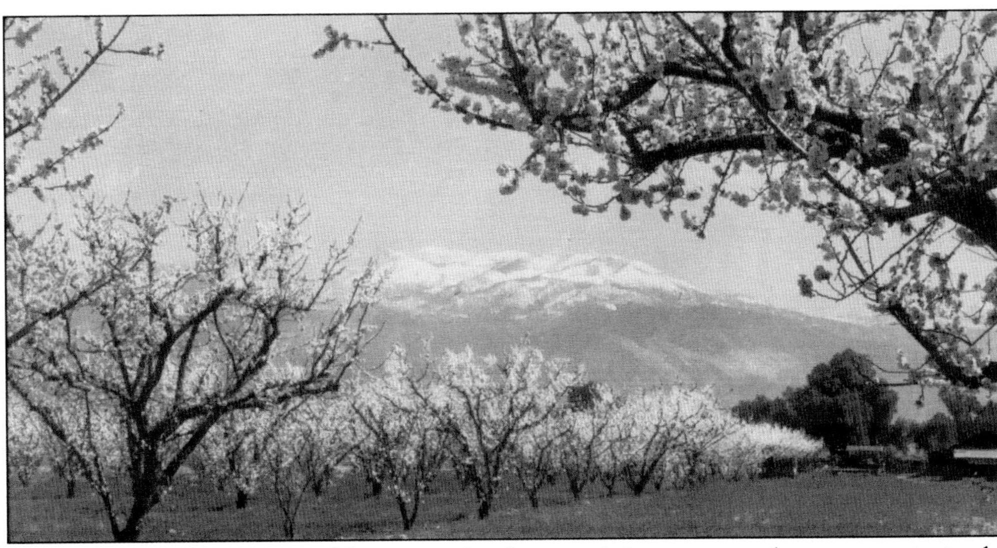

An apricot grove blooms east of downtown San Jacinto while snowcapped mountains rise in the distance. In 1944, there were 5,500 acres of apricot groves in the San Jacinto Valley. That land dropped to 25 acres on two ranches in 2007. The fruit ripens in June or July and is all picked by hand. (Courtesy San Jacinto Museum.)

S. L. Muller stands next to a 40-pound field box of picked apricots in 1927. Apricots are picked in peck buckets, placed in boxes, and hauled to a processing shed. Many workers cut the apricots in half to remove seeds and then place them on redwood trays that hold 10 or 20 pounds in a room for fumigation. Afterward, the trays are placed in rows on the ground to dry from the sun. After about three days, the dried fruit is ready for packaging. (Courtesy San Jacinto Museum.)

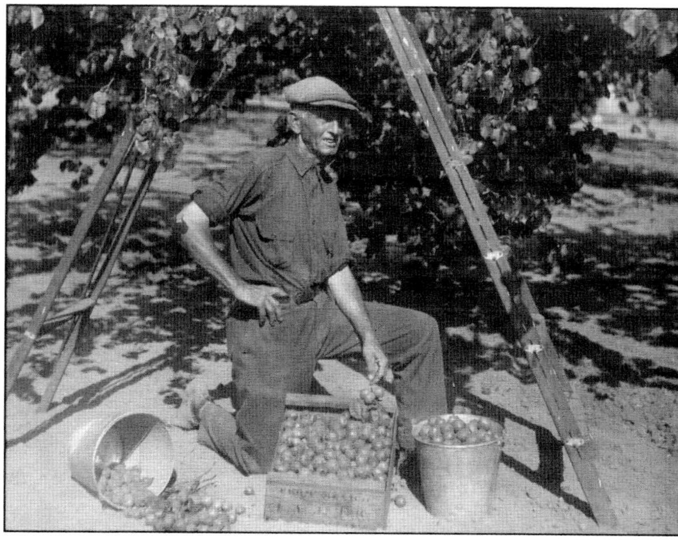

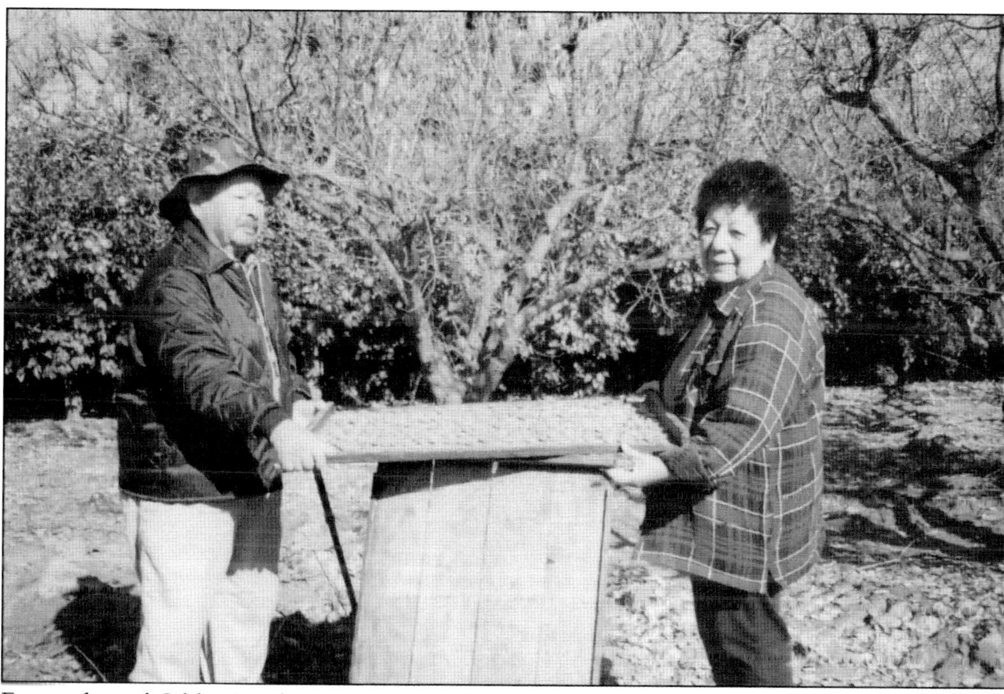

Fernando and Ofelia Savala carry a tray of dried apricots in their 16-acre grove on the east side of Hewitt, between Washington and Commonwealth. In 1940, Fernando came from Mexico at the age of 15 to pick apricots. During World War II, he enlisted in the U.S. Army and married Ofelia. The two owned their own ranch by the 1960s. On their ranch, they continue to operate the last fruit stand in the valley, selling fruit and vegetables. (Courtesy Jack Warneke.)

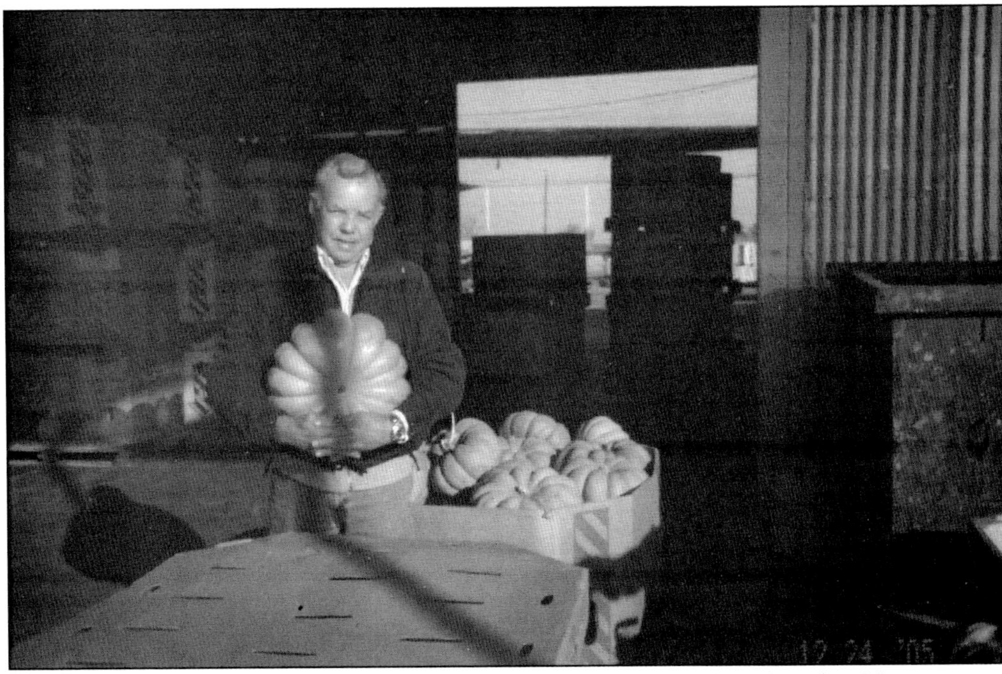

Ignacio Cordero holds a Castillo squash prior to shipment into Los Angeles. He emigrated from Mexico in 1957, first working in the valley's apricot groves. In 1971, he formed C&R Farms with his sons. The company is a grower and shipper of produce from the family farm. (Courtesy Jack Warneke.)

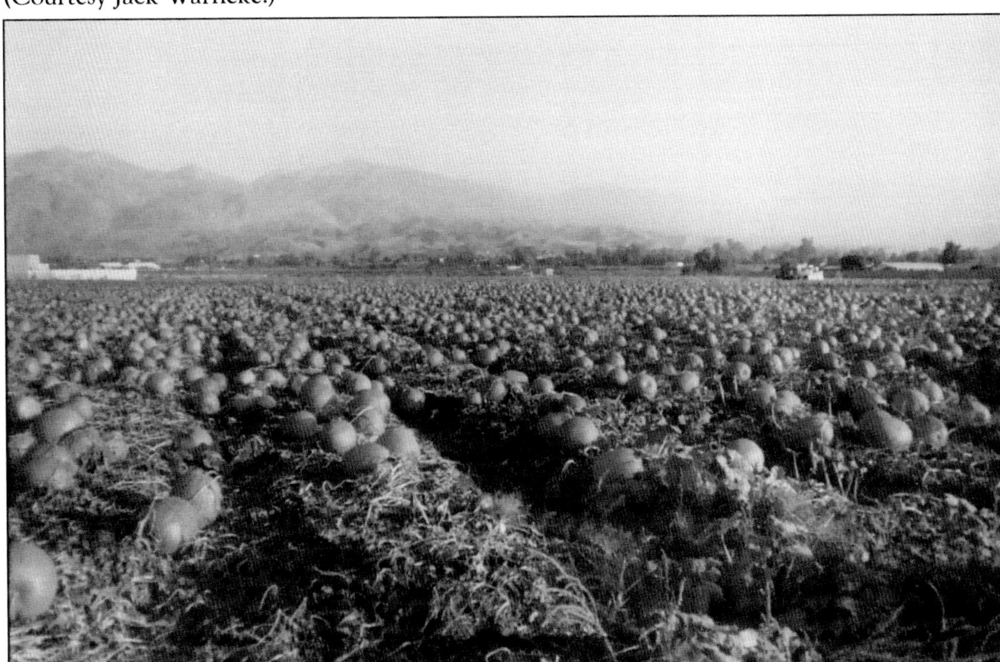

A field of pumpkins owned by C&R Farms occupies land in east San Jacinto, south of Mountain Avenue near Hemet Street. The company, specializing in watermelons and pumpkins, maintains processing facilities at the corner of Sanderson and Esplanade. (Courtesy Ignacio Cordero.)

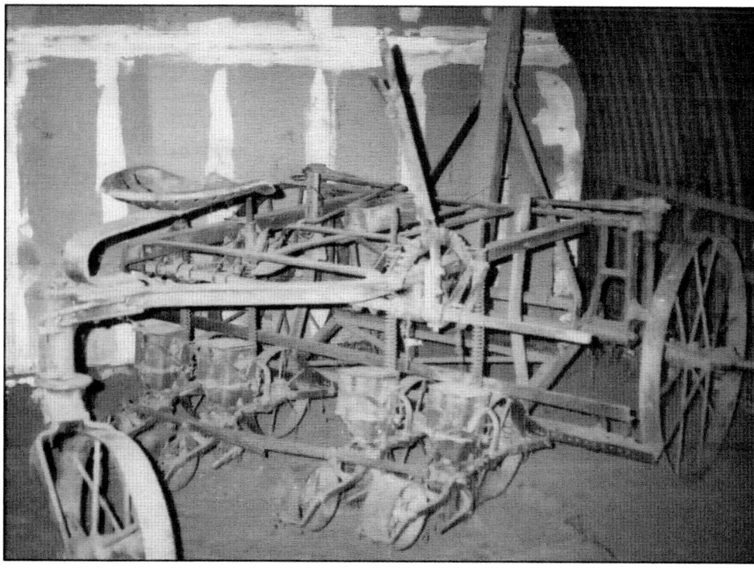

This four-row horse-drawn vegetable planter was used by Clarence Planchon in the 1920s and 1930s. It was manufactured in Ventura, California. Clarence owned Planchon's Groceries and Meat Market and the Union 76 station at the corner of Ramona Boulevard and Young Street in the 1950s and 1960s. (Courtesy Ken Holtzclaw.)

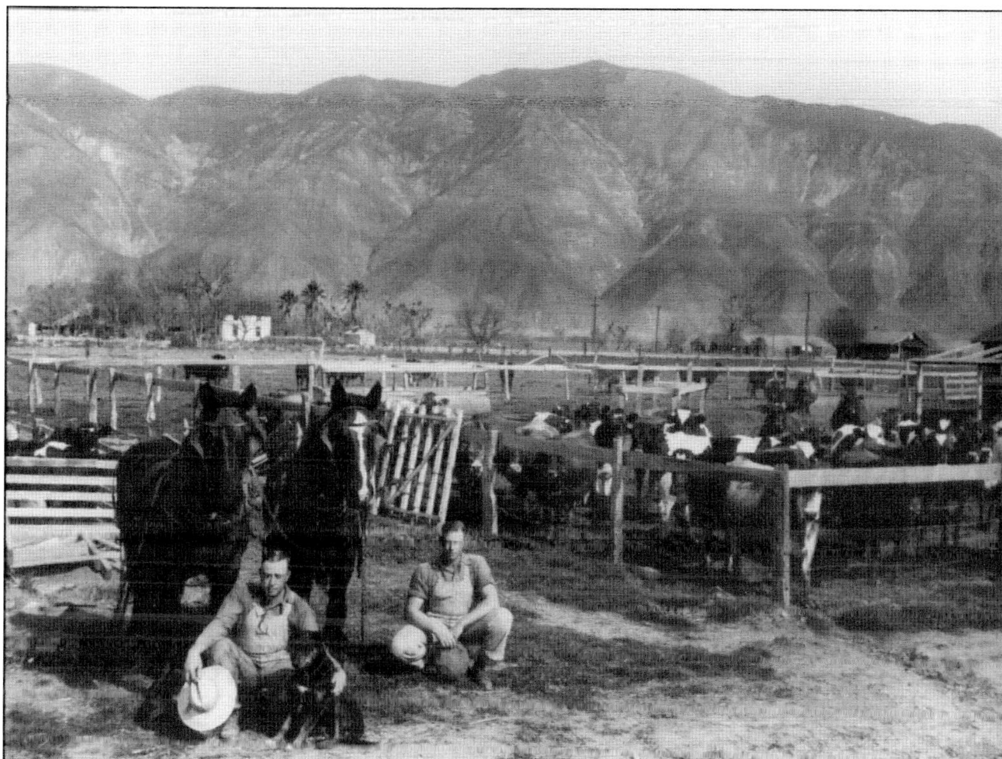

The Eastman Dairy was located on north San Jacinto Avenue near the Ramona Expressway. Bill (left) and Dave Eastman are pictured here with some of their cows. The first dairy in San Jacinto dates back to 1894, when Davis and Rankin came from Chicago to start their business. (Courtesy San Jacinto Museum.)

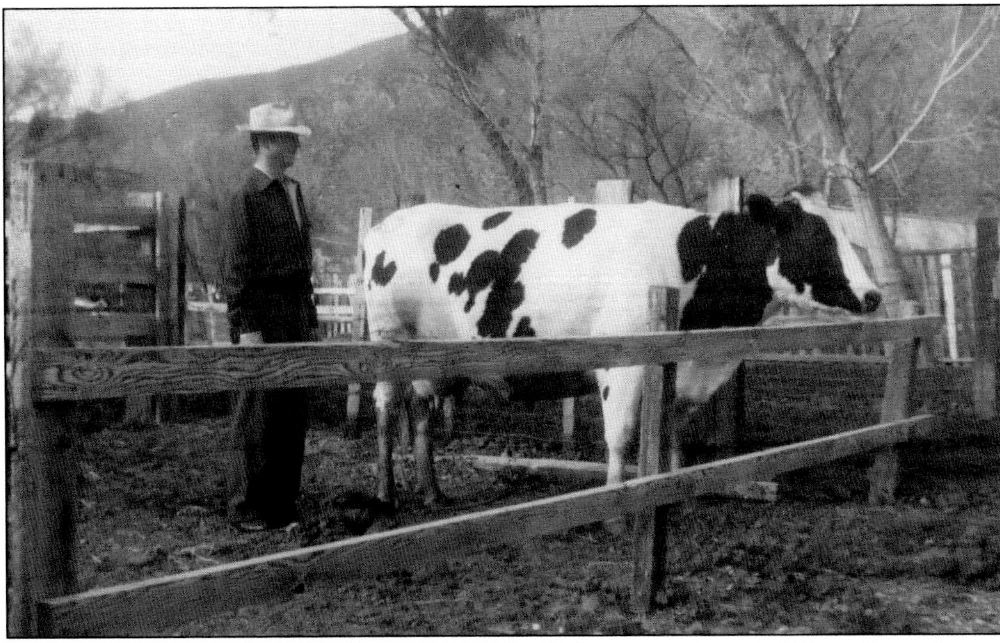

In this 1930s photograph, Bill Nelson stands with a Holstein cow from the Nelson Dairy, located on the north side of the San Jacinto River next to Gilman Hot Springs. Most of the dairies at this time had around 20 milking cows. Clayton Record Sr. started Rancho Record on De Anza Drive in 1922 with 22 cows. (Courtesy Becky Rose Schlosser.)

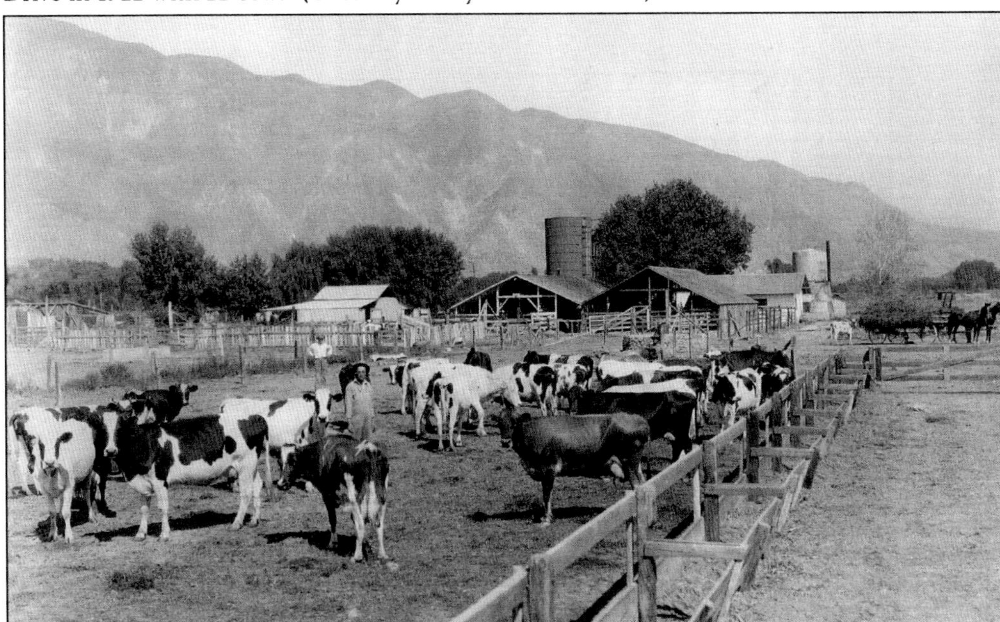

Mark Warden's dairy, seen here, was situated along Record Road west of State Street. Cliff Rose moved to San Jacinto in 1937 and found employment at the Warden Dairy. He later became the owner of Rose's Hardware and Gifts, a shop on the south side of Main Street. Rose was elected to the San Jacinto City Council in 1988. He is the brother-in-law of Bill Nelson and the father of Becky Rose Schlosser. (Courtesy San Jacinto Museum.)

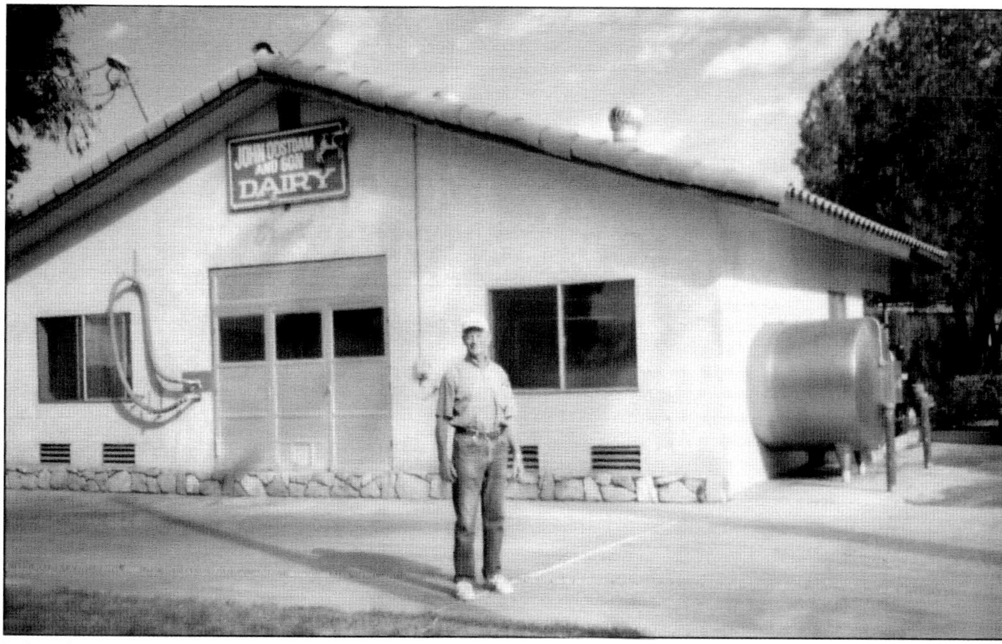

John O'ostram stands in front of the milking barn at the John O'ostram and Son Dairy, located on Ramona Boulevard west of Potter Road. The operation is an example of a modern dairy built after the 1960s, when the herd of cows was greater than 1,000 head. Milking on a large farm like this is performed 24 hours a day. (Courtesy Jack Warneke.)

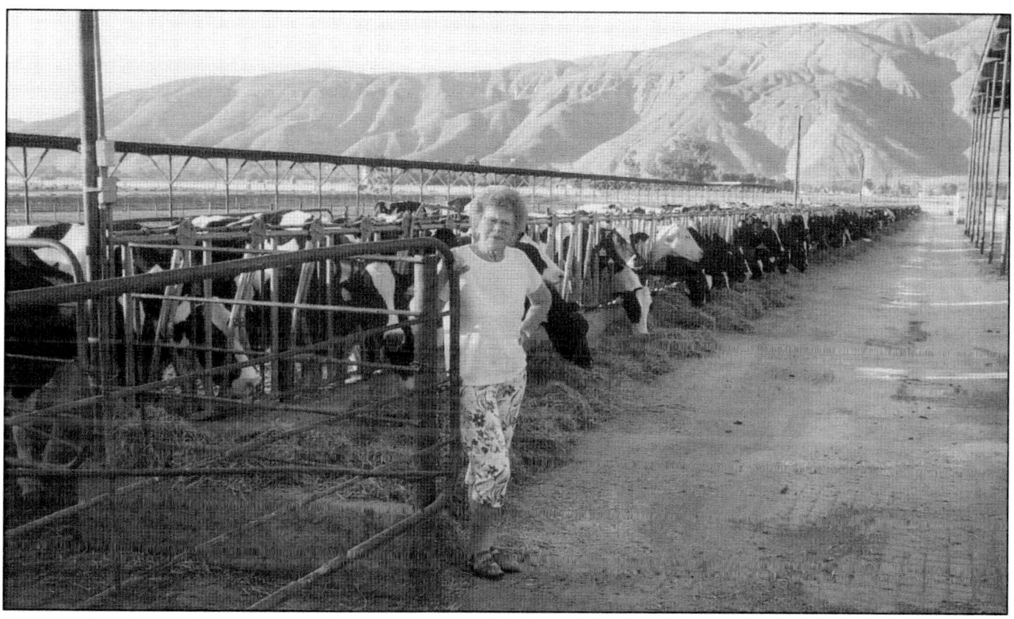

It is evidently feeding time at the O'ostram Dairy, as the stanchions are filled with cows eating hay. Joan O'ostram stands by the line of dairy cows. In 1984, there were 31 dairies in San Jacinto with a total of 22,700 cows. (Courtesy Joan O'ostram.)

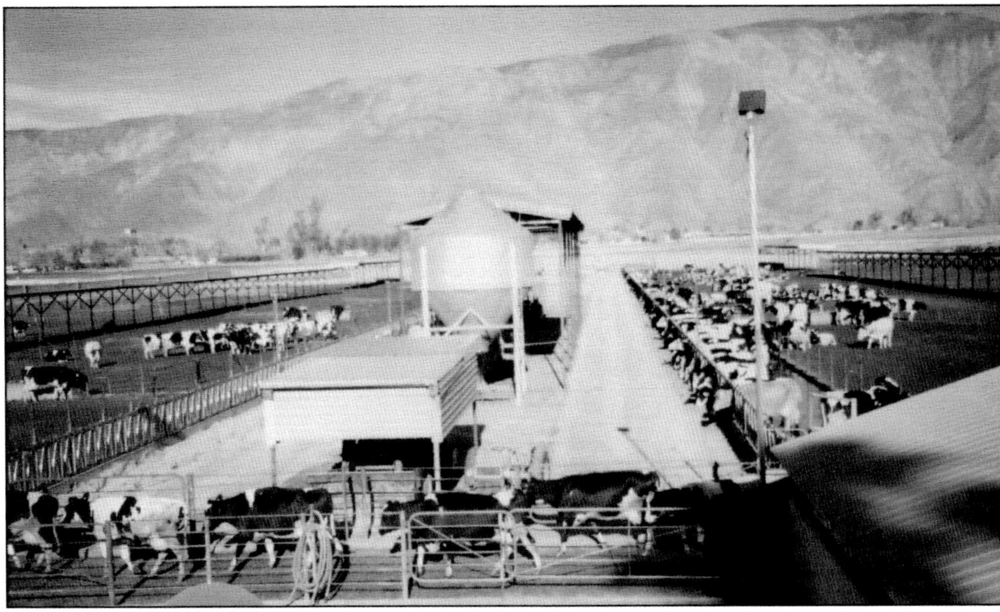

This photograph reveals the extent of the O'ostram Dairy. The cows at the bottom are just coming from the milking barn to go into the coral and be fed. John and Joan's son Art O'ostram married Betty Youngsma, and now the two manage the Youngsma Dairy on Warren Road. (Courtesy Jack Warneke.)

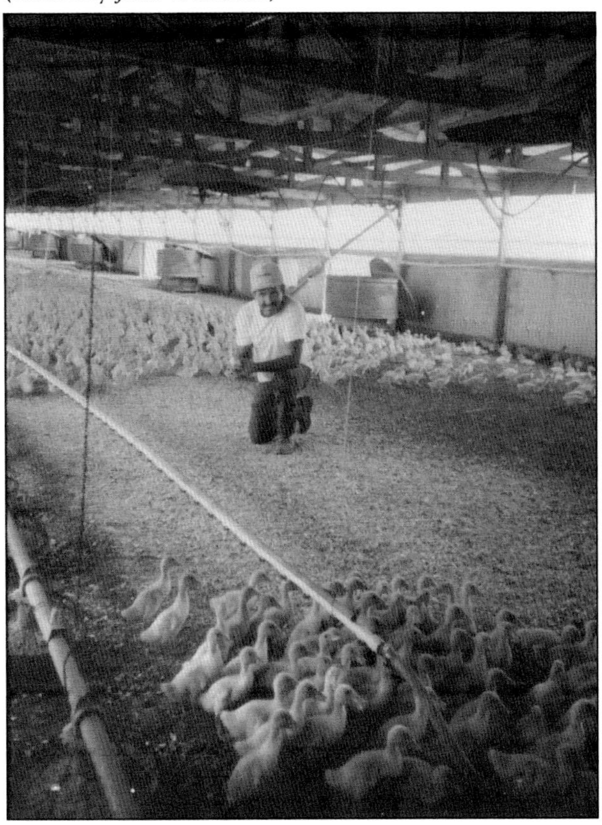

Gordon Hurst's duck ranch occupies land on the east side of Sanderson and north of Esplanade. Gordon is pictured in the duck house among a large flock of young ducks. Harry Hurst's son Gordon stopped growing turkeys and switched to ducks in the 1980s. Gordon's brother Bill also had a duck ranch in Hemet following the termination of the turkey-raising business. (Courtesy Mary Grace Hurst.)

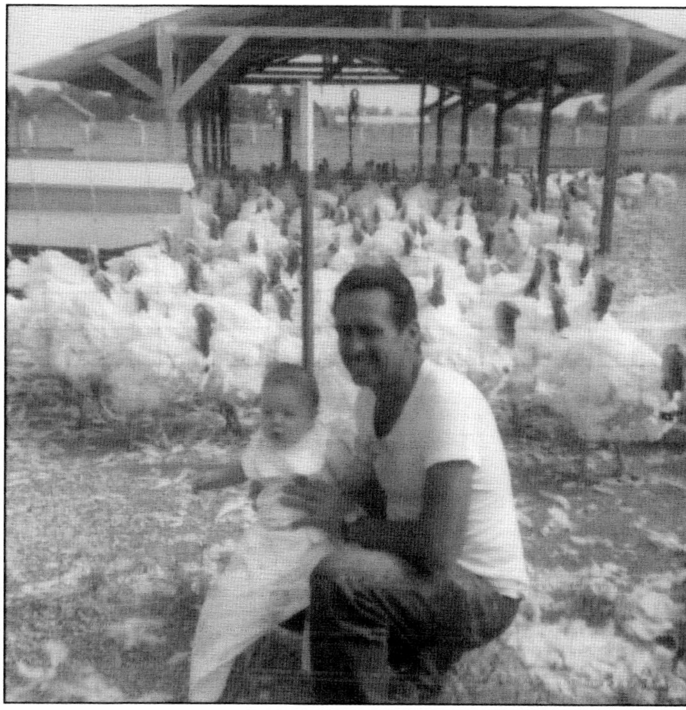

Harry and Mary Hurst moved from the San Fernando Valley to San Jacinto in 1957. Here Harry holds his grandson Joseph while showing him a flock of white turkeys. The couple raised turkeys from 1962 until 1981, when Harry died. They had 10 children, and the 3 sons—Gordon, John, and Bill—continued the business until 1985. Another turkey grower in San Jacinto was Lawrence Gates, who started the Gates Ranch on De Anza Drive in 1944. His son David maintained the operation from 1970 to 1986. (Courtesy Mary Grace Hurst.)

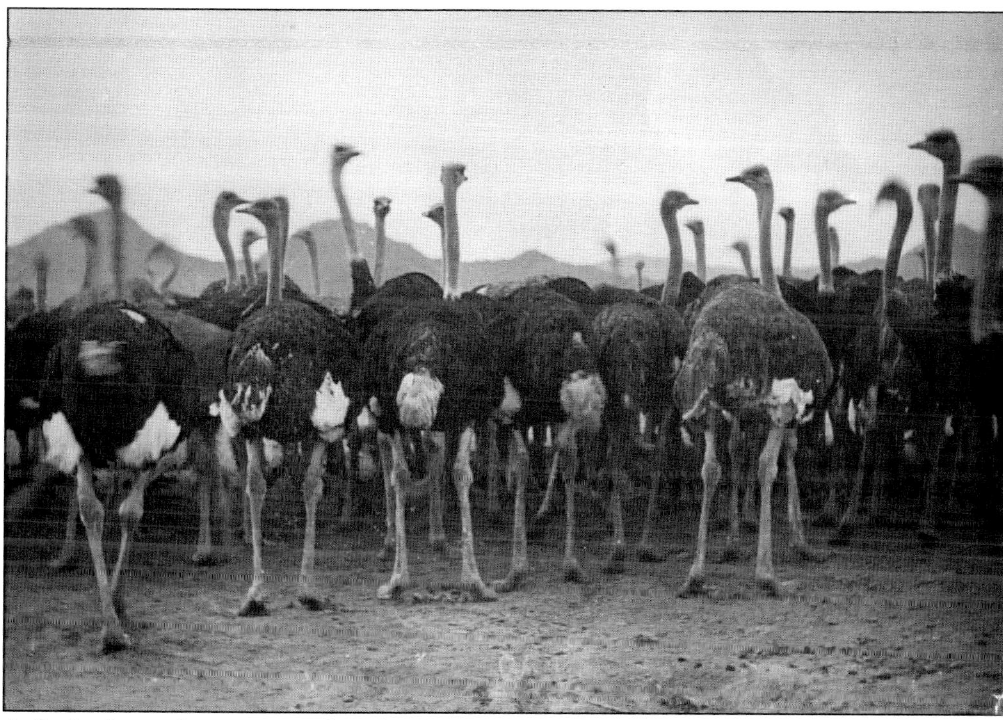

A flock of ostriches is pictured at the Cawston Ostrich Ranch, near present-day Cawston and Cottonwood Avenues, in the early 1900s. At the time, the feathers were prized for decoration in the house and also in ladies' hats, making the raising of ostriches a lucrative endeavor. (Courtesy San Jacinto Museum.)

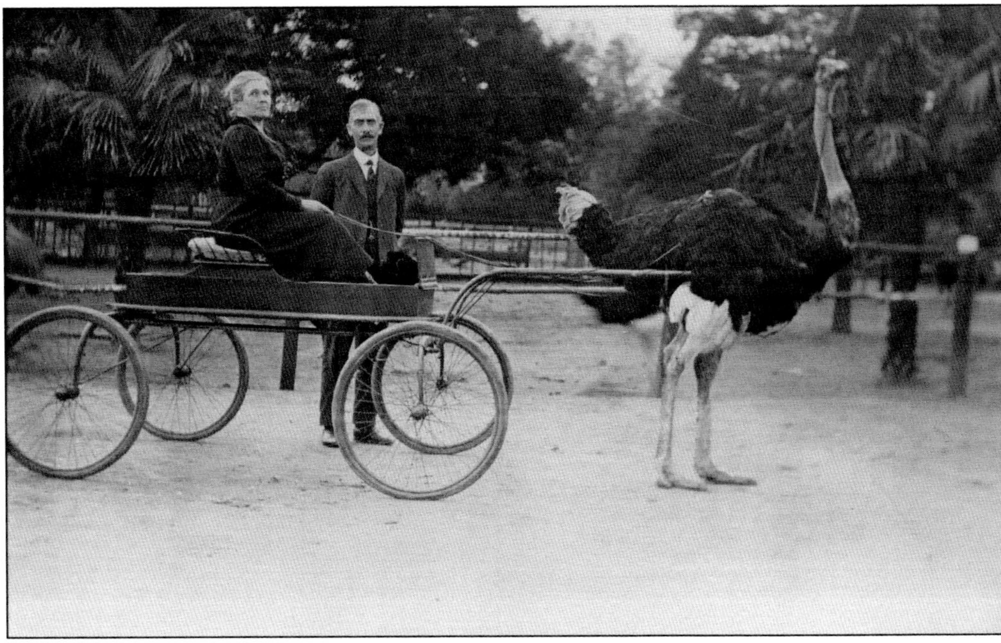

A novel use of ostriches can perhaps be deduced from this early-1900s photograph. Here the ostrich and buggy may have been props for a souvenir photography business. The lady holding the reins is Ida Warneke, apparently preparing to go on a ride as her husband, Christopher, looks on. (Courtesy Jack Warneke.)

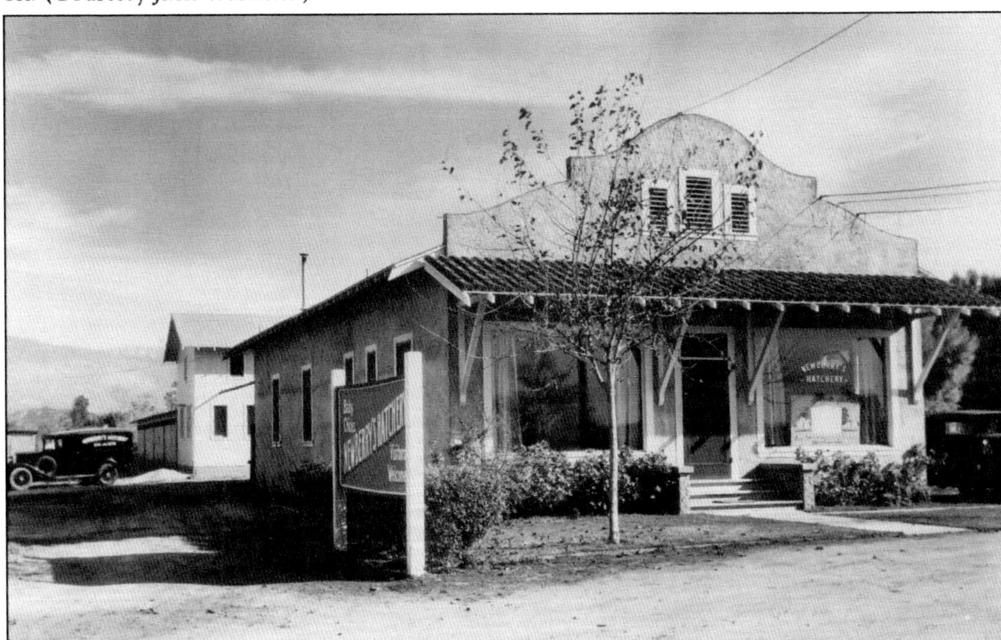

Newberry's Hatchery was located on San Jacinto Avenue from the 1930s to the 1950s. The sign out front reads, "Newberry's Hatchery. Baby Chicks and Visitors Welcome." During this era, hatcheries were popular not only for large chicken growers but also for individual households that wanted to grow chickens for eggs and meat. (Courtesy San Jacinto Museum.)

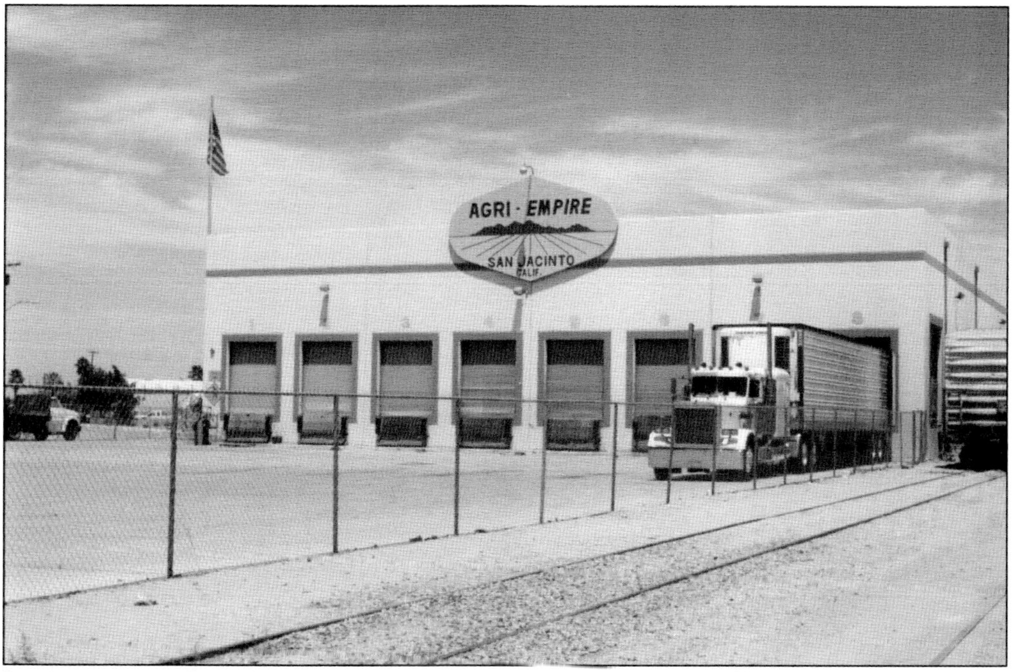

Jim Minor came from the Moreno Valley and, in 1943, took out an $800 loan to establish the San Jacinto Packing Company at Seventh and Main Streets. The Agri-Empire Corporation was formed from that company in 1970 and diversified into raising cattle. This packinghouse was built in 1991. (Courtesy San Jacinto Museum.)

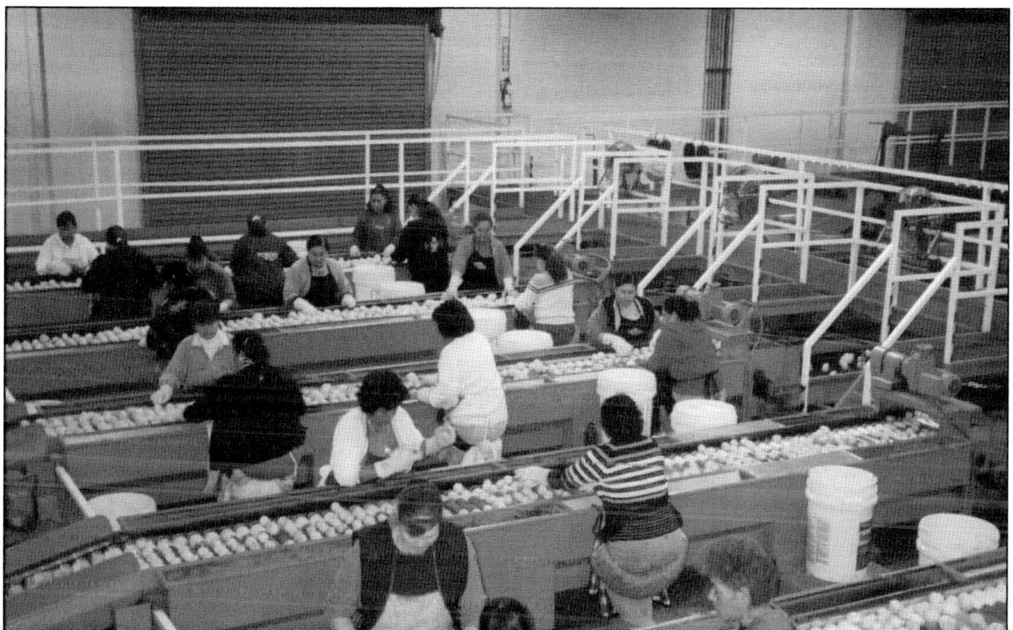

In the Agri-Empire potato packinghouse, potatoes are washed and graded. Note the activity of the workers as they grade the potatoes passing by on a conveyor. By 1968, the company was responsible for 30 percent of the potatoes grown in Southern California. (Courtesy San Jacinto Museum.)

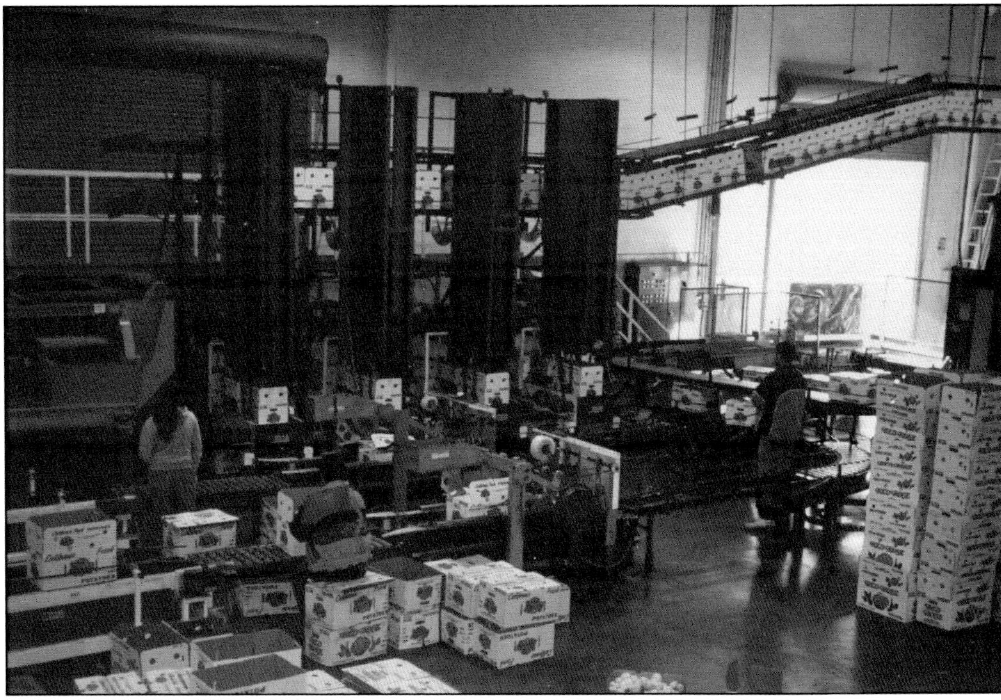

Here Agri-Empire's graded potatoes are packed into 40-pound cardboard boxes. Note the conveyor in the rear that is moving full boxes out of the room for shipment. Most of the potatoes are shipped by truck, but occasionally a freight train still comes to town. (Courtesy San Jacinto Museum.)

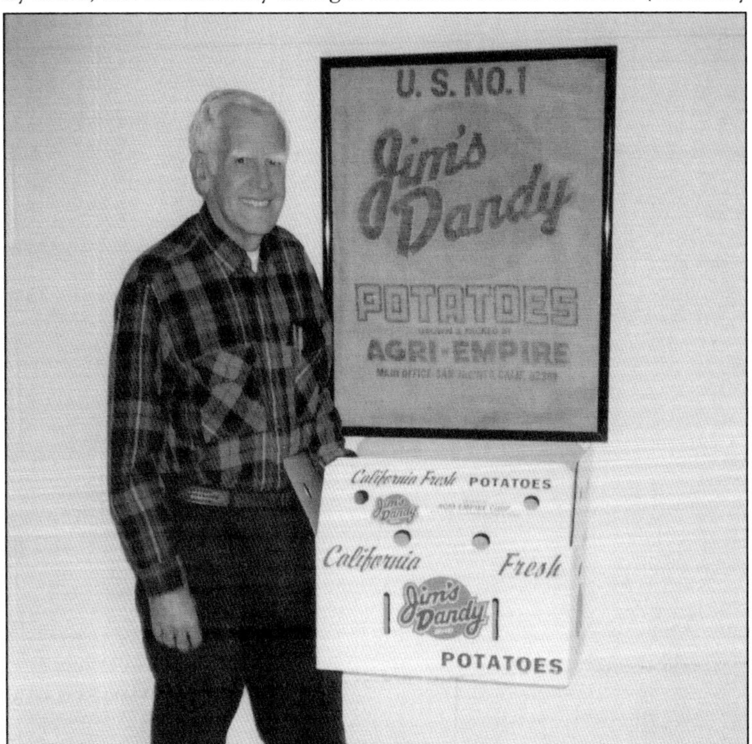

Jack Warneke holds a Jim's Dandy potato packing box directly under a wall-mounted burlap sack depicting the same brand. Burlap sacks were originally designed to hold 100 pounds, making them difficult to physically move and handle. The boxes are designed to hold only 40 pounds. The Jim Dandy label is named for founder James Minor. His son Larry is now the manager of operations. (Courtesy Ken Holtzclaw.)

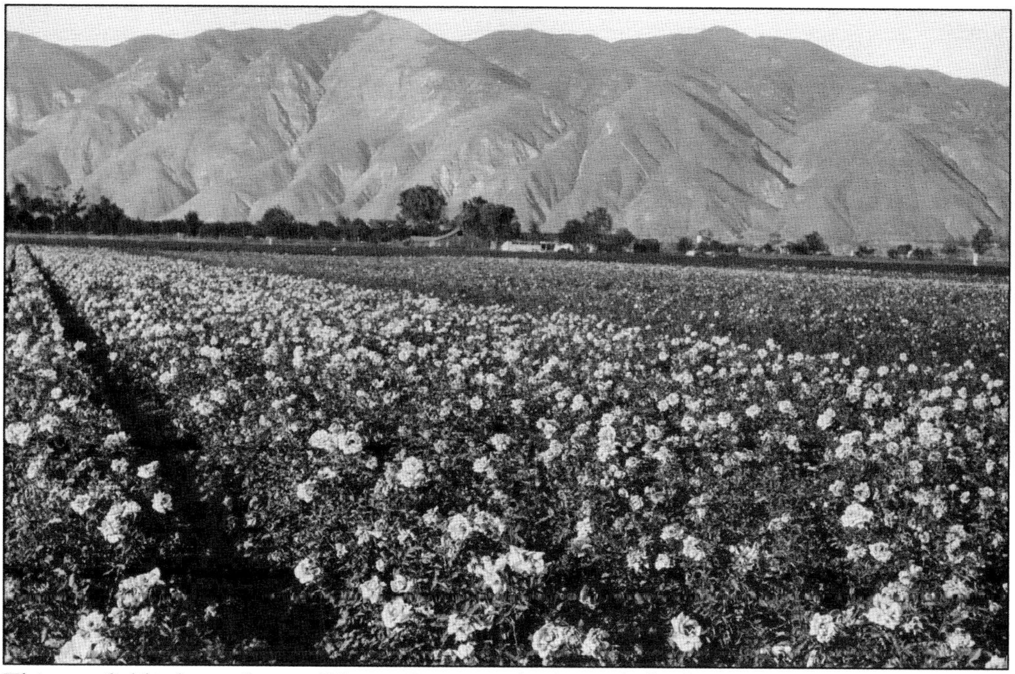

This rose field is located east of Hewitt Street on the farm of Charles W. Howard, who established the Howard Rose Company in 1908. He was joined by a partner, Ernest Lindquist, in 1911. The partners also owned a plant nursery under the name Hemet Wholesale until 1978. Rose production lasted from the 1920s to the 1970s. (Courtesy San Jacinto Museum.)

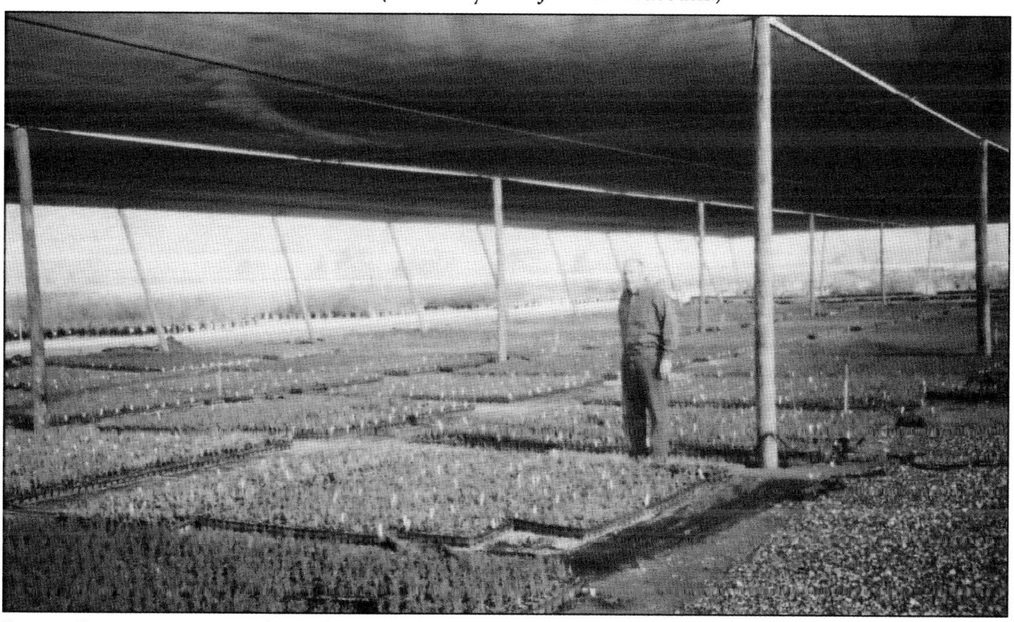

James Conner is pictured at Alta Nursery, situated on North Alessandro between the Ramona Expressway and the San Jacinto River. Conner bought equipment from Hemet Wholesale after its termination in 1978 and used it to start the nursery in 1979. He grew a wide range of plants in containers to be sold to retail stores. The plants began as vegetative cuttings or seeds, as seen here. When of sufficient size, they were transplanted to larger containers. (Courtesy Jack Warneke.)

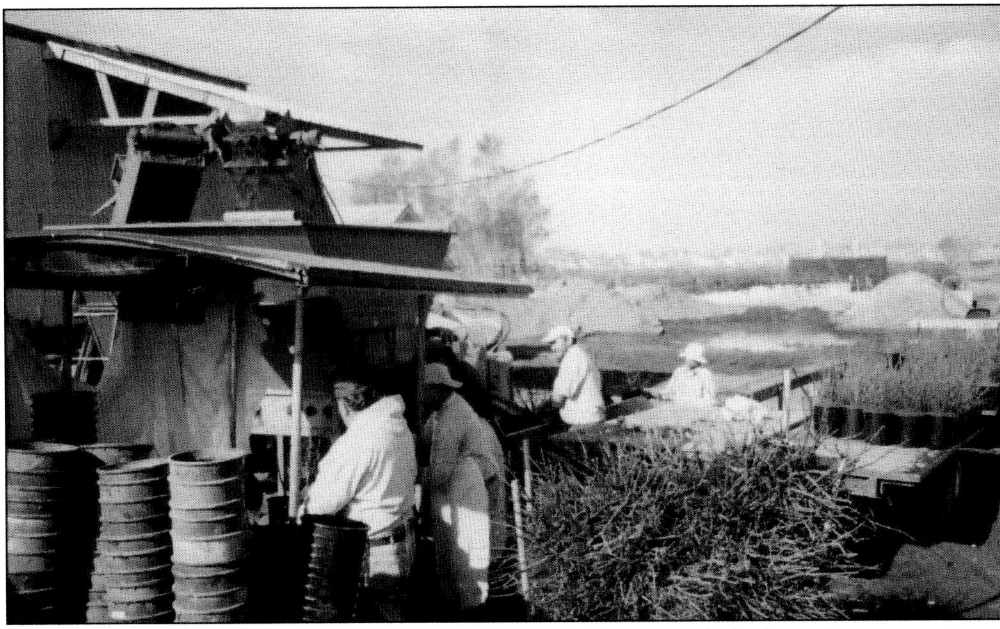

Shown here is a "canning operation," in which nursery plants are shifted into larger containers. Three-gallon containers are placed on a conveyor belt and, as they move to the right, are filled with a planting mix of wood shavings, peat moss, and sand. The plant is then inserted into the soil mix, at which time a worker sets the container on a trailer bed for transfer to the field. (Courtesy Jack Warneke.)

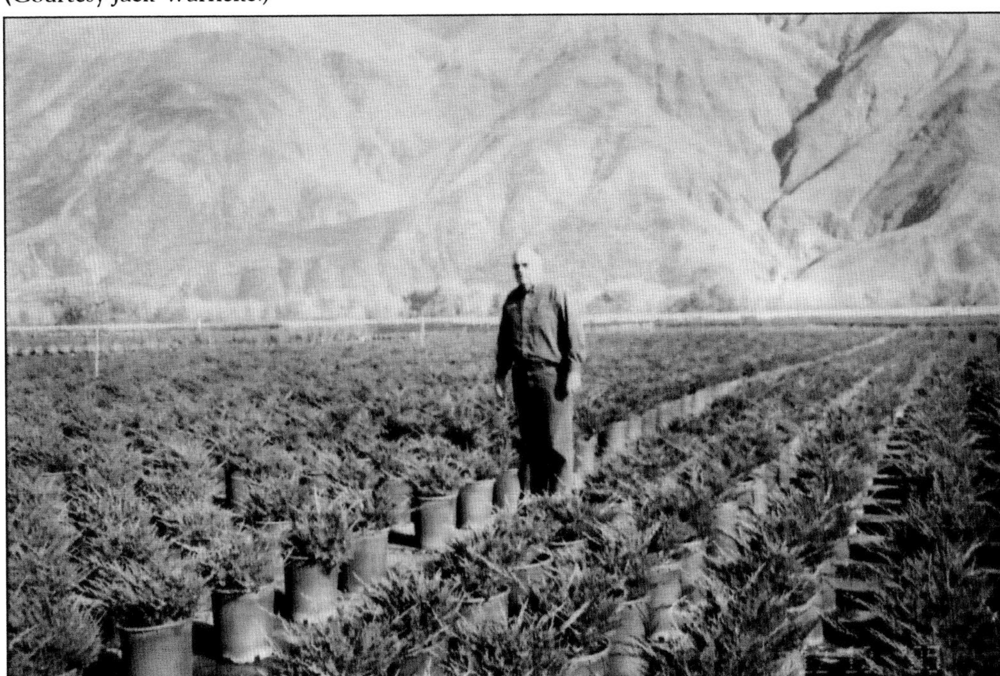

James Conner stands in the field area of Alta Nursery. The final process is growing the plants to maturity in the containers in which they will be sold. The field's juniper plants are irrigated by aboveground sprinklers. The San Jacinto River is in the background. (Courtesy Jack Warneke.)

Harry Hoffman (center) writes on a pad several years after selling the Soboba Theater in 1941. The view shows the interior of the auction barn at the San Jacinto Auction, located at Lyon Avenue and De Anza Drive. Harry and Virginia Hoffman bought the Sunset Ranch on De Anza Drive in 1937 and raised Thoroughbred horses. In 1944, they started the San Jacinto Auction, which remained in operation until 1990. (Courtesy San Jacinto Museum.)

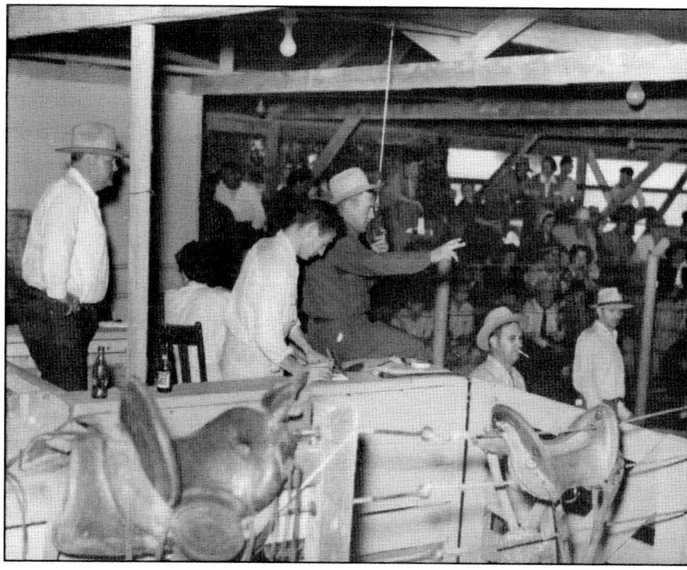

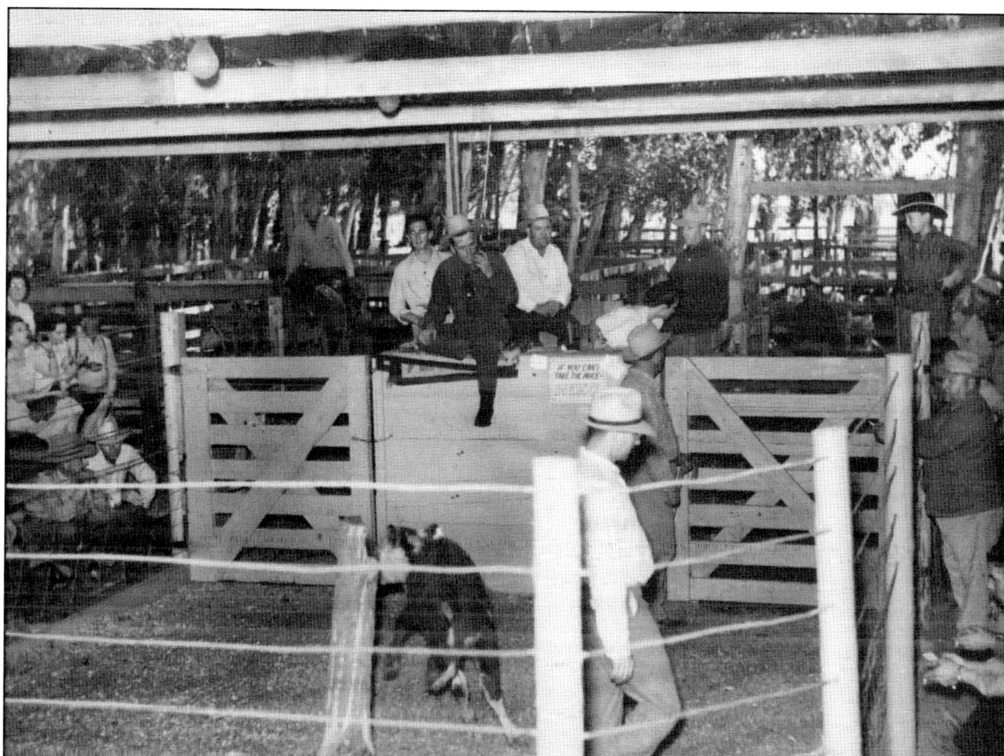

A calf is auctioned at one of the San Jacinto Auction's outdoor pens. On the stand are, from left to right, Harry Hoffman, auctioneer Hoyt Banks, Charles Curtis, and clerk Rennie Porter. S. B. Sidders (left) and C. T. Burtt are pictured in the sales ring. Auctions were held each Saturday and generally lasted all day. (Courtesy San Jacinto Museum.)

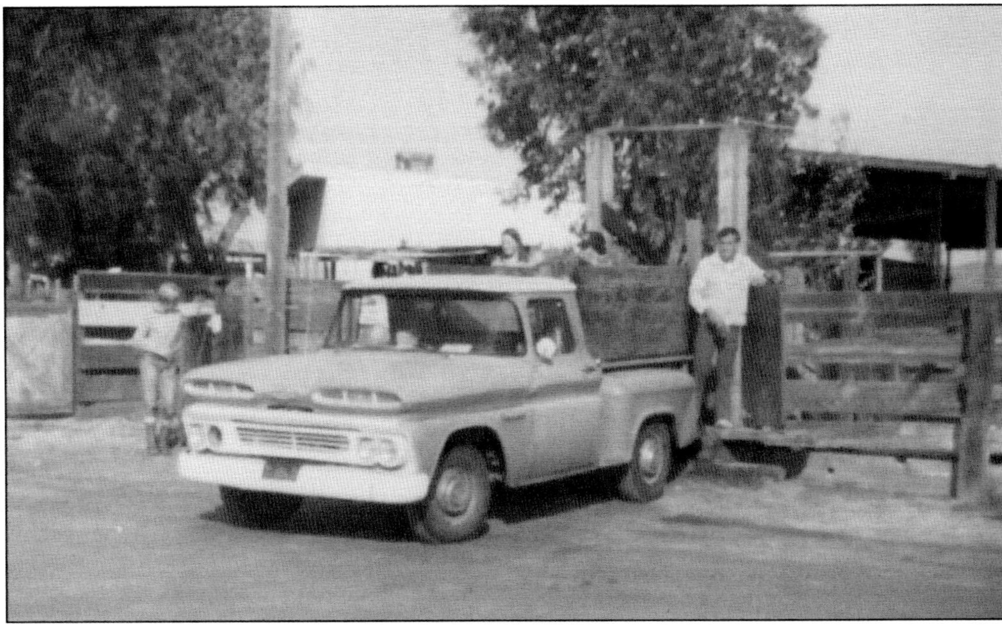

Jack Warneke (right) helps his son Steve unload the pigs that were raised as a Future Farmers of America (FFA) project in connection with his school. The San Jacinto Auction barn appears in the background. Also taking place on the grounds every weekend was a large swap meet. Bob Young owned a building supply shop (to the left of Jack's 1960 Chevy pickup) and also auctioned items on Saturdays. (Courtesy Jack Warneke.)

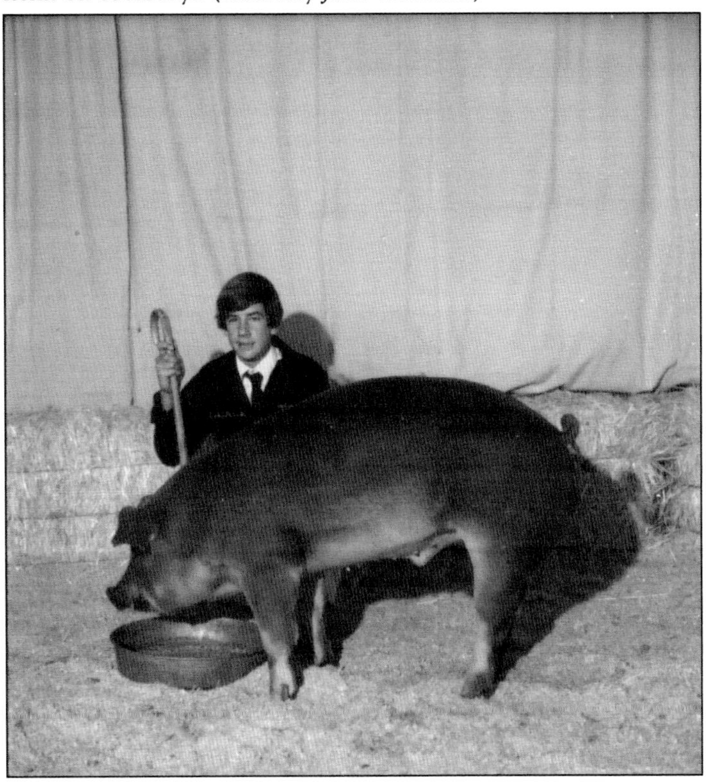

Steve Warneke is shown at the Lake Perris Farmer's Fair with his market hog in 1977. Steve took over his brother Harry's FFA pig project in 1974 and received a FFA State Farmer Award in 1978. When Harry was in the organization in 1970, San Jacinto High School did not have a farm on which students could raise animals. Consequently, Jack Warneke drew up the plans for a school farm, and the FFA Parent Booster Club began the operation on the high school campus. The school farm was demolished in 2005 to allow for new classrooms. (Courtesy Jack Warneke.)

Six

SPECIAL EVENTS

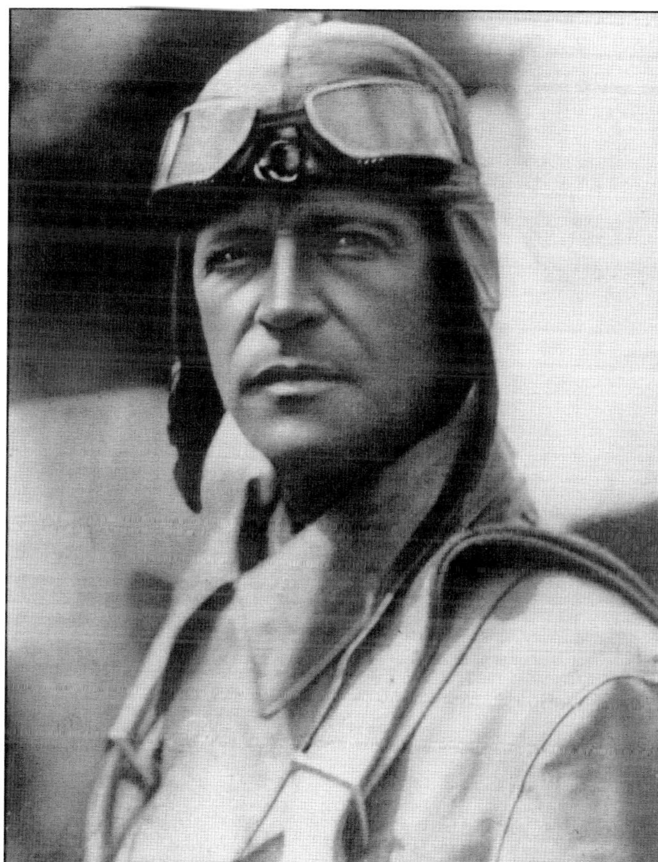

Joseph Stalin intended to establish a world-class aviation program for the Soviet Union in the 1930s. As a result, Mikhail Gromov piloted the Russian ANT-25 plane that landed in San Jacinto on July 14, 1937. Gromov was in the third aircraft to attempt a nonstop long-distance flight over the North Pole. The first had been lost in the Arctic, while the second had landed at Pearson Field in Vancouver, Washington, with engine problems. Gromov made it all the way to San Diego, but fog along the coast forced him to look inland. March Field was also foggy, but he spotted a clear area in the San Jacinto Valley. At 6:00 a.m., he made two passes over Earl Smith's dairy and then landed in the pasture north of Cottonwood Avenue and west of Sanderson Avenue. (Courtesy San Jacinto Museum.)

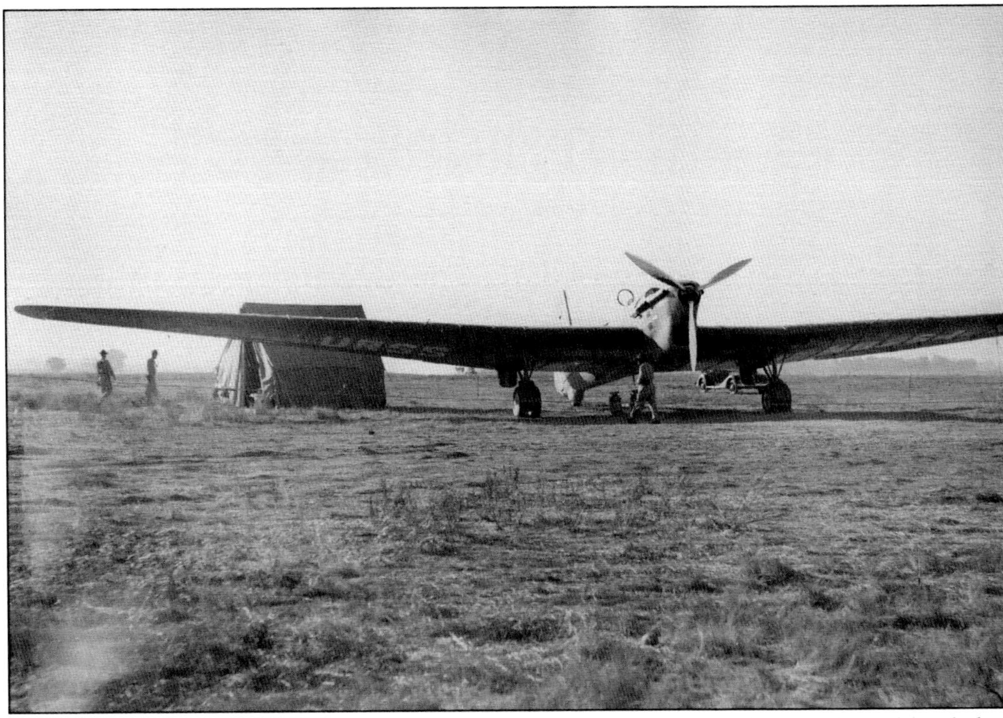

This Russian ANT-25 aircraft flew nonstop from Moscow over the North Pole and landed in San Jacinto in July 1937. The crew consisted of pilot Mikhail Gromov, copilot Andrei Yumashev, and navigator Sergei Danilin. The men flew 6,305 miles in 62 hours, breaking the record held by the French. The aircraft was disassembled and shipped back to a Moscow museum, where it was destroyed during World War II. (Courtesy San Jacinto Museum.)

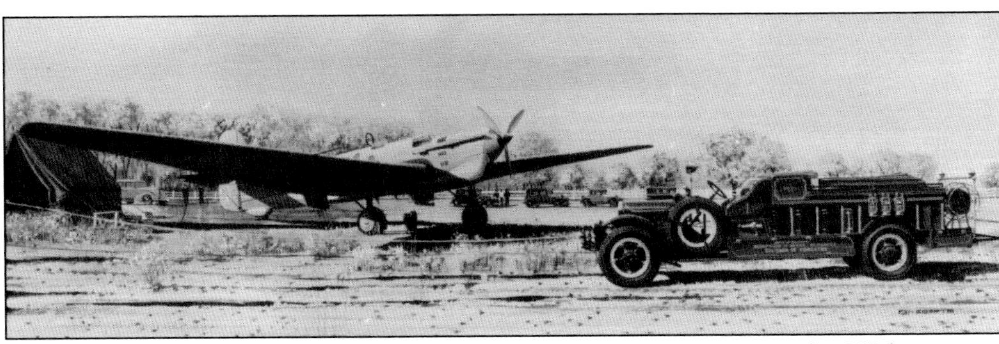

Seen in Earl Smith's dairy pasture, the aircraft had a 113-foot wingspan and a 950-horsepower engine. The tent on the left served as the March Field guard headquarters, and the fire truck aided the city of San Jacinto. The many cars in the background paid Earl Smith 25¢ to view the aircraft. An estimated 4,000 people witnessed the event. At the time, San Jacinto had a population of only 1,600, so visitors came from afar. (Courtesy San Jacinto Museum.)

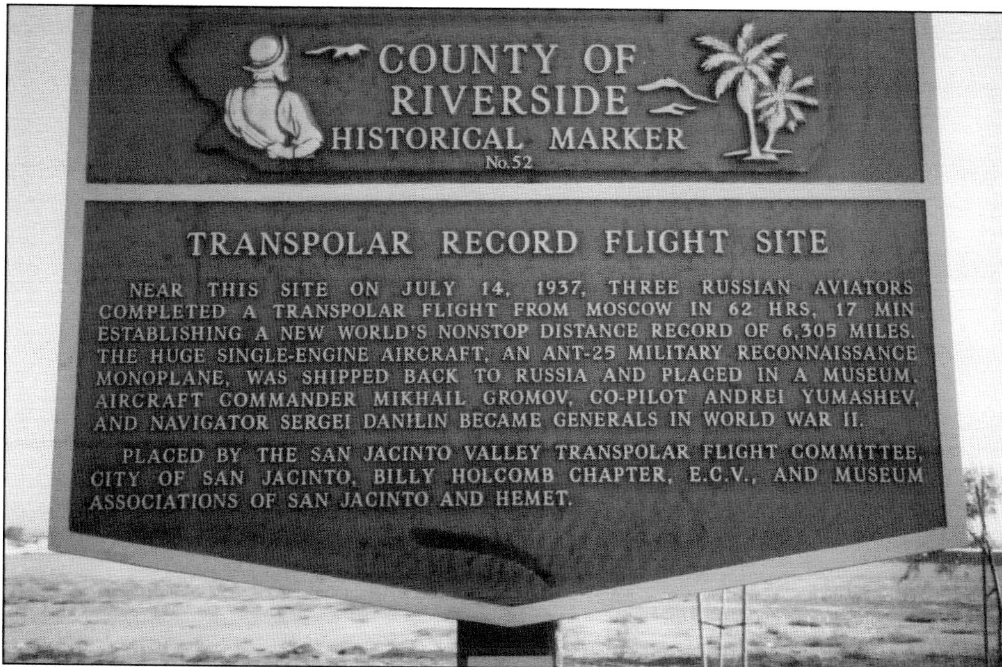

This commemorative plaque was unveiled in July 2007 for the 70th anniversary of the Russian ANT-25 nonstop flight from Moscow. The plaque is located along Cottonwood Avenue at the new San Jacinto Fire Station, across from the actual landing site. It has been designated County of Riverside Historical Marker No. 52. (Courtesy Ken Holtzclaw.)

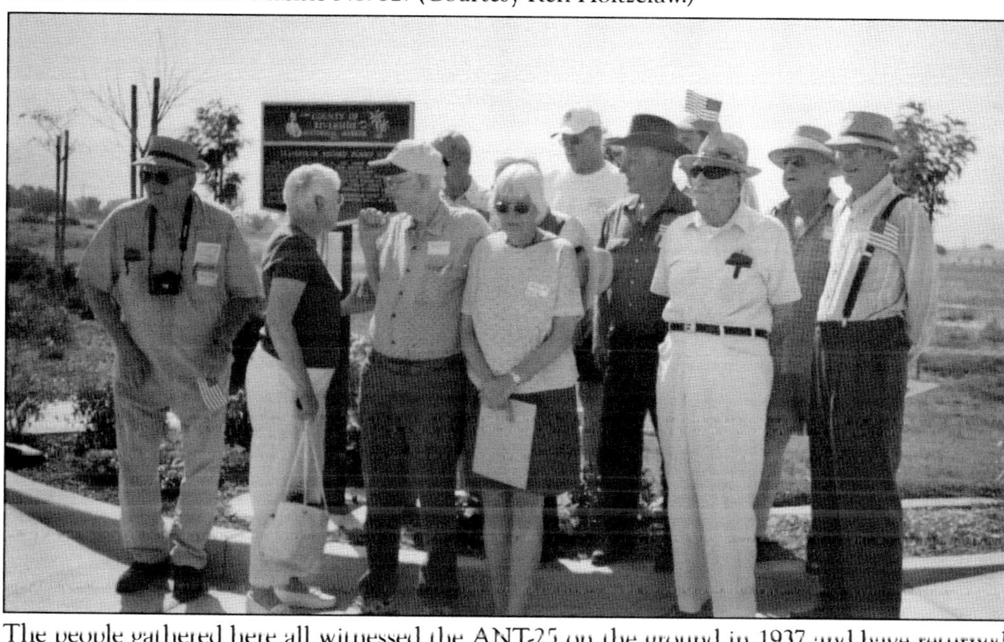

The people gathered here all witnessed the ANT-25 on the ground in 1937 and have returned for the event's 70th anniversary. Pictured from left to right are Howard Miller, Rilla Strickney Carlson, Harvey Peebles, Doug Brown, Betty Jo Dunham, Ronald Ashley, George Ott, Nelson Dilworth, Paul Marsh, James Darvey, and James Dilworth. Floy Rose and Walter L. Harvey are hidden from view. (Courtesy Nancy Warneke.)

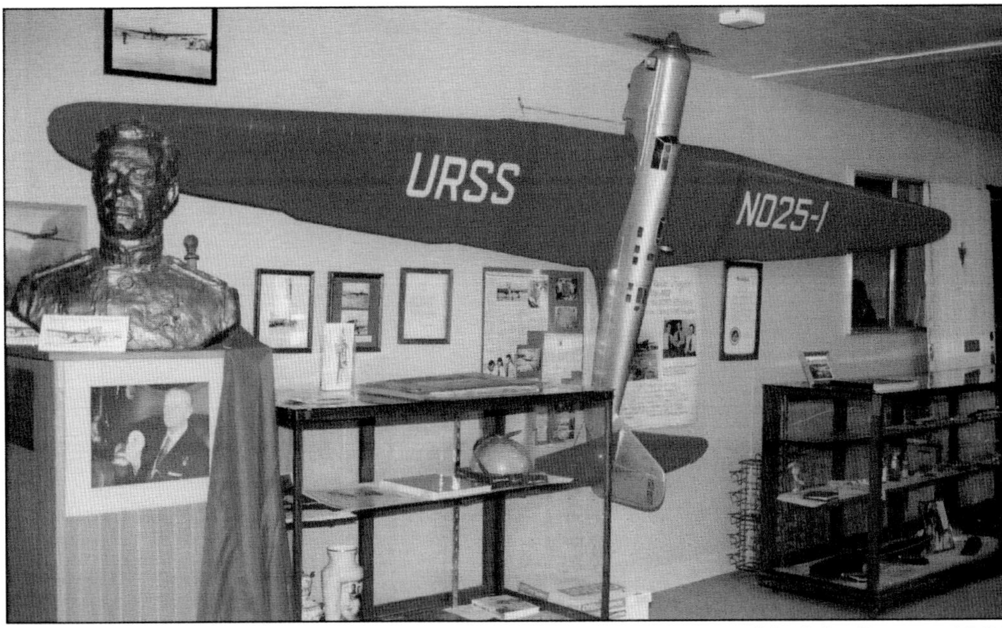

Russian objects are displayed along with this San Jacinto Museum model of the Russian ANT-25, which includes a bust of pilot Mikhail Gromov. Nina Gromov, Mikhail's widow, arranged to have the bust cast in Moscow. John Proctor, a San Diego pilot who flew around the world in 1993, delivered it to California. (Courtesy Mary Collier.)

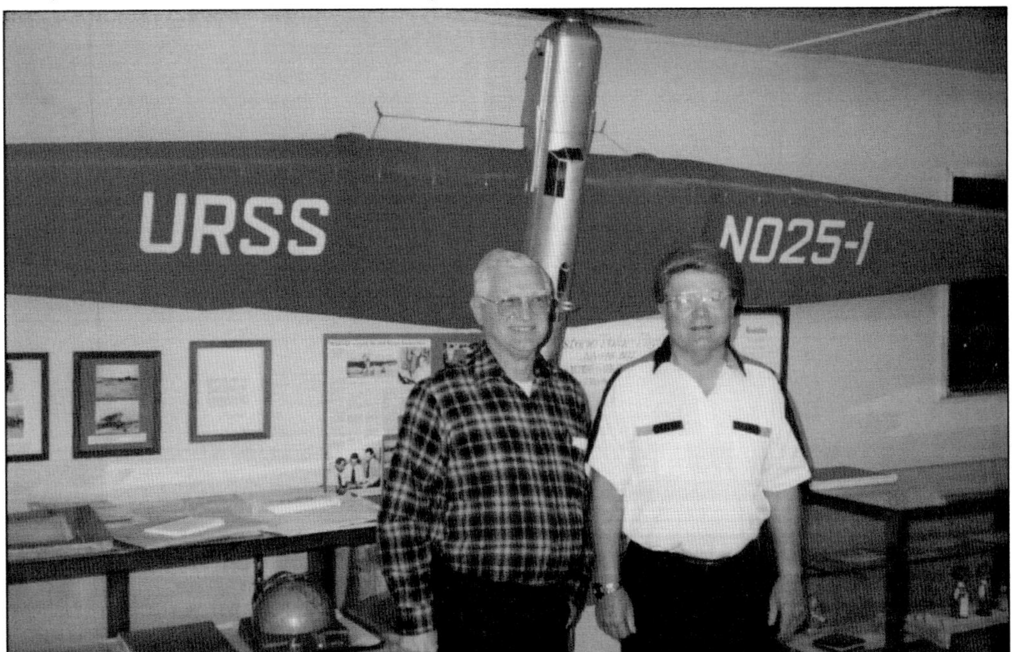

This plane, built on a one-to-seven scale of the original Russian ANT-25, is flyable. Ed Erfurth of Hesperia (left) created the model in 1986 to commemorate the record flight. Bruce Scales of Hemet bought the model and flew it at a model air show in Las Vegas in 1995. Scales donated the plane to the San Jacinto Museum in 2007. (Courtesy Russ Jacobs.)

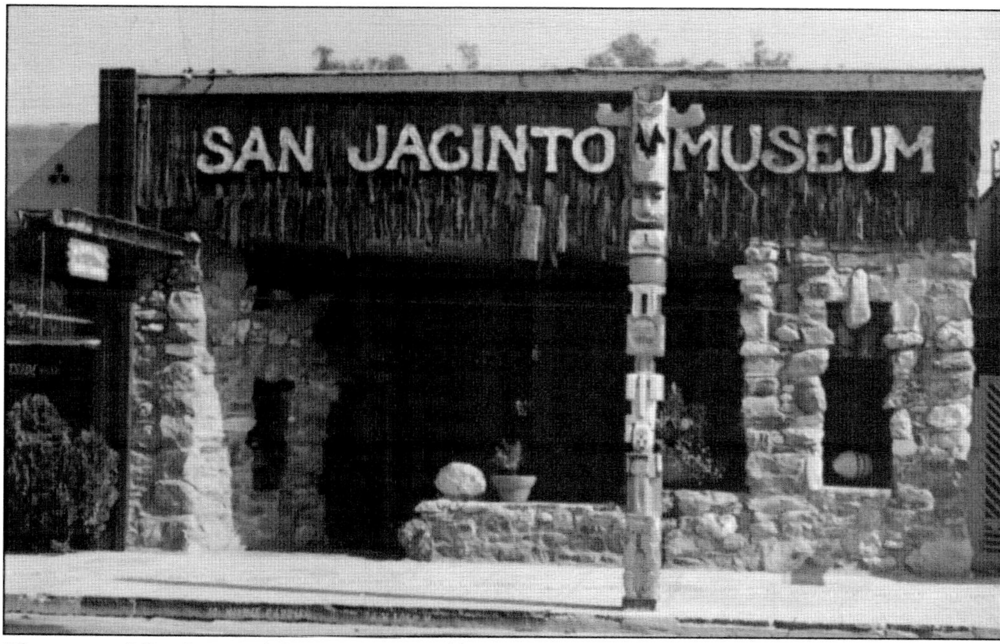

The original San Jacinto Museum, pictured here, was founded in 1939. Located on the north side of Main Street, the building was actually designed to be a restaurant. The rock work was done by Kenneth Kriege, who also did the rock work at the Pioneer Hotel. This structure was condemned in 2003. (Courtesy San Jacinto Museum.)

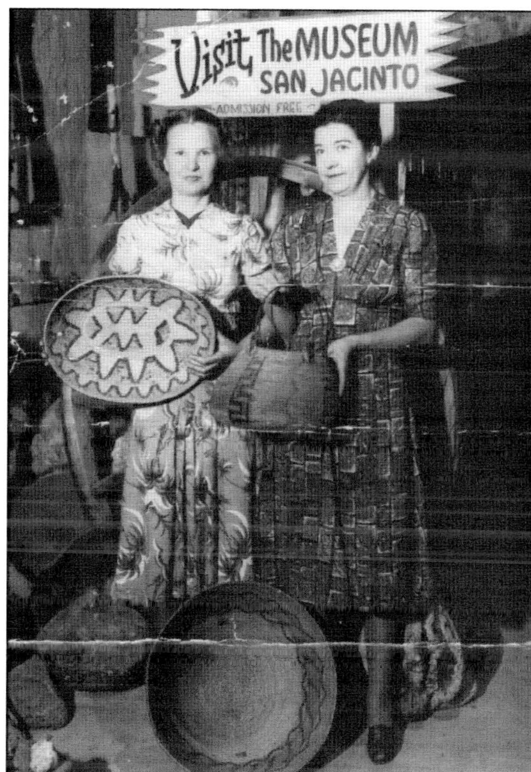

The San Jacinto Woman's Club founded the San Jacinto Museum in 1939. Here two founding members, Muriel Michell Shields (left) and Linda "Lulu" O'Loan Lockwood, show off the Native American basket collection on display in the new museum. Linda "Lulu" O'Loan Lockwood is the daughter of George O'Loan, the butcher at the local meat market. The San Jacinto Museum is only one of two municipal museums in Riverside County. The other is the Riverside City Museum. (Courtesy Charles Van Fleet.)

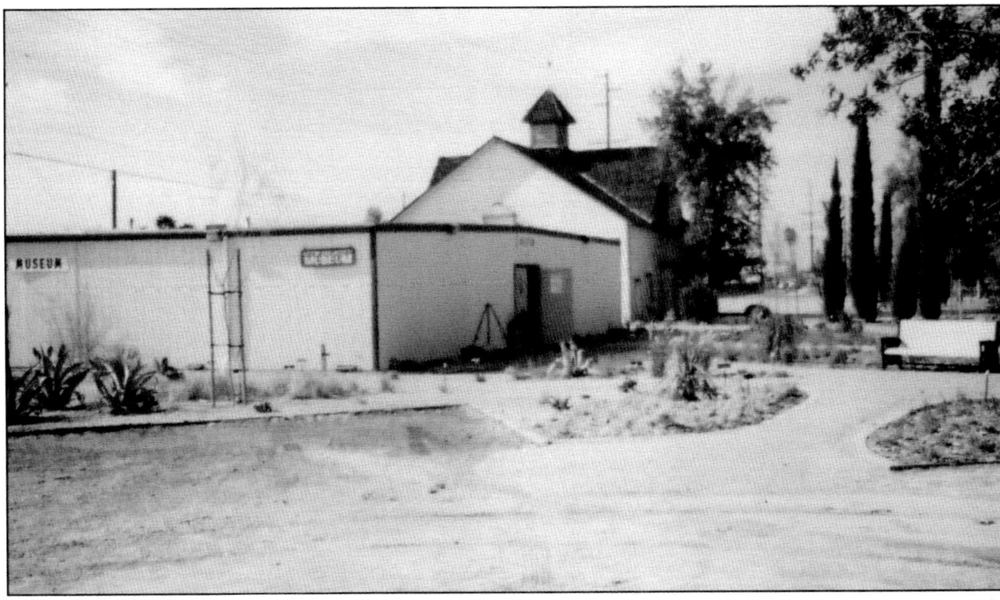

The San Jacinto City Museum is situated on the Francisco Estudillo Heritage Park grounds. It stands on the site of a former well and adjacent to the carriage house. In 1978, a citizens' committee formed the San Jacinto Valley Museum Association, which supports the city museum through public awareness and fund-raising. The organization purchased the new museum building (pictured) for the City of San Jacinto in 2005. (Courtesy Jack Warneke.)

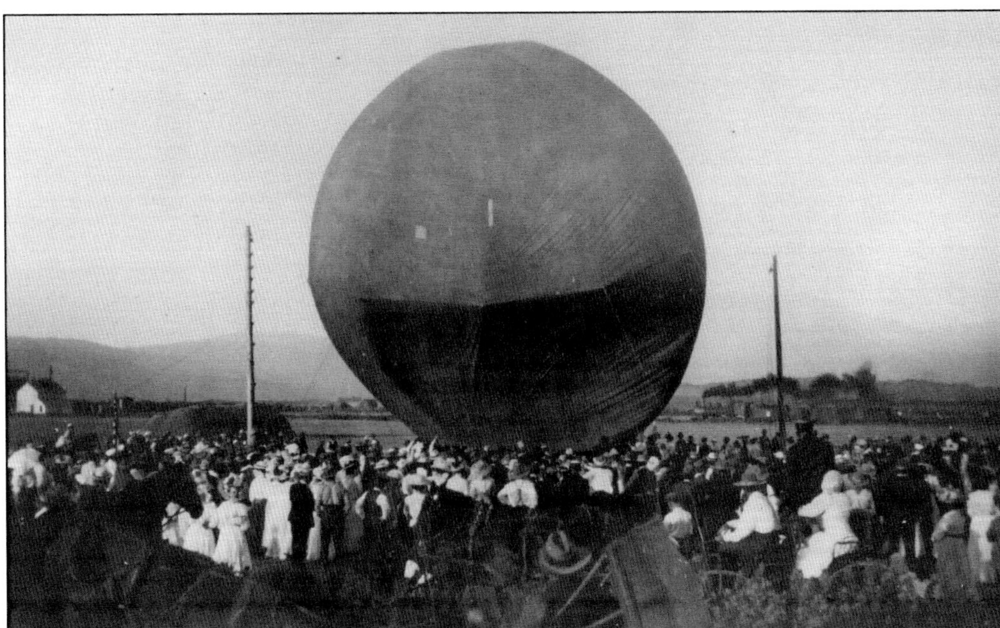

Balloon rides were offered in San Jacinto around 1905 and proved quite popular. In this view, people arrive in horse-drawn buggies in the foreground, while a train transports tourists in the background. (Courtesy Clarence Swift collection.)

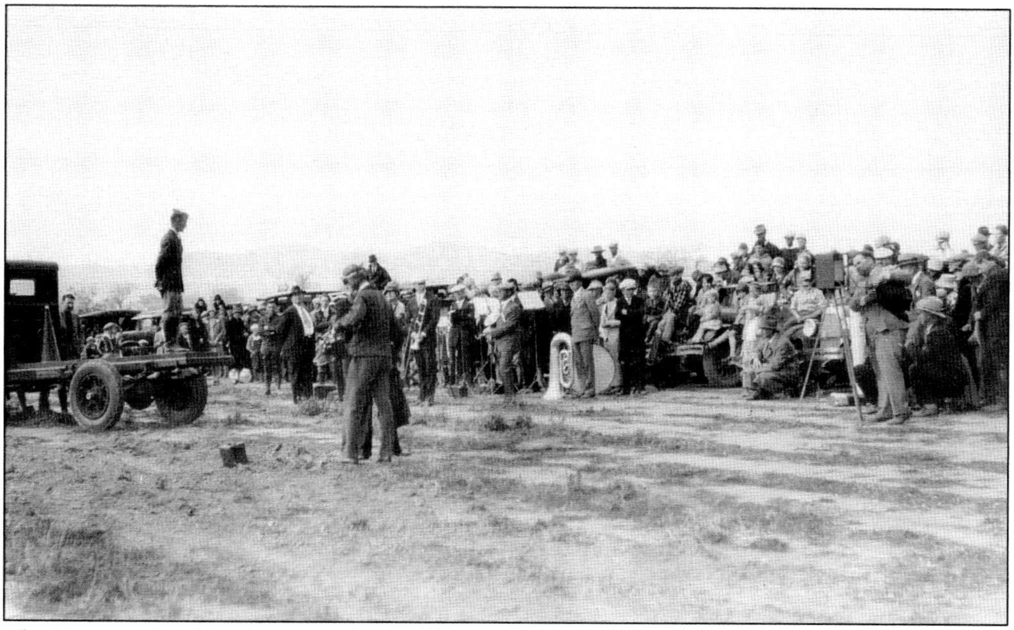

The Harmon Field landing strip, located between San Jacinto and Santa Fe Avenues and north of Midway, was dedicated in 1929. Here a March Field officer makes comments from the bed of a truck. The airstrip was no longer in use by 1940. After World War II, Bill Martin had the Hemacinto Drive-in Movie Theater built on the site. Across San Jacinto Avenue was the Midway Drive-in Restaurant, providing the first fast food in the valley. (Courtesy San Jacinto Museum.)

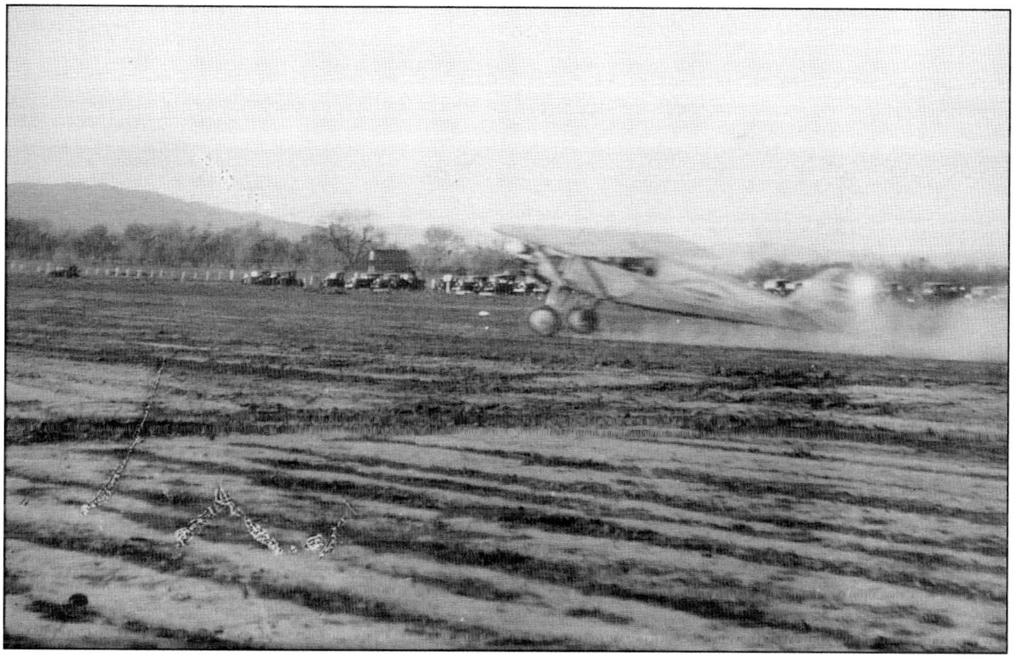

An aircraft takes off during the dedication of Harmon Field in 1929. The airstrip was on a 45-degree diagonal, extending from San Jacinto Avenue southwest to Santa Fe Avenue and just south of the present Blue Fountain Mobile Home Park. Note the rural environment of the area at the time. (Courtesy San Jacinto Museum.)

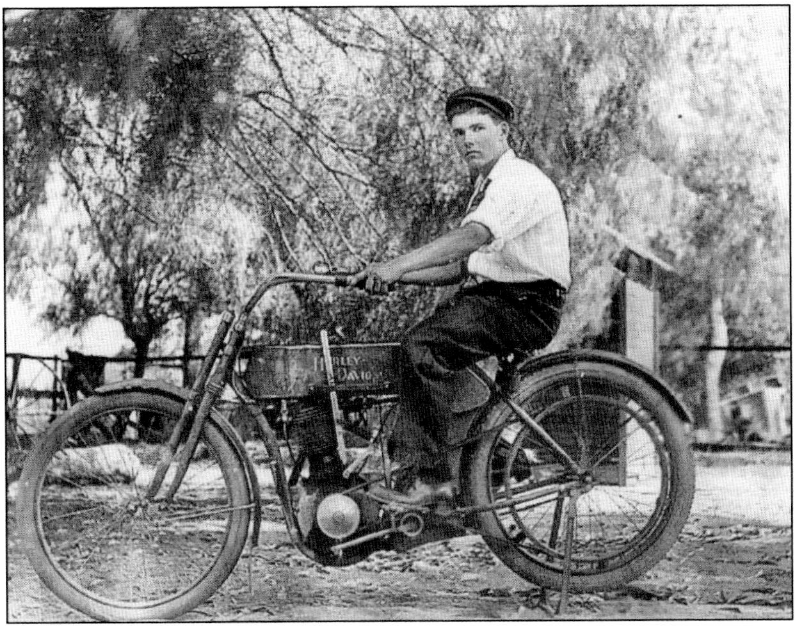

In 1915, Joe Barrows sits on his 1912 Harley Davidson motorcycle, the most modern version of its day. Barrows also liked to ride in airplanes and later became a pilot who flew at Harmon Field when it opened in San Jacinto. (Courtesy San Jacinto Museum.)

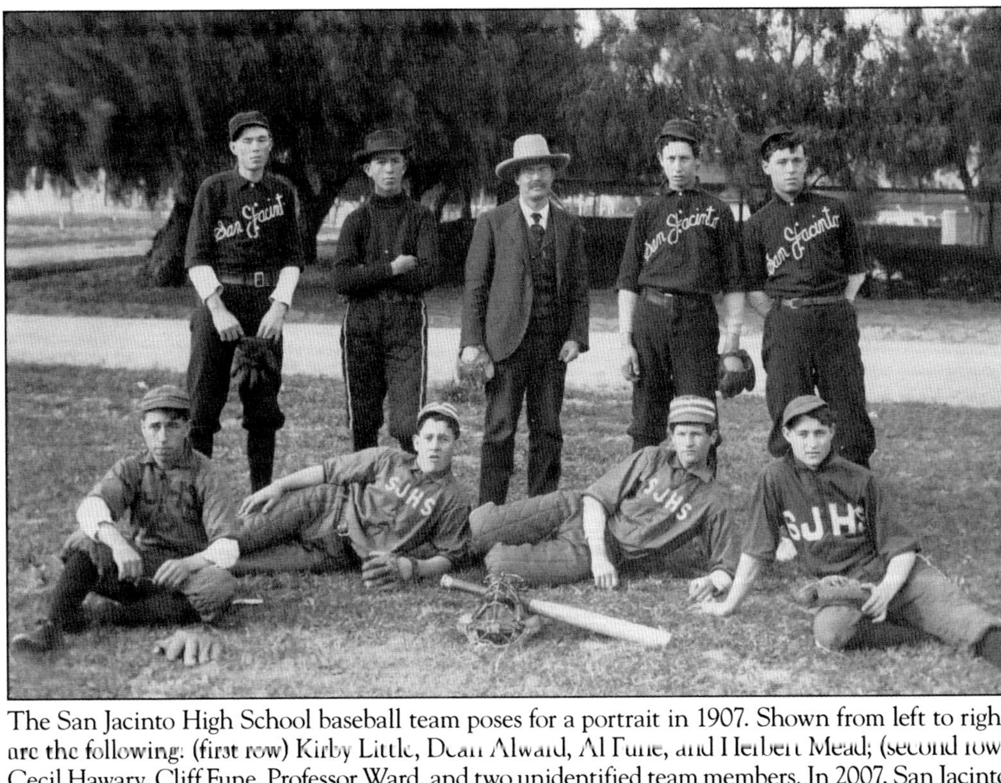

The San Jacinto High School baseball team poses for a portrait in 1907. Shown from left to right are the following: (first row) Kirby Little, Dean Alward, Al Fune, and Herbert Mead; (second row) Cecil Hawary, Cliff Fune, Professor Ward, and two unidentified team members. In 2007, San Jacinto High School won its first California Division championship. (Courtesy San Jacinto Museum.)

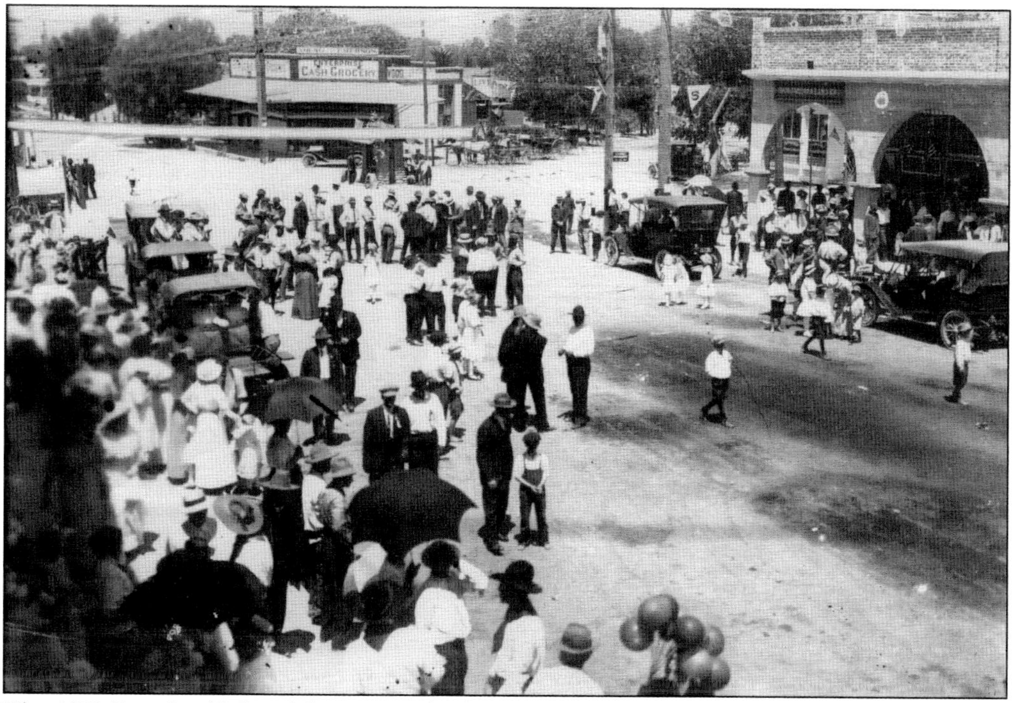

The 1910 Fourth of July celebration took place at Five Corners in San Jacinto, where banners were tied to power poles. This view shows Main Street at the corner of San Jacinto Avenue. Note the water well in the center of the intersection. The celebration appears to be a gala event. (Courtesy San Jacinto Museum.)

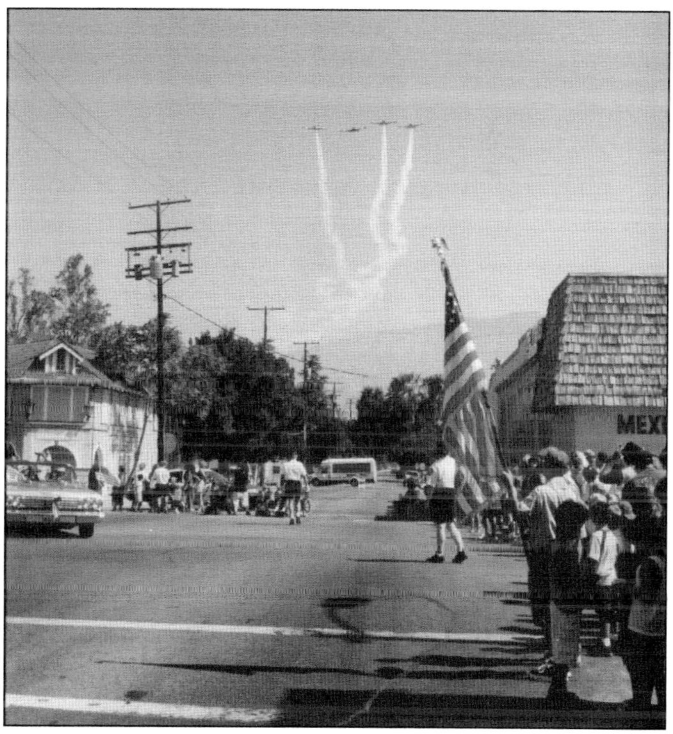

The 2001 Fourth of July festivities in San Jacinto featured a flyover of four aircraft to start the parade. This view looks north on San Jacinto Avenue, showing the Vosburg Hotel on the left. The approaching car is coming from Ramona Boulevard. (Courtesy San Jacinto Museum.)

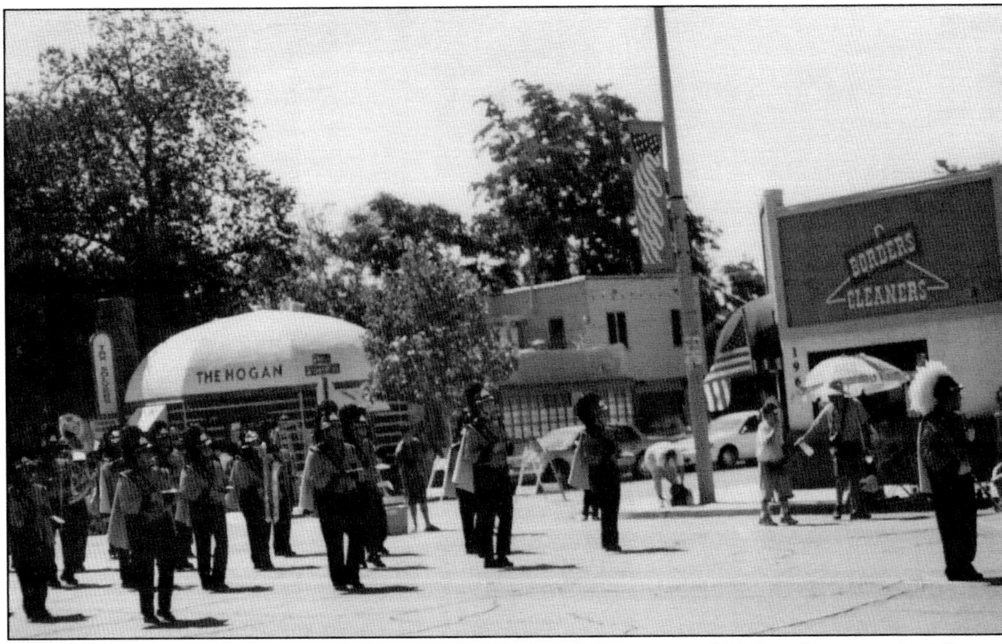

San Jacinto city officials revived the Fourth of July celebration in 2000 with a parade followed by events at Francisco Estudillo Heritage Park. This year, the San Jacinto High School band lined up on Main Street to start the parade. Note the Hogan Gift Shop at the corner of Sheriff Avenue, with Borders Cleaners on the other corner. The building behind the Hogan is one of Oscar Hofmann's Hopi Pueblo–style structures of the 1930s. (Courtesy Jack Warneke.)

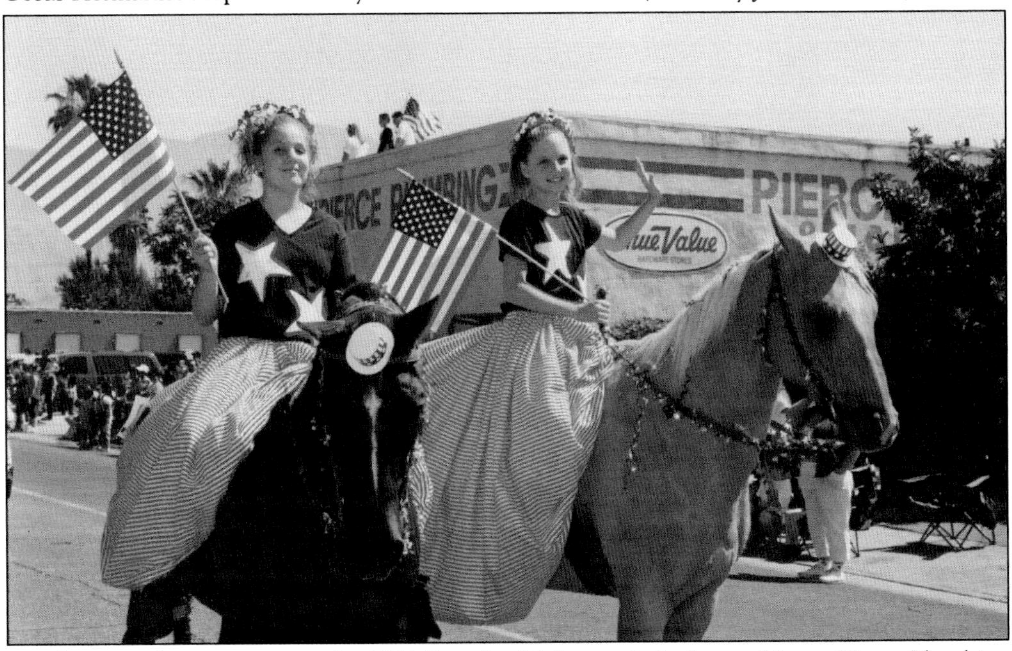

Two happy girls participate in the 2001 Fourth of July parade in front of Larry Pierce Plumbing on San Jacinto Avenue. In addition to running the retail store, Pierce also performed contract plumbing for businesses and residences. It is interesting to note that the girls are not wearing hats, but the horses are. (Courtesy San Jacinto City.)

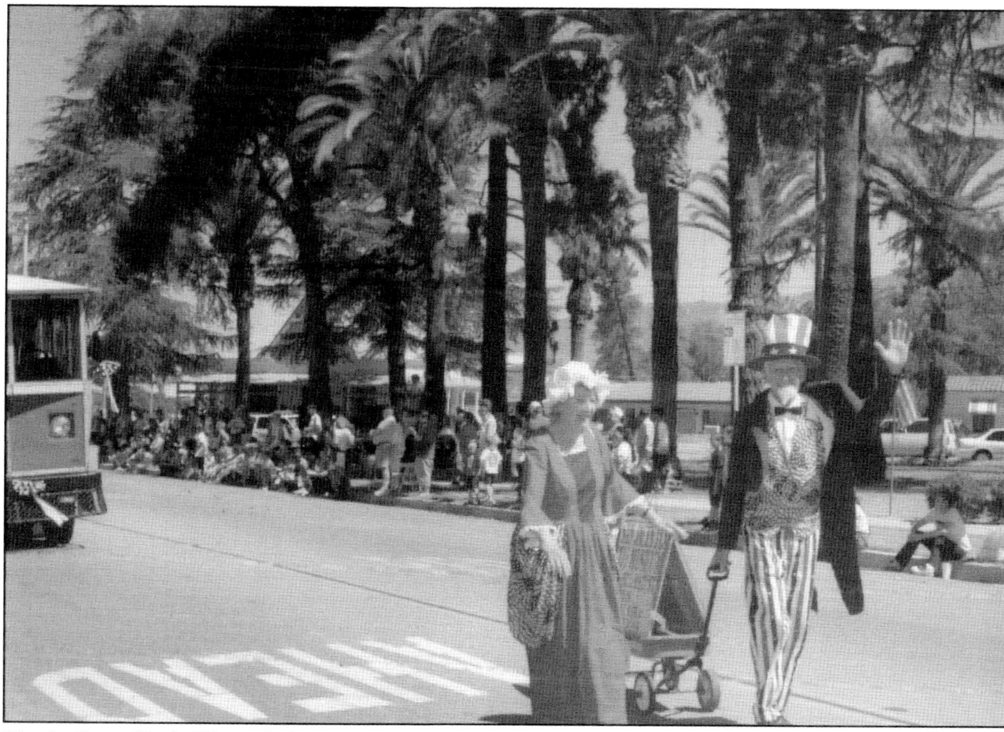

Uncle Sam (Jack Warneke) waves to the 2001 Fourth of July parade crowd while walking alongside Betsy Ross (Nancy Warneke) on Ramona Boulevard. A backdrop of the beautiful Druding Veterans Memorial Park appears behind them. In 2007, Jack and Nancy Warneke had been in each parade since it was revived in 2000. (Courtesy San Jacinto City.)

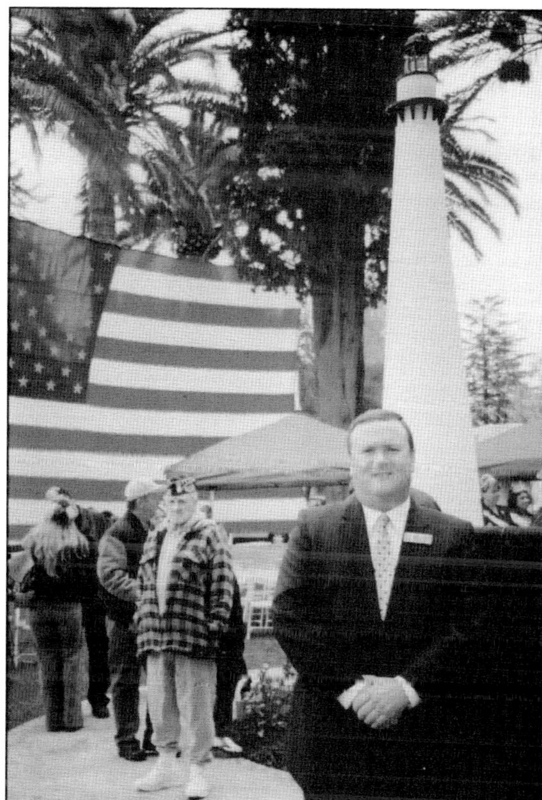

Mayor James Ayers stands in front of the new Coast Guard Memorial in Druding Veterans Memorial Park during its December 2007 dedication at the corner of Ramona Boulevard and Pico. While vice mayor in 2001, Ayers began dedicating memorials to the U.S. Military and proved instrumental in acquiring a U.S. Army M-60 tank for the U.S. Army Memorial to All Army Veterans, which stands proudly in the park. (Courtesy Jack Warneke.)

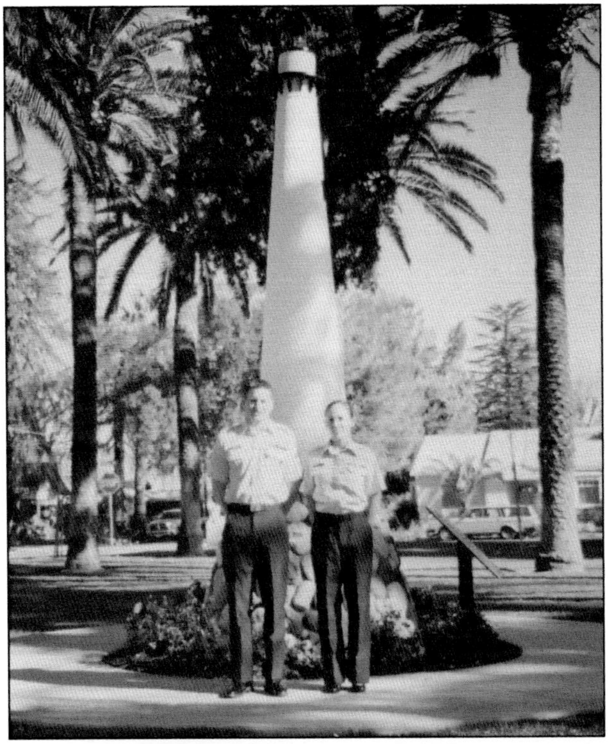

Two members of the U.S. Coast Guard, Petty Officer 3rd Class Brandon Tucker (left) and Petty Officer 3rd Class Melinda Warneke Tucker, stand in front of a replica of the Fenwick Lighthouse in Delaware, dedicated to members of the coast guard. Melinda's brothers Fred and Bill appear in the photograph of the U.S. Navy Memorial. (Courtesy Jack Warneke.)

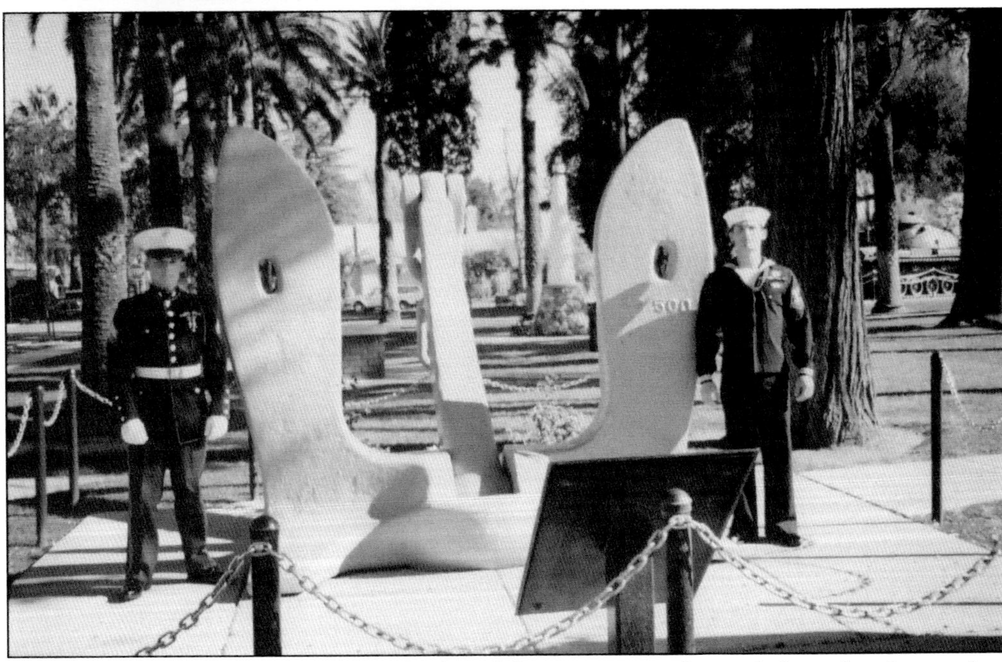

This anchor, taken from the USS *Cleveland* amphibious transport ship, is dedicated to the members of the U.S. Navy. Standing before the memorial is Corp. Bill Warneke (left), a U.S. Marine and a veteran of the Iraq War. Bill is the brother of Frederick Warneke (right), a petty officer 2nd Class and a navy seal. Visible in the background is the U.S. Coast Guard Memorial Lighthouse, and on the right is the U.S. Army Memorial Tank. (Courtesy Jack Warneke.)

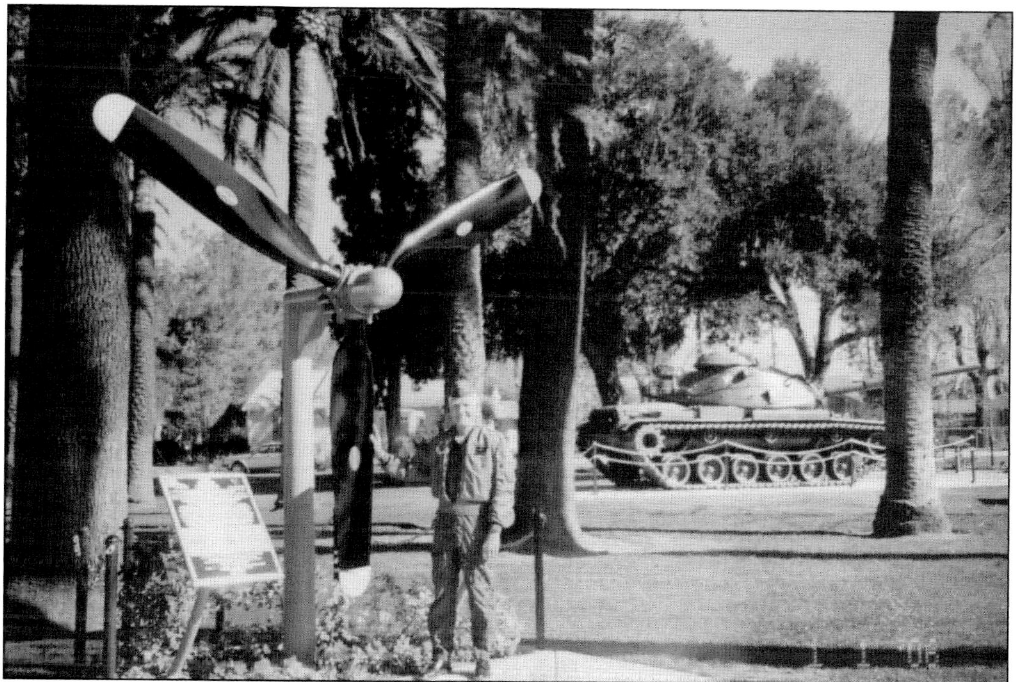

Taken from a World War II B-17 "Flying Fortress" bomber, this propeller is dedicated to the members of the U.S. Air Force. Standing beside the propeller is Lt. Col. Jack Warneke, a retired Air Force Reserve pilot. Druding Park was named after Frank Druding, who landscaped the area. In 2001, the park was renamed Druding Veterans Memorial Park. (Courtesy Melinda Warneke Tucker.)

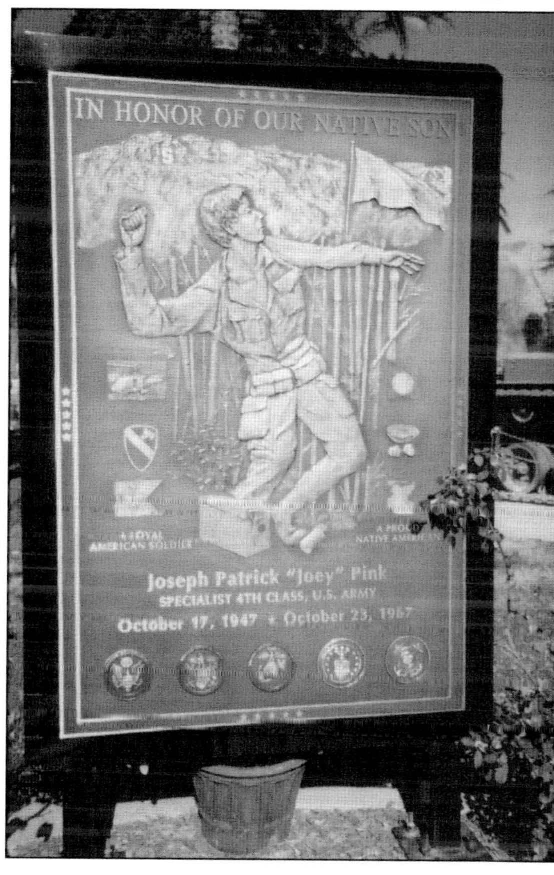

This plaque, In Honor of Our Native Son, is a memorial to Joseph Pink, a member of the Soboba tribe of Luiseño Indians. It has been installed in Druding Veterans Memorial Park in his honor. "Joey" Pink was the only San Jacinto casualty of the Vietnam War. He was killed in combat near Da Nang, Vietnam, on October 23, 1967, one week after his 20th birthday. (Courtesy Jack Warneke.)

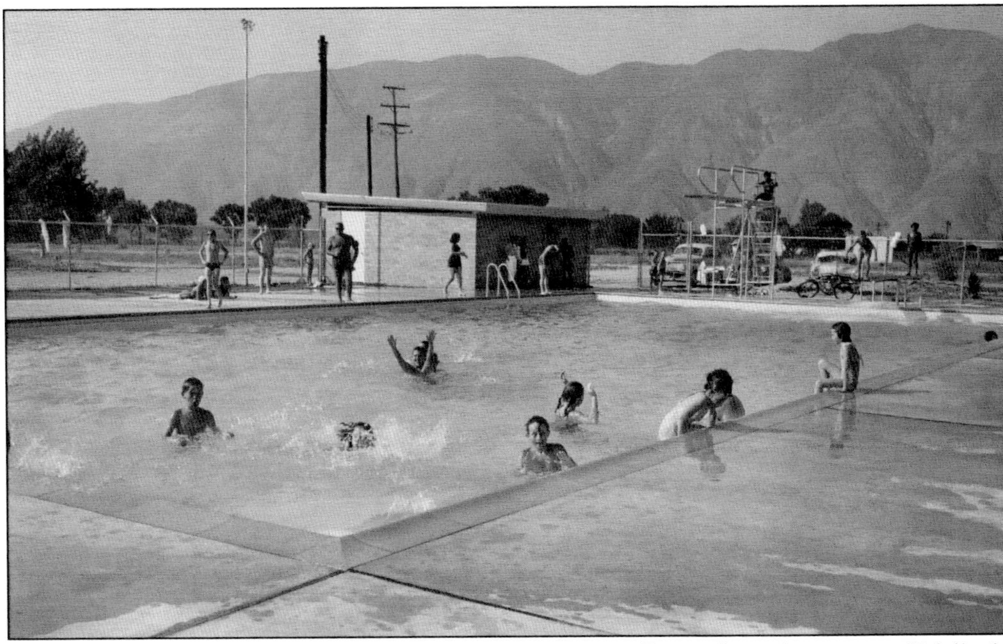

The San Jacinto swimming pool opened in the 1940s in Sallee Park, at the corner of Idyllwild Drive and Tahquitz Road. Note the high dive at the far end of the pool and the mountain range behind the swimming pool. Sallee Park was named after Frazier Sallee, a judge in the early 1900s. (Courtesy San Jacinto Museum.)

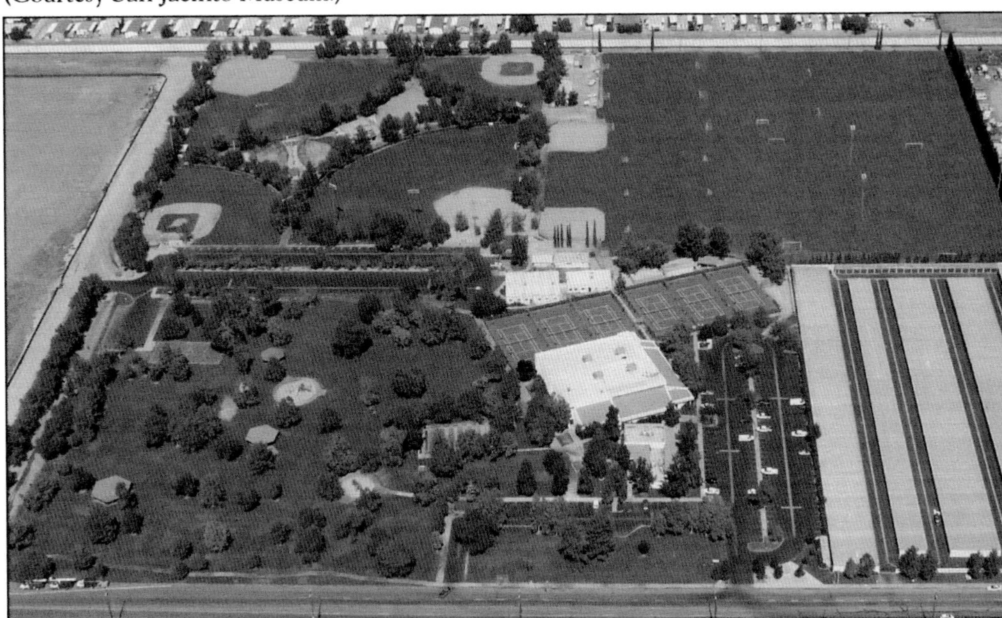

This aerial view depicts the Valley Wide Recreation and Park District, located on the north of Esplanade between State Street and Pine Avenue. In the upper section are four baseball fields (left), two softball fields (center), and soccer fields. The lower left has been designated the picnic and park area. The gymnasium building is visible in the center, adjacent to the tennis courts. (Courtesy Valley Wide Park District.)

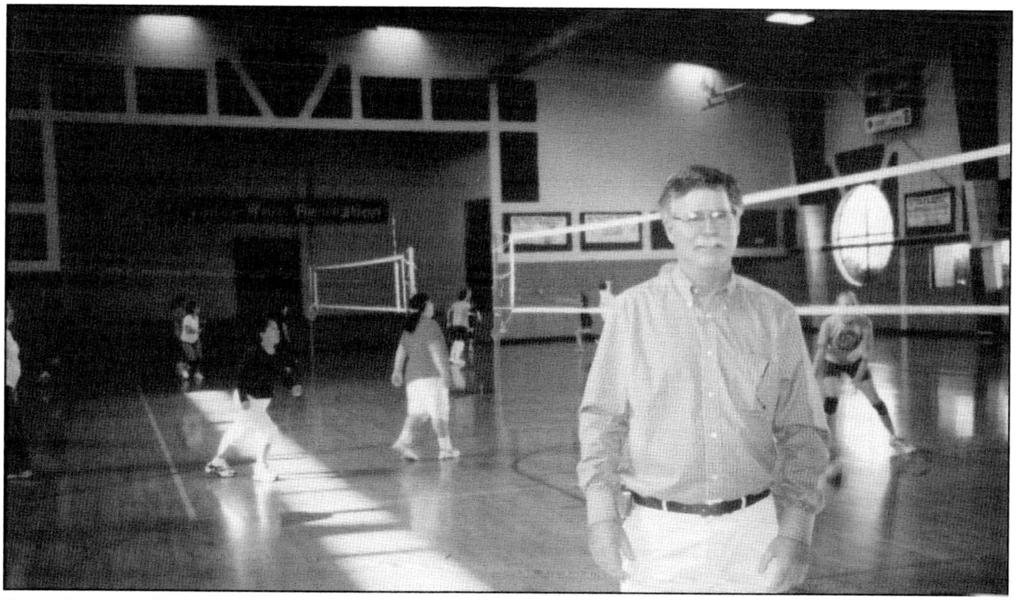

Sam Goepp, the manager of the Valley Wide Recreation and Park District, stands inside the gymnasium, where a volleyball game is in progress. While serving as director for more than 20 years, he has seen the district grow to 66 parks and playing fields in the San Jacinto Valley. The area extends from San Jacinto to Valle Vista, Winchester, French Valley, and Menifee. (Courtesy Jack Warneke.)

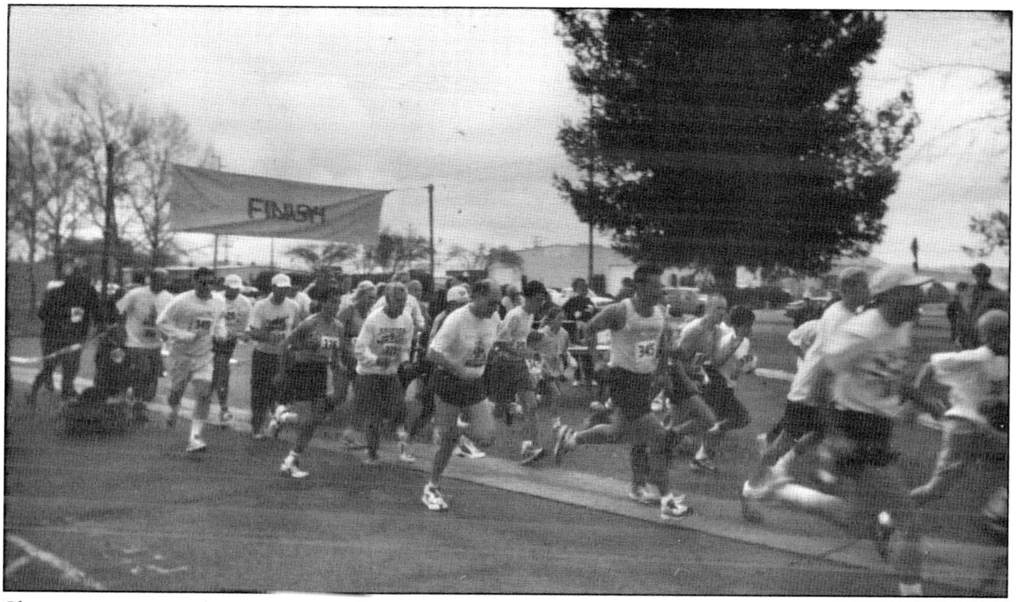

Shown in 1999 is the five-kilometer Easter Bunny Hop, an event sponsored by the Valley Wide Recreation and Park District. Steve Warneke is fourth from left at the start line. Jack Warneke wears a long-sleeve white shirt at the lower right corner of the finish sign. Nancy Warneke, seventh from left of the start line also participates in the race, but is obscured. During the 1980s and 1990s, Valley Wide held five-kilometer races in both the spring and the fall—the Bunny Hop in the spring and the Turkey Trot in the fall. In 2008, the Bunny Hop will be revived. (Courtesy Jack Warneke.)

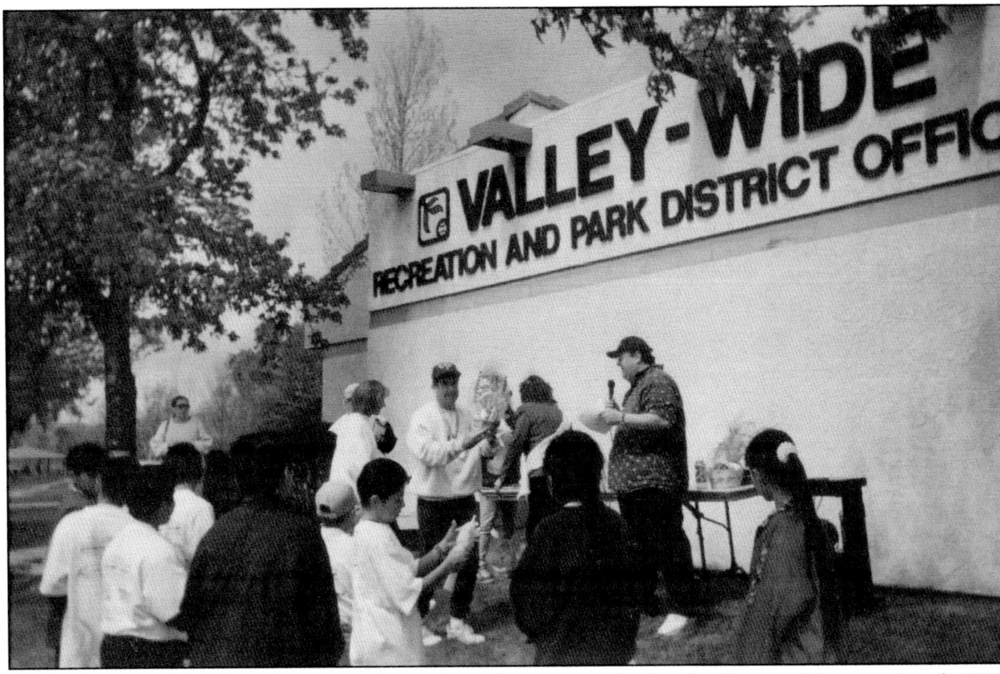

Ron Hoffman, holding the microphone, hands out awards for the Bunny Hop in April 1999. Steve Warneke, wearing a cap, receives his first award: an Easter basket and a medal attached to a ribbon around his neck. Jack Warneke won first place in the division for men aged 60 to 70 with a time of 22 minutes and 50 seconds. Nancy won second place for women aged 60 to 70. (Courtesy Jack Warneke.)

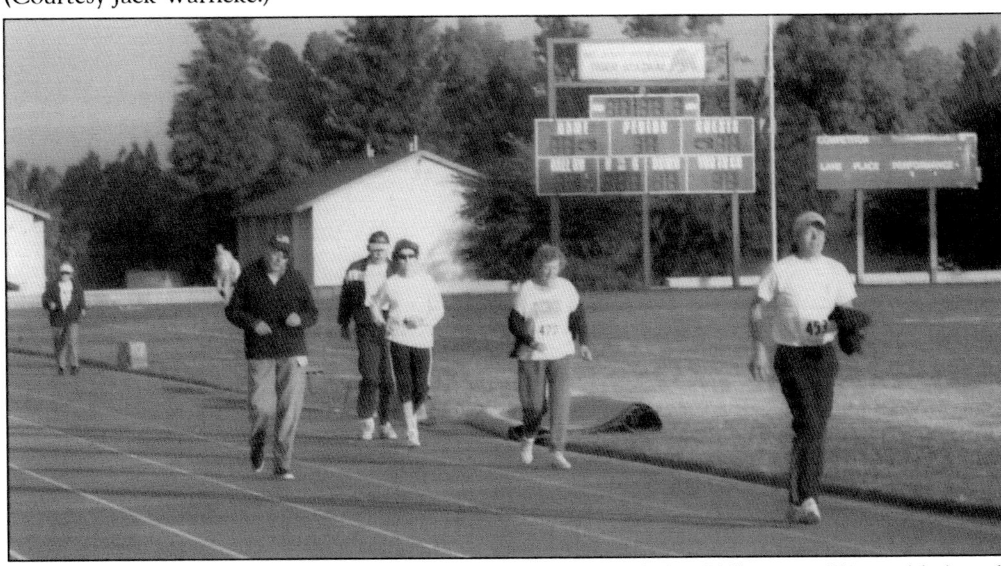

The Valley Wide Recreation and Park District has sponsored the Oldlympics (50 or older) each fall since the mid-1980s. Spanning a 10-day period, the events include swimming, bowling, horseshoes, tennis, softball, shuffleboard, golf, billiards, and track and field. The track and field events are held at the San Jacinto High School track. This photograph shows the two-mile walk competition, with Nancy Warneke fifth from the left. (Courtesy Valley Wide Recreation and Park District.)

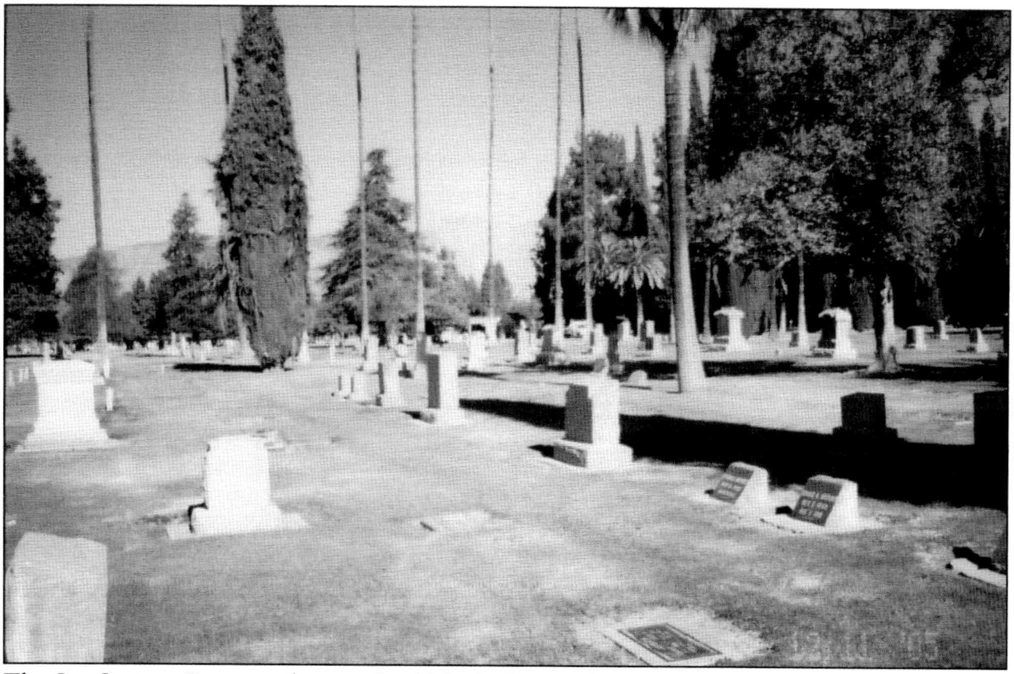

The San Jacinto Cemetery lies north of Menlo Avenue between San Jacinto Avenue and Santa Fe Street. The aboveground monuments occupy the older section of the cemetery. All new burials have monuments that are at ground level for the convenience of park maintenance. (Courtesy Jack Warneke.)

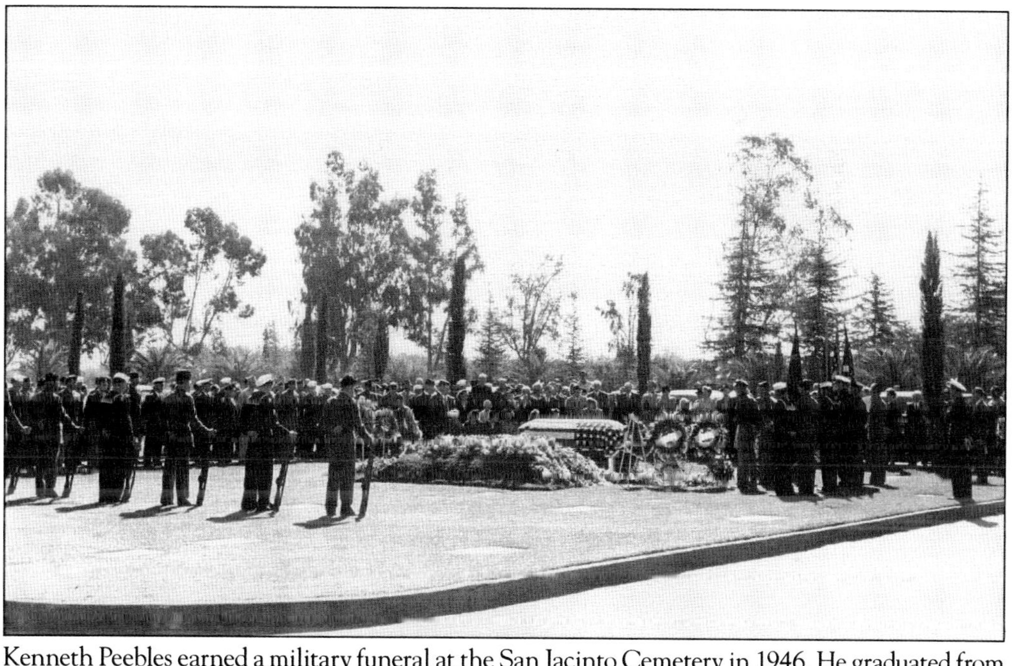

Kenneth Peebles earned a military funeral at the San Jacinto Cemetery in 1946. He graduated from San Jacinto High School in 1939 and enlisted in the U.S. Navy in 1942, at the beginning of World War II. A Japanese sniper killed him while he was a corpsman helping wounded marines during the invasion of Tarawa in the Gilbert Islands in the fall of 1943. (Courtesy San Jacinto Museum.)